THE BERLITZ
SELF-TEACHER:
GERMAN

EDITED BY THE STAFF OF

THE BERLITZ SCHOOLS OF LANGUAGES

UNDER THE DIRECTION OF

ROBERT STRUMPEN-DARRIE

AND

CHARLES F. BERLITZ

D1529356

Grosset & Dunlap · *Publishers* · NEW YORK

INTRODUCTION

A very strange paradox exists in connection with languages and the learning of them. On the one hand, the ability to speak two or more languages reasonably well is *prima facie* evidence of better-than-average intelligence. On the other hand, learning a language is a very easy business. The proof of it is that every living human being who is not an utter idiot speaks one!

The trick lies in how you go about it. It would seem reasonable to use somewhat the same system to learn a new language as you did to acquire your own. This idea built up the Berlitz Schools of Languages from a one-room studio in Providence, Rhode Island, to a globe-circling institution with over 300 branches.

In a word, you learn to *speak* a language *by speaking it*—and in no other way. That is how Germans learn German, and that is how you learned English.

You will succeed with the BERLITZ SELF-TEACHER to the extent that you speak. Do not deceive yourself into thinking you have "arrived" when you find yourself able to read or translate the German text. You master German only in the degree to which you can express *your* ideas in it. The ability to interpret the thoughts of others is only the first step.

One way of using the BERLITZ SELF-TEACHER is to pair off with someone else, or to organize a small group. After reading over the lesson in advance for meaning and pronunciation, each student then reads aloud, direct from the German text. The lesson is divided into convenient portions by agreement among the students. After each student has practiced reading aloud, one of them assumes the role of instructor and questions the others from the exercises called THINKING IN GERMAN. When all can answer these questions without hesitation, each student should invent ten or twelve new questions, based on the same or preceding lessons, and then put these questions to the others. Afterwards, answers to the exercise questions should be written out and corrected from the keys in the appendix.

When a group of you are learning together, do not succumb to the "community-sing" temptation. Each student must speak individually, so that he can hear himself and the others, and profit thereby.

Make no mistake, however! This book is designed primarily for the student working alone. He must do exactly what pairs or groups do, covering each operation for himself. If you are embarrassed by the sound of your own voice, hide in the pantry! Put a sack over your head! No matter what form of defense mechanism you set up, see to it that you *speak out!* Do not mumble or whisper.

Your attention is directed to the glossary in the back of the book. Use it sparingly, if at all. With few exceptions, all the words are made clear in the lesson texts, and only occasionally have we sneaked a new one into the THINKING IN GERMAN, just to keep you on your toes.

The authors have enjoyed preparing the BERLITZ SELF-TEACHER, because they are confident that, properly used, it can provide you with a flying start toward a working knowledge of German—and an extra dividend of good, clean fun.

NOTE ON PRONUNCIATION

HAVE YOU NOTICED that many foreigners, among them the Germans, have some difficulty in learning to pronounce the English *th?* They say *tink* for *think* and *dis* for *this.* The reason is that the *th* sound does not exist in German. Until a German sees and hears an English speaking person pronounce *th,* he cannot know how to arrange his tongue, teeth and jaws to reproduce the sound.

You may expect a similar experience in dealing with German pronunciation. In developing a phonetic system for this book, we have sometimes compromised with strict accuracy to gain simplicity, because, no matter how many symbols we dream up to indicate shades and tones of sounds, you can still not be sure until you hear the sounds spoken.

Here are some tips on the important German sounds.

All German letters are pronounced as in English with the following exceptions:

VOWELS: A — *ah* — invariably like *ah.*

E — *ay* — always like *ay,* but not pronounced after "I", where it merely prolongs the length of the "I", and gives it the sound of *ee* in "see".

I — *ee* — pronounced like the "I" in "sit", except when followed by "E" or "H". Then *ee.*

U — *oo* — always like *oo.*

CONSONANTS: C — *tsay* — like "TS", except before "A", "O" and "U": then like "K".

G — *gay* — always hard like the English "G" in "gold", except at the end of a word, after *i;* then like *kh.*

vii

H — *hah* — not pronounced after vowels (AH–
      EH–IH–OH–UH). Merely
      lengthens the vowel sound.

J — *yot* — always like the English "Y" in
      "York".

S — *ess* — at the beginning of a word or syl-
      lable, like the English "Z". Always
      like "SH" before "T" and "P", at
      the beginning of a word or syllable.
      Between two consonants, always
      like "SS".

Ex: Spanien — SHPAH-*n'yehn* — Spain
     Stern   — *shtairn*   — star
     Fenster — FEN-*st'r*   — window.

V — *faou* — always like "F", except in a few
      foreign words.

W — *vay* — always like the English "V".

Y — EW-*psee-lon* — always like the *Umlaut ü,*
      as explained later.

Z — *tsett* — always like "TSS".

THE UMLAUT: There are three "Umlauts": ä–*ay;* ö–*uh;* ü–*ew.*
      The *Umlaut ü* is equivalent to the French "U"
      and is pronounced by pursing the lips as to
      whistle and saying "EE". We represent it ar-
      bitrarily as *ew.*

THE DIPHTHONGS: EI and AI are always pronounced like long
      "I" in English.

Ex: Mai — *Migh* — May
     Ei — *Igh* — egg.

EU — *oy* — invariably like "OY".

ÄU — *oy* — composed of the *Umlaut Ä*
      and *U,* always pronounced
      like "OY".

Ex: Fräulein — FROY-*line* — Miss.

ÜBUNG NR. 1

Was ist das?
Vahss ist dahs?
What is this?

Der Bleistift
Dehr BLIGH-*shtift*
The pencil

der Schlüssel
dehr SHLEW-*s'l*
the key

die Feder
dee FAY-*d'r*
the pen

die Schachtel
dee SHAKH-*t'l*
the box

das Buch
dahs Bookh
the book

das Papier
*dahs Pah-*PEER
the paper

Ist das der Bleistift?
Ist dahs dehr BLIGH-*shtift?*
Is this the pencil?

Ja, das ist der Bleistift.
Yah, dahs ist dehr BLIGH-*shtift.*
Yes, this is the pencil.

Ist das die Feder? **Nein, das ist nicht die Feder, das ist der Bleistift.**
Ist dahs dee FAY-*d'r?* *Nine, dahs ist nikht dee* FAY-*d'r, dahs ist dehr*
BLIGH-*shtift.*
Is this the pen? No, this is not the pen, this is the pencil.

REMEMBER the difference between *der, die, das*. Words that take *der* are said to be masculine, those that take *die* are feminine, and those that take *das* are called neuter.

1

der Stuhl	der Tisch	die Lampe
dehr Shtool	*dehr Tish*	*dee* LAHM-*peh*
the chair	the table	the lamp

Ist das die Lampe? **Nein, das ist nicht die Lampe, das ist der Tisch.**
Ist dahs de LAHM-*peh?* *Nine, dahs ist nikht dee* LAHM-*peh, dahs ist dehi Tish.*
Is this the lamp? No, it is not the lamp, it is the table.

NOTE: The word *das* has several meanings. It means "the", "this", "that" and sometimes "it".

die Tür	das Fenster	das Bild
dee Tewr	*dahs* FEN-*st'r*	*dahs Bilt*
the door	the window	the picture

der Boden	die Decke	die Wand
dehr BOH-*d'n*	*dee* DEK-*keh*	*dee Vahnt*
the floor	the ceiling	the wall

Was ist das? **Das ist die Tür, die Wand, das Bild, etc.**
Vahss ist dahs? *Dahs ist dee Tewr, dee Vahnt, dahs Bilt, etc.*
What is this? It is the door, the wall, the picture, etc.

Sehr gut!
Zair goot!
Very good!

1	2	3	4	5
eins	zwei	drei	vier	fünf
eye'nss	*tsvigh*	*drigh*	*feer*	*fewnf*

HINTS on Pronunciation: *W* sounds like our "v". The *U* with two dots over it is called *UMLAUT U* and is pronounced like "ee" with the lips pursed as in whistling. Practice it! As this sound does not exist in English, we represent it—quite arbitrarily—by "ew" in our pronunciations. *ST* is pronounced like "sht" in the beginning of a word or a syllable. Ex. *Bleistift—Fenster.* BLIGH-*shtift—*FEN-*st'r.*
Master the German "ch". It is important and has no equivalent in English. It is an aspirated, guttural and prolonged "k", represented in our phonetics by "kh". Practice saying, "Ach, du lieber Augustin!"

THINKING IN GERMAN

Answer the following questions aloud; then write the answers and check them in the key beginning on page 249.

1. Ist das das Buch?

2. Ist das der Bleistift?

3. Ist das der Tisch?

4. Was ist das?

5. Ist das die Schachtel?

6. Ist das das Fenster?

7. Ist das die Tür?

8. Was ist das?

9. Ist das der Schlüssel?

10. Ist das der Stuhl?

11. Ist das die Lampe?

12. Was ist das?

13. Ist das der Bleistift?

14. Ist das die Schachtel?

15. Ist das der Schlüssel?

16. Was ist das?

17. Ist das der Tisch?

18. Ist das der Stuhl?

19. Ist das die Tür?

20. Was ist das?

ÜBUNG NR. 2

Die Kleider
Dee KLIGH-*d'r*
Clothing

Was ist das?
Vahss ist dahs?
What is this?

das Hemd
dahs Hemt
the shirt

der Kragen
dehr KRAH-g'*n*
the collar

die Hose
dee HOH-*zeh*
the trousers

Das ist der Hut.
Dahs ist dehr Hoot.
It is the hat.

der Mantel
dehr MAHN-*t'l*
the overcoat

der Schuh
dehr shoo
the shoe

die Krawatte
*dee Krah-*VAH-*teh*
the tie

der Rock
dehr Rokk
the coat

der Handschuh
dehr HAHNT-*shoo*
the glove

das Kleid
dahs Klight
the dress

die Tasche
dee TAH-*sheh*
the pocket

die Handtasche
dee HAHNT-*tah-sheh*
the hand-bag

das Taschentuch
dahs TAH-*shen-tookh*
the handkerchief

4

Ist das der Rock? Nein, das ist nicht der Rock, das ist die Hose.
Ist dahs dehr Rokk? *Nine, dahs ist nikht dehr Rokk, dahs ist dee*
HOH-zeh.
Is this the coat? No, it is not the coat, it is the trousers.

NOTE: All nouns in German begin with a capital letter, whether at the beginning of a sentence or not.

Ist das der Hut oder der Kragen?   Das ist der Kragen.
Ist dahs dehr Hoot OH-d'r dehr KRAH-g'n?   *Dahs ist dehr KRAH-g'n.*
Is this the hat or the collar?   It is the collar.

Ist das die Krawatte oder das Taschentuch?
Ist dahs dee Krah-VAH-teh OH-d'r dahs TAH-shen-tookh?
Is this the tie or the handkerchief?

Das ist weder die Krawatte noch das Taschentuch, das ist der Handschuh.
Dahs ist VAY-d'r dee Krah-VAH-teh nokh dahs TAH-shen-tookh, dahs ist dehr
HAHNT-shoo.
This is neither the tie nor the handkerchief, it is the glove.

Ist das das Kleid oder der Mantel?
Ist dahs dahs Klight OH-d'r dehr MAHN-t'l?
Is this the dress or the overcoat?

Nein, das ist weder das Kleid noch der Mantel, das ist das Hemd.
Nine, dahs ist VAY-d'r dahs Klight nokh dehr MAHN-t'l, dahs ist dahs Hemt.
No, it is neither the dress nor the overcoat, it is the shirt.

6	7	8	9	10
sechs	sieben	acht	neun	zehn
zeks	*ZEE-b'n*	*ahkht*	*noin*	*tsain*

HINT on Pronunciation: The *S* when written before a vowel is pronounced like the English "z".

THINKING IN GERMAN
(Answers on page 250)

1. Was ist das?
2. Ist das der Schuh oder der Handschuh?
3. Ist das die Krawatte oder das Taschentuch?

4. Was ist das?
5. Ist das das Taschentuch oder der Handschuh?
6. Ist das der Bleistift?

7. Was ist das?
8. Ist das das Kleid?
9. Ist das der Mantel?
10. Ist das der Rock oder die Hose?
11. Ist das die Krawatte?
12. Ist das der Hut oder der Mantel?

ÜBUNG NR. 3

Die Farben
Dee FAHR-*b'n*
The colors

Schwarz	**weiss**	**rot**	**blau**
Shvahrtss	*vice*	*roht*	*blaou*
Black	white	red	blue
grün	**gelb**	**braun**	**grau**
grewn	*ggelp*	*braoun*	*graou*
green	yellow	brown	gray

Der Schuh ist schwarz.
Dehr Shoo ist shvahrtss.
The shoe is black.

Die Krawatte ist gelb.
*Dee Krah-*VAH-*teh ist ggelp.*
The tie is yellow.

Der Kragen ist weiss.
Dehr KRAH-*g'n ist vice.*
The collar is white.

Der Handschuh ist braun.
Dehr HAHNT-*shoo ist braoun.*
The glove is brown.

7

Der Rock ist grau.
Dehr Rokk ist graou.
The coat is gray.

Das Kleid ist grün.
Dahs Klight ist grewn.
The dress is green.

Die Hose ist blau.
Dee HOH-zeh ist blaou.
The trousers are blue.

Wie ist der Schuh?
Vee ist dehr Shoo?
How is the shoe?

Der Schuh ist schwarz.
Dehr Shoo ist shvahrtss.
The shoe is black.

Wie ist der Kragen?
Vee ist dehr KRAH-g'n?
How is the collar?

Der Kragen ist weiss.
Dehr KRAH-g'n ist vice.
The collar is white.

Das Buch ist grün und gelb.
Dahs Bookh ist grewn oont ggelp.
The book is green and yellow.

Die Krawatte ist blau und weiss.
Dee Krah-VAH-teh ist blaou oont vice.
The tie is blue and white.

Wie ist *der* Bleistift?
Vee ist dehr BLIGH-shtift?
How is the pencil?

Er **ist schwarz.**
Air ist shvahrtss.
It is black.

Wie ist *die* Feder?
Vee ist dee FAY-d'r?
How is the pen?

Sie **ist schwarz.**
Zee ist shvahrtss.
It is black.

Wie ist *das* Buch?
Vee ist dahs Bookh?
How is the book?

Es **ist schwarz.**
Ess ist shvahrtss.
It is black.

NOTE: When the Germans say: *Wie ist das Buch?*—"How is the book?"—they are not asking about its health but for a description of its color, dimensions, etc.

Wie ist der Tisch,
Vee ist dehr Tish,
How is the table,

der Stuhl,
dehr Shtool,
the chair,

die Wand,
dee Vahnt,
the wall,

das Kleid?
dahs Klight?
the dress?

Ist der Bleistift rot?
Ist dehr BLIGH-shtift roht?
Is the pencil red?

Ja, er ist rot.
Yah, air ist roht.
Yes, it is red.

Ist die Feder braun?
Ist dee FAY-d'r braoun?
Is the pen brown?

Nein, sie ist nicht braun.
Nine, zee ist nikht braoun.
No, it is not brown.

Ist das Buch grün oder blau?
Ist dahs Bookh grewn OH-d'r blaou?
Is the book green or blue?

Es ist blau.
Ess ist blaou.
It is blue.

REMEMBER: The pronouns for inanimate objects vary according to their genders. The table is not "it" but "he"— *er—*, and speaking of a door you must use "she" *—sie.*

Der Bleistift ist blau.	**Die Feder ist blau.**	**Das Buch ist blau.**
Dehr BLIGH-*shtift ist blaou.*	*Dee* FAY-*d'r ist blaou.*	*Dahs Bookh ist blaou.*
The pencil is blue.	The pen is blue.	The book is blue.

Das ist der rote Bleistift.
Dahs ist dehr ROH-*teh* BLIGH-*shtift.*
This is the red pencil.

Das ist der grüne Bleistift.
Dahs ist dehr GREW-*neh* BLIGH-*shtift.*
This is the green pencil.

Das ist die rote Feder.
Dahs ist dee ROH-*teh* FAY-*d'r.*
This is the red pen.

Das ist die grüne Feder.
Dahs ist dee GREW-*neh* FAY-*d'r.*
This is the green pen.

Das ist das rote Buch.
Dahs ist dahs ROH-*teh Bookh.*
This is the red book.

Das ist das grüne Buch.
Dahs ist dahs GREW-*neh Bookh.*
This is the green book.

REMEMBER: If the definite article (*der, die, das*) and an adjective precede the noun as in "The green door"*—Die grüne Tür,* the adjective takes a final *e.*

Dieser Bleistift ist rot,
DEEZ'*r* BLIGH-*shtift ist roht,*
This pencil is red,

dieser ist schwarz.
DEEZ'*r ist shvahrtss.*
this one is black.

Diese Krawatte ist blau,
DEE-*zeh Krah-*VAH-*teh ist blaou,*
This tie is blue,

diese ist grün.
DEE-*zeh ist grewn.*
this one is green.

Dieses Papier ist weiss,
DEEZ'*s Pah-*PEER *ist vice,*
This paper is white,

dieses ist gelb.
DEEZ'*s ist ggelp.*
this one is yellow.

Das ist der rote Bleistift,
Dahs ist dehr ROH-*teh* BLIGH-*shtift,*
This is the red pencil,

das ist der schwarze.
dahs ist dehr SHVAHR-*tseh.*
this is the black one.

Das ist die blaue Krawatte,
Dahs ist dee BLAOU-*eh Krah-*VAH-*teh,*
This is the blue tie,

das ist die grüne.
dahs ist dee GREW-*neh.*
this is the green one.

Das ist das weisse Papier,
Dahs ist dahs VIGH-*sseh Pah*-PEER,
This is the white paper,

da; ist das gelbe.
dahs ist dahs GGEL-*beh.*
this is the yellow one.

IMPORTANT NOTE: A predicate adjective (used after the verb "to be") is invariable in form, regardless of the gender of the subject. Ex. "The thick book is green."— *Das dicke Buch ist grün.*

Welcher Bleistift ist das?
VEL-*kher* BLIGH-*shtift ist dahs?*
Which pencil is this?

Das ist der rote Bleistift.
Dahs ist dehr ROH-*teh* BLIGH-*shtift.*
This is the red pencil.

Wie ist dieser Bleistift?
Vee ist DEEZ'*r* LLIGH-*shtift?*
How is this pencil?

Er ist rot.
Air ist roht.
It is red.

Welches Buch ist das?
VEL-*khes Bookh ist dahs?*
Which book is this?

Wie ist das Buch?
Vee ist dahs Bookh?
How is the book?

11	12	13	14	15
elf	**zwölf**	**dreizehn**	**vierzehn**	**fünfzehn**
elf	*tsvuhlf*	DRIGH-*tsain*	FEER-*tsain*	FEWNF-*tsain*

THINKING IN GERMAN

(Answers on page 250)

1. Ist die Feder blau?
2. Wie ist die Feder?
3. Ist die Feder rot?
4. Ist die Feder weiss oder schwarz?

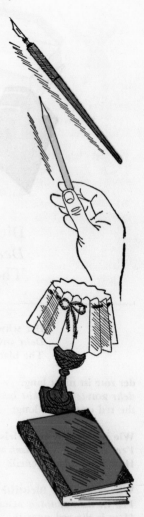

5. Was ist das?
6. Ist das der Bleistift?
7. Ist der Bleistift rot?
8. Ist er schwarz?
9. Wie ist er?

10. Ist das der Tisch?
11. Ist das die Tür?
12. Was ist das?
13. Wie ist die Lampe?
14. Ist sie rot?
15. Ist sie grau?
16. Ist sie blau?

17. Welches Buch ist das?
18. Ist das das rote Buch?
19. Ist das das gelbe Buch?
20. Wie ist es?
21. Ist dieses Buch schwarz?

ÜBUNG NR. 4

Die Dimensionen
*Dee Dee-mens-*YOH-*nen*
The dimensions

Der schwarze Bleistift ist lang,
Dehr SHVAHR-*tseh* BLIGH-*shtift ist lahnk,*
The black pencil is long,

der rote ist nicht lang;	**er ist kurz.**
dehr ROH-*teh ist nikht lahnk;*	*air ist koorts.*
the red one is not long;	it is short.
Wie ist der schwarze Bleistift?	**Er ist lang.**
Vee ist dehr SHVAHR-*tseh* BLIGH-*shtift?*	*Air ist lahnk.*
How is the black pencil?	It is long.
Wie ist der rote Bleistift?	**Er ist kurz.**
Vee ist dehr ROH-*teh* BLIGH-*shtift?*	*Air ist koorts.*
How is the red pencil?	It is short.
Die gelbe Schachtel ist lang.	**Die schwarze Schachtel ist kurz.**
Dee GGEL-*beh* SHAKH-*t'l ist lahnk.*	*Dee* SHVAHR-*tseh* SHAKH-*t'l ist koorts.*
The yellow box is long.	The black box is short.

12

Ist das gelbe Kleid kurz?
Ist dahs GGEL-*beh Klight koorts?*
Is the yellow dress short?

Ist das schwarze Kleid lang?
Ist dahs SHVAHR-*tseh Klight lahnk?*
Is the black dress long?

Ist das gelbe Kleid kurz oder lang?
Ist dahs GGEL-*beh Klight koorts* OH-*d'r lahnk?*
Is the yellow dress short or long?

Welcher Bleistift ist lang, der schwarze oder der rote?
VEL-*kher* BLIGH-*shtift ist lahnk, dehr* SHVAHR-*tseh* OH-*d'r dehr* ROH-*teh?*
Which pencil is long, the black one or the red one?

Der schwarze ist lang.
Dehr SHVAHR-*tseh ist lahnk.*
The black one is long.

Das braune Buch ist breit;
Dahs BRAOU-*neh Bookh ist bright;*
The brown book is wide;

das schwarze ist nicht breit;
dahs SHVAHR-*tseh ist nikht bright;*
the black one is not wide;

es ist schmal.
ess ist shmahl.
it is narrow.

Wie ist das braune Buch?
Vee ist dahs BRAOU-*neh Bookh?*
How is the brown book?

Ist es breit oder schmal?
Ist ess bright OH-*d'r shmahl?*
Is it wide or narrow?

Welches ist das schmale Buch?
VEL-*khes ist dahs* SHMAH-*leh Bookh?*
Which one is the narrow book?

Das Fenster ist breit.
Dahs FEN-*st'r ist bright.*
The window is wide.

Die Tür ist schmal.
Dee Tewr ist shmahl.
The door is narrow.

Ist die gelbe Schachtel schmal oder breit?
Ist dee GGEL-*beh* SHAHKH-*t'l shmahl* OH-*d'r bright?*
Is the yellow box narrow or wide?

Ist das Fenster schmal?
Ist dahs FEN-*st'r shmahl?*
Is the window narrow?

Wie ist das rote Buch?
Vee ist dahs ROH-*teh Bookh?*
How is the red book?

Wie ist das gelbe Kleid?
Vee ist dahs GGEL-*beh Klight?*
How is the yellow dress?

Welcher Bleistift ist kurz und schmal?
VEL-*kher* BLIGH-*shtift ist koorts oont shmahl?*
Which pencil is short and narrow?

Das braune Buch ist lang und breit,
Dahs BRAOU-*neh Bookh ist lahnk oont bright,*
The brown book is long and wide,

es ist gross.
ess ist grohss.
it is big.

Das rote Buch ist kurz und schmal,
Dahs ROH-*teh Bookh ist koorts oont shmahl,*
The red book is short and narrow,

es ist klein.
ess ist kline.
it is small.

Ist das gelbe Kleid gross?
Ist dahs GGEL-*beh Klight grohss?*
Is the yellow dress big?

Ist die schwarze Schachtel klein?
Ist dee SHVAHR-*tseh* SHAKH-*t'l kline?*
Is the black box small?

Ist das Fenster gross oder klein?
Ist dahs FEN-*st'r grohss* OH-*d'r kline?*
Is the window big or small?

Ist der Tisch gross?
Ist dehr Tish grohss?
Is the table big?

Welches Kleid ist gelb, das kleine oder das grosse?
VEL-*khes Klight ist ggelp, dahs* KLIGH-*neh* OH-*d'r dahs* GROH-*sseh?*
Which dress is yellow, the small one or the large one?

REMEMBER: You have already seen that the adjective preceded by *DER, DIE* or *DAS* takes a final *e* before the nouns. This is also true if the noun is left out. Ex: "The black car."—*Das schwarze Auto.* "The black *one*" would be *Das schwarze.*

Berlin ist gross.
*Behr-*LEEN *ist grohss.*
Berlin is big.

Potsdam ist klein.
POTS-*dahm ist kline.*
Potsdam is small.

Ist Wien klein?
Ist Veen kline?
Is Vienna small?

Nein, es ist nicht klein, es ist gross.
Nine, ess ist nikht kline, ess ist grohss.
No, it is not small, it is big.

Wie ist Salzburg?
Vee ist ZAHLTS-*boork?*
How is Salzburg?

Salzburg ist nicht gross, es ist klein.
ZAHLTS-*boork ist nikht grohss, ess ist kline.*
Salzburg is not big, it is small.

Ist Deutschland gross?
Ist DOITSH-*lahnt grohss?*
Is Germany big?

Ist Cuba klein?
Ist KOO-*bah kline?*
Is Cuba small?

Ist Amerika gross oder klein?
*Ist Ah-*MEH-*ree-kah grohss* OH-*d'r kline?*
Is America large or small?

NOTE: Names of cities and countries are almost always neuter.

16	17	18	19	20
sechzehn	siebzehn	achtzehn	neunzehn	zwanzig
SEKH-*tsain*	ZEEP-*tsain*	AKHT-*tsain*	NOIN-*tsain*	TSVAHN-*tsikh*

THINKING IN GERMAN

(Answers on page 250)

1. Ist das rote Buch lang?

2. Ist es breit?

3. Ist es gross?

4. Ist das grüne Buch kurz?

5. Ist es schmal?

6. Ist es klein?

7. Wie ist das grosse Buch?

8. Welches ist das kleine Buch?

9. Wie ist das lange Kleid?

10. Welches Kleid ist kurz?

11. Wie ist das kurze Kleid?

12. Ist es schwarz oder blau?

13. Ist das breite Fenster blau oder rot?

14. Welches Fenster ist schmal?

15. Ist das blaue Fenster klein?

16. Wie ist das kleine Fenster, grün oder rot?

17. Ist das grüne Buch breit?

18. Welches Buch ist schmal?

19. Ist das grosse Fenster blau oder schwarz?

20. Ist das gelbe Kleid klein und kurz?

21. Wie ist das grüne Buch, kurz oder lang?

22. Welches ist das breite Fenster, das rote oder das blaue?

23. Ist das rote Buch kurz?

ÜBUNG NR. 5

Wer ist das?
Vair ist dahs?
Who is that?

Ein Herr	eine Dame	ein Fräulein
Ine Herr	EYE-*neh* DAH-*meh*	*ine* FROY-*line*
A gentleman	a lady	a young lady

Ist das ein Herr?	Ist das eine Dame?	Ist das ein Fräulein?
Ist dahs ine Herr?	*Ist dahs* EYE-*neh* DAH-*meh?*	*Ist dahs ine* FROY-*line?*
Is this a gentleman?	Is this a lady?	Is this a young lady?

NOTE to Student: *Ein* (masculine or neuter), *eine* (feminine) mean "a" or "one". It may startle you to know that girls and young ladies are *grammatically* neuter in German. Hence: *Das Mädchen* "the girl", *das Fräulein* "the young lady". This is because all diminutives (words ending in -*chen* and -*lein*) are neuter. *Mädchen*—literally "little maid", *Fräulein*—literally "little woman".

Das ist Herr Berlitz.	Das ist Frau Berlitz.
Dahs ist Herr BEHR-*lits.*	*Dahs ist Fraou* BEHR-*lits.*
This is Mr. Berlitz.	This is Mrs. Berlitz.

16

Das ist Fräulein Berlitz.
Dahs ist FROY-*line* BEHR-*lits.*
This is Miss Berlitz.

Ist das Herr Berlitz?
Ist dahs Herr BEHR-*lits?*
Is this Mr. Berlitz?

Ja, das ist Herr Berlitz.
Yah, dahs ist Herr BEHR-*lits.*
Yes, this is Mr. Berlitz.

Nein, das ist nicht Herr Berlitz.
Nine, dahs ist nikht Herr BEHR-*lits.*
No, this is not Mr. Berlitz.

Ist das Frau Berlitz?
Ist dahs Fraou BEHR-*lits?*
Is this Mrs. Berlitz?

Nein, das ist nicht Frau Berlitz,
Nine, dahs ist nikht Fraou BEHR-*lits,*
No, this is not Mrs. Berlitz,

das ist Frau Truman.   **Sie sind der Schüler,**   **ich bin der Lehrer.**
dahs ist Fraou TROO-*mahn.*   *Zee zint dehr* SHEW-*l'r,*   *ikh bin dehr* LAY-*r'r.*
this is Mrs. Truman.   You are the pupil,   I am the teacher.

WATCH OUT for *Sie—sie—sie!*—"you"—"she"—"they". The same word has different meanings. *Sie* with a capital S means "you" in the formal address, sie means "she" when used in the singular and *sie* means "they" referring to the 3rd. person of the plural. So you can tell by the size of the *s* and by the verb used in connection with the pronoun which *sie* is meant. However, at the beginning of a sentence, the *s* is always capitalized. So you just have to conclude from the sense of the sentence whether it means "you," "she" or "they."

Herr Schmidt ist Deutscher.
Herr Shmitt ist DOIT-*sher.*
Mr. Schmidt is German.

Herr Jones ist Amerikaner.
*Herr Jones ist Ah-meh-ree-*KAH-*n'r.*
Mr. Jones is American.

Herr Dupont ist Franzose.
*Herr Dew-*POHN *ist Fran-*TSOH-*zeh.*
Mr. Dupont is French.

Herr Weidinger ist Schweizer.
Herr VY-*din-g'r ist* SHVIGH-*tser.*
Mr. Weidinger is Swiss.

Sind Sie Deutscher?
Zint Zee DOIT-*sher?*
Are you German?

Bin ich Amerikaner?
*Bin ikh Ah-meh-ree-*KAH-*n'r?*
Am I American?

Sie sind Amerikanerin.
*Zee zint Ah-meh-ree-*KAH-*neh-rin.*
You are American.

Sind Sie Italienerin?
*Zint Zee Ee-tahl-*YAY-*neh-rin?*
Are you Italian?

Herr Cripps ist Engländer.
Herr Kripps ist ENNG-*len-der.*
Mr. Cripps is English.

Don Quixote ist Spanier.
*Dohn Kee-*SHOT *ist* SHPAHN-*yer.*
Don Quixote is Spanish.

NOTE to Student: The ending *—er* indicates the male **sex** like in *Lehrer, Amerikaner, Schüler.* The ending *—in* indicates the female like *Lehrerin, Amerikanerin, Schülerin.*

Wer bin ich?
Vair bin ikh?
Who am I?

Sie sind der Lehrer.
Zee zint dehr LAY-*r'r.*
You are the teacher.

Wer sind Sie?
Vair zint zee?
Who are you?

Ich bin die Schülerin.
Ikh bin dee SHEW-*leh-rin.*
I am the pupil.

Bin ich Herr Einstein?
Bin ikh Herr INE-*shtine?*
Am I Mr. Einstein?

Nein, Sie sind nicht Herr Einstein.
Nine, Zee zint nikht Herr INE-*shtine.*
No, you are not Mr. Einstein.

Sind Sie Frau Dietrich?
Zint Zee Fraou DEET-*rikh?*
Are you Mrs. Dietrich?

Nein, ich bin nicht Frau Dietrich.
Nine, ikh bin nikht Fraou DEET-*rikh.*
No, I am not Mrs. Dietrich.

Ist das Fräulein Garbo?
Ist dahs FROY-*line* GAR-*boh?*
Is this Miss Garbo?

Nein, das ist nicht Fräulein Garbo.
Nine, dahs ist nikht FROY-*line* GAR-*boh.*
No, this is not Miss Garbo.

Wer ist diese Dame?
Vair ist DEE-*zeh* DAH-*meh?*
Who is this lady?

Das ist Frau Diemand.
Dahs ist Fraou DEE-*mahnt.*
That is Mrs. Diemand.

Wer ist dieses Fräulein?
Vair ist DEEZ's FROY-*line?*
Who is this young lady?

Das ist Fräulein Engel.
Dahs ist FROY-*line* ENG'l.
This is Miss Engel.

Wie ist dieser Hut?
Vee ist DEEZ'r *Hoot?*
How is this hat?

Er ist schwarz.
Air ist shvahrtss.
It is black.

Wie ist diese Krawatte?
Vee ist DEE-*zeh Krah-*VAH-*teh?*
How is this tie?

Sie ist braun.
Zee ist braoun.
It is brown.

Wie ist dieses Kleid?
Vee ist DEEZ's *Klight?*
How is this dress?

Es ist blau.
Ess ist blaou.
It is blue.

REMEMBER: "This"—*Dieser, diese, dieses,* varies its endings according to the gender of the noun following it. Ex. *Dieser Herr, diese Frau, dieses Fräulein.*

21	22	23
einundzwanzig	**zweiundzwanzig**	**dreiundzwanzig**
INE-*oont-tsvahn-tsikh*	TSVIGH-*oont-tsvahn-tsikh*	DRIGH-*oont-tsvahn-tsikh*

24	25
vierundzwanzig	**fünfundzwanzig**
FEER-*oont-tsvahn-tsikh*	FEWNF-*oont-tsvahn-tsikh*

THINKING IN GERMAN

(Answers on page 251)

1. Wer sind Sie?
2. Sind Sie Amerikaner?—Sind Sie Amerikanerin?
3. Sind Sie der Lehrer?
4. Sind Sie Deutscher?—Sind Sie Deutsche?
5. Ich bin Herr Juhn. Ich bin der Lehrer. Wer bin ich?
6. Bin ich der Lehrer?
7. Bin ich Amerikaner?
8. Bin ich Spanier?
9. Ist Marlene Dietrich Deutsche oder Amerikanerin?
10. Ist Sonja Henie Italienerin?
11. Ist Clark Gable Deutscher?
12. Sind Sie Engländer?—Sind Sie Engländerin?
13. Wer ist Franzose, Cary Grant oder Maurice Chevalier?
14. Ist Frau Chiang Kai-Shek Chinesin oder Japanerin?
15. Ist Cripps Amerikaner?
16. Ist Carmen Miranda Deutsche?
17. Ist dieser Hut klein oder gross?
18. Ist dieser Kragen breit oder schmal?
19. Sind Sie der Schüler oder der Lehrer?—die Schülerin oder die Lehrerin?

ÜBUNG NR. 6

Wo ist es?
Voh ist ess?
Where is it?

Das Buch ist *auf* dem Tisch.
Dahs Bookh ist aouf daim Tish.
The book is on the table.

Wo ist der Hut?
Voh ist dehr Hoot?
Where is the hat?

Wo ist Herr Schmidt?
Voh ist Herr Shmitt?
Where is Mr. Schmidt?

Wo ist die Feder?
Voh ist dee FAY-d'r?
Where is the pen?

Wo ist das Papier?
Voh ist dahs Pah-PEER?
Where is the paper?

Der Hut ist auf dem Stuhl.
Dehr Hoot ist aouf daim Shtool.
The hat is on the chair.

Er ist auf dem Stuhl.
Air ist aouf daim Shtool.
It is on the chair.

Er ist an dem Fenster.
Air ist ahn daim FEN-st'r.
He is at the window.

Sie ist auf dem Papier.
Zee ist aouf daim Pah-PEER.
It is on the paper.

Es ist in dem Buch.
Ess ist in daim Bookh.
It is in the book.

20

Wo ist das Taschentuch?
Voh ist dahs TAH-*shen-tookh?*
Where is the handkerchief?

Es ist in der Tasche.
Ess ist in dehr TAH-*sheh.*
It is in the pocket.

Wo ist die Schachtel?
Voh ist dee SHAKH-*t'l?*
Where is the box?

Sie ist *unter* dem Tisch.
Zee ist OON-*t'r daim Tish.*
It is under the table.

Das Fenster ist *vor* mir.
Dahs FEN-*st'r ist fohr meer.*
The window is in front of me.

Die Tür ist *hinter* mir.
Dee Tewr ist HINT'r *meer.*
The door is behind me.

Der Tisch ist vor Ihnen.
Dehr Tish ist fohr EE-*nen.*
The table is before you.

Die Wand ist hinter Ihnen.
Dee Vahnt ist HINT'r *EE-nen.*
The wall is behind you.

 IMPORTANT NOTE: With the prepositions "on", "in", "under", "before", "at", "behind", "beside", etc.; *auf, in, unter, vor, an, hinter, neben,* etc., we encounter the dative case. Don't let this frighten you as all it means is that the form of the article *der, die, das,* changes into *dem, der, dem,* when it follows one of these prepositions in the constructions illustrated above. Ex. *Der Tisch — unter dem Tisch. Die Tür — hinter der Tür. Das Buch — in dem Buch.*

Ist der Tisch vor Ihnen?
Ist dehr Tish fohr EE-*nen?*
Is the table before you?

Ja, der Tisch ist vor mir.
Yah, dehr Tish ist fohr meer.
Yes, the table is before me.

Ist der Stuhl vor mir?
Ist dehr Shtool fohr meer?
Is the chair before me?

Nein, der Stuhl ist nicht vor Ihnen.
Nine, dehr Shtool ist nikht fohr EE-*nen.*
No, the chair is not before you.

Sind Sie vor mir?
Zint Zee fohr meer?
Are you before me?

Ja, ich bin vor Ihnen.
Yah, ikh bin fohr EE-*nen.*
Yes, I am before you.

Was ist hinter mir?
Vahss ist HINT'r *meer?*
What is behind me?

Das Fenster ist hinter Ihnen.
Dahs FEN-*st'r ist* HINT'r *EE-nen.*
The window is behind you.

Was ist hinter Ihnen?
Vahss ist HINT'r *EE-nen?*
What is behind you?

Die Wand ist hinter mir.
Dee Vahnt ist HINT'r *meer.*
The wall is behind me.

Wo ist das Buch?
Voh ist dahs Bookh?
Where is the book?

Es ist vor mir.
Ess ist fohr meer.
It is before me.

Wo ist die Schachtel?
Voh ist dee SHAKH-*t'l?*
Where is the box?

Sie ist hinter Ihnen.
Zee ist HINT'r *EE-nen.*
It is behind you.

REMEMBER: The dative forms of *ich* and *Sie* are *mir* and *Ihnen*. Ex: "Who is behind you?"—*Wer ist hinter Ihnen?*; "You are behind me."—*Sie sind hinter mir.*

Wo bin ich?	**Sie sind hinter dem Tisch.**
Voh bin ikh?	*Zee zint* HINT'*r daim Tish.*
Where am I?	You are behind the table.
Wer bin ich?	**Sie sind der Lehrer.**
Vair bin ikh?	*Zee zint dehr* LAY-*r'r.*
Who am I?	You are the teacher.

Wo sind Sie?	**Ich bin an der Tür.**	**Ist der Stuhl vor Ihnen?**
Voh zint Zee?	*Ikh bin ahn dehr Tewr.*	*Ist dehr Shtool fohr* EE-*nen?*
Where are you?	I am at the door.	Is the chair before you?

Nein, der Stuhl ist nicht vor mir, er ist hinter mir.
Nine, dehr Shtool ist nikht fohr meer, air ist HINT'*r meer.*
No, the chair is not before me, it is behind me.

Der schwarze Hut ist vor Ihnen auf dem Stuhl.
Dehr SHVAHR-*tseh Hoot ist fohr* EE-*nen aouf daim Shtool.*
The black hat is before you on the chair.

Ist er hinter Ihnen?
Ist air HINT'*r* EE-*nen?*
Is it behind you?

Berlin ist in Deutschland.	**New York ist in Amerika.**
*Behr-*LEEN *ist in* DOITSH-*lahnt.*	*New York ist in Ah-*MEH-*ree-kah.*
Berlin is in Germany.	New York is in America.
London ist in England.	**Paris ist in Frankreich.**
London ist in ENNG-*lahnt.*	*Pah-*REES *ist in* FRAHNK-*righkh.*
London is in England.	Paris is in France.
Ist Berlin in Frankreich?	**Nein, es ist in Deutschland.**
*Ist Behr-*LEEN *in* FRAHNK-*righkh?*	*Nine, ess ist in* DOITSH-*lahnt.*
Is Berlin in France?	No, it is in Germany.

26	27	28
sechsundzwanzig	siebenundzwanzig	achtundzwanzig
ZEKS-*oont-tsvahn-tsikh*	ZEEB'*n-oont-tsvahn-tsikh*	AHKHT-*oont-tsvahn-tsikh*

29	30
neunundzwanzig	dreissig
NOIN-*oont-tsvahn-tsikh*	DRIGH-*ssikh*

THINKING IN GERMAN

(Answers on page 251)

 1. Wo ist das Buch?
 2. Ist es auf dem Tisch?
 3. Ist es unter dem Stuhl?
 4. Wo ist die Feder?
 5. Ist sie auf dem Buch?
 6. Wo ist das Fenster?
 7. Wo ist der Lehrer?
 8. Ist der Professor unter dem Tisch?
 9. Ist er vor dem Tisch?
10. Was ist hinter Ihnen?
11. Ist die Tür in der Wand?
12. Ist das Papier in dem Buch?
13. Wo ist die Schachtel?
14. Was ist in der Schachtel?
15. Ist der Schlüssel auf dem Tisch?
16. Ist dieses Buch gross oder klein?
17. Ist der Hut auf dem Stuhl gross oder klein?
18. Ist Berlin in Deutschland?
19. Wo ist New York?
20. Wo sind Sie?

ÜBUNG NR. 7

Was tut der Lehrer?
Vahss toot dehr LAY-r'r?
What is the teacher doing?

Ist das der Lehrer?
Ist dahs dehr LAY-r'r?
Is this the teacher?

Ja, das ist der Lehrer.
Yah, dahs ist der LAY-r'r.
Yes, this is the teacher.

Was tut der Lehrer?
Vahss toot dehr LAY-r'r?
What is the teacher doing?

Er steht hinter dem Tisch.
Air shtait HINT'r *daim Tish.*
He is standing behind the table.

Der Lehrer geht.
Dehr LAY-r'r *gait.*
The teacher is going.

Fräulein Roth geht nicht.
FROY-*line Roht gait nikht.*
Miss Roth is not going.

Das schwarze Buch liegt,
Dahs SHVAHR-*tseh Bookh leegt,*
The black book is lying (down),

das rote steht.
dahs ROH-*teh shtait.*
the red one is standing.

24

Der Lehrer nimmt das rote Buch.
Dehr LAY-*r'r nimt dahs* ROH-*teh Bookh.*
The teacher takes the red book.

Was nimmt er?
Vahss nimt air?
What does he take?

Nehmen Sie das Buch?
NAY-*men Zee dahs Bookh?*
Do you take the book?

Der Bleistift liegt hier, die Feder dort.
Dehr BLIGH-*shtift leegt here, dee* FAY-*d'r dohrt.*
The pencil is lying here, the pen there.

Wo sitzen Sie?
Voh ZITS'*n Zee?*
Where are you sitting?

Sie stehen dort,
Zee SHTAY'*n dohrt,*
You are standing there,

Wer steht dort?
Vair shtait dohrt?
Who is standing there?

Der Lehrer nimmt das Buch.
Dehr LAY-*r'r nimt dahs Bookh.*
The teacher takes the book.

Der Schüler stellt das Buch hin.
Dehr SHEW-*l'r shtellt dahs Bookh hin.*
The pupil stands the book up.

Der Lehrer öffnet das Buch.
Dehr LAY-*r'r* UHFF-*net dahs Bookh.*
The teacher opens the book.

Was tut der Lehrer?
Vahss toot dehr LAY-*r'r?*
What is the teacher doing?

Öffnet er das Buch oder schliesst er es?
UHFF-*net air dahs Bookh* OH-*d'r shleesst air ess?*
Does he open the book or does he close it?

Er schliesst es.
Air shleesst ess.
He closes it.

Sitzt er oder steht er?
Zitst air OH-*d'r shtait air?*
Is he sitting or standing?

Steht die Lampe oder liegt sie?
Shtait dee LAHM-*peh* OH-*d'r leegt zee?*
Is the lamp standing or lying (down)?

Nein, ich nehme nicht das Buch.
Nine, ikh NAY-*meh nikht dahs Bookh.*
No, I do not take the book.

Steht die Lampe hier?
Shtait dee LAHM-*peh here?*
Is the lamp standing here?

Bin ich hier oder dort?
Bin ikh here OH-*d'r dohrt?*
Am I here or there?

ich sitze hier.
ikh ZIT-*seh here.*
I am sitting here.

Stehe ich dort?
SHTAY-*heh ikh dohrt?*
Am I standing there?

Er legt das Buch hin.
Air laigt dahs Bookh hin.
He puts the book down.

Er nimmt das Papier.
*Air nimt dahs Pah-*PEER.
He takes the paper.

Er schliesst es.
Air shleesst ess.
He closes it.

Sie schliessen das Buch.
Zee SHLEE-*ss'n dahs Bookh*
You close the book.

Öffnen Sie die Tür?
UHFF-nen Zee dee Tewr?
Do you open the door?

Nein, ich öffne sie nicht.
Nine, ikh UHFF-neh zee nikht.
No, I do not open it.

Bitte, schliessen Sie die Tür!
BIT-teh, SHLEE-ss'n Zee dee Tewr!
Please, close the door!

Was tun Sie?
Vahss toon Zee?
What are you doing?

Ich schliesse die Tür.
Ikh SHLEE-sseh dee Tewr.
I close the door.

Legen Sie das Papier hin!
LAY-g'n Zee dahs Pah-PEER hin!
Put the paper down!

Nehmen Sie die Feder!
NAY-men Zee dee FAY-d'r!
Take the pen!

Was tun Sie?
Vahss toon Zee?
What are you doing?

Ich lege das Papier hin und nehme die Feder.
Ikh LAY-ggeh dahs Pah-PEER hin oont NAY-meh dee FAY-d'r.
I put down the paper and take the pen.

Schliesse ich die Tür?
SHLEE-sseh ikh dee Tewr?
Do I close the door?

Nein, Sie schliessen sie nicht.
Nine, Zee SHLEE-ss'n zee nikht.
No, you do not close it.

Öffnen Sie bitte das Fenster!
UHFF-nen Zee BIT-teh dahs FEN-st'r!
Please open the window!

Was tun Sie?
Vahss toon Zee?
What are you doing?

Ich öffne das Fenster.
Ikh UHFF-neh dahs FEN-st'r.
I open the window.

Nehmen Sie das Buch und gehen Sie!
NAY-m'n Zee dahs Bookh oont GAY'n Zee!
Take the book and go!

Ich nehme das Buch und gehe.
Ikh NAY-meh dahs Bookh oont GAY-heh.
I take the book and go.

REMEMBER: The imperative form of the verb is used when you tell someone to do something, as in the next to last sentence. It is convenient to remember that the imperative form is the same as the present form with *Sie* except that the *Sie* comes after the verb. Ex: "You go"—*Sie gehen.*

"Go!"—*Gehen Sie!*

Das ist der Bleistift.
Dahs ist dehr BLIGH-*shtift.*
This is the pencil.

Nehmen Sie den Bleistift!
NAY-*m'n Zee dain* BLIGH-*shtift!*
Take the pencil!

Das ist der Hut.
Dahs ist dehr Hoot.
This is the hat.

Was tun Sie?
Vahss toon Zee?
What are you doing?

Was tue ich?
Vahss TOO-*eh ikh?*
What am I doing?

Steht der Schuh oder liegt er?
Shtait dehr Shoo OH-*d'r leegt air?*
Is the shoe standing or lying?

Was tun Sie?
Vahss toon Zee?
What are you doing?

Nehme ich den Hut?
NAY-*meh ikh dain Hoot?*
Do I take the hat?

Nehmen Sie den Hut?
NAY-*m'n Zee dain Hoot?*
Do you take the hat?

Schliessen Sie die Tür?
SHLEE-*ss'n Zee dee Tewr?*
Do you close the door?

Schliesse ich die Tür?
SHLEE-*sseh ikh dee Tewr?*
Do I close the door?

Ich nehme den Bleistift.
Ikh NAY-*meh dain* BLIGH-*shtift.*
I take the pencil.

Legen Sie den Bleistift hin!
LAY-*g'n Zee dain* BLIGH-*shtift hin!*
Put the pencil down!

Nehmen Sie den Hut!
NAY-*m'n Zee dain Hoot!*
Take the hat!

Sie nehmen den Hut.
Zee NAY-*m'n dain Hoot.*
You take the hat.

Ich lege den Mantel hin.
Ikh LAY-*ggeh dain* MAHN-*t'l hin.*
I put the coat down.

Sie legen den Mantel hin.
Zee LAY-*g'n dain* MAHN-*t'l hin.*
You put the coat down.

Er liegt dort.
Air leegt dohrt.
It is lying there.

Stellen Sie den Schuh hin!
SHTEL-*l'n Zee dain Shoo hin!*
Put the shoe down!

Ich stelle ihn hin.
Ikh SHTEL-*leh een hin.*
I put it down.

Ja, Sie nehmen ihn.
Yah, Zee NAY-*m'n een.*
Yes, you take it.

Nein, ich nehme ihn nicht.
Nine, ikh NAY-*meh een nikht.*
No, I do not take it.

Ja, ich schliesse sie.
Yah, ikh SHLEE-*sseh zee.*
Yes, I close it.

Nein, Sie schliessen sie nicht.
Nine, Zee SHLEE-*ss'n zee nikht.*
No, you do not close it.

Öffnen Sie das Fenster?
UHFF-*n'n Zee dahs* FEN-*st'r?*
Do you open the window?

Ja, ich öffne es.
Yah, ikh UHFF-*neh ess.*
Yes, I open it.

Öffne ich das Fenster?
UHFF-*neh ikh dahs* FEN-*st'r?*
Do I open the window?

Nein, Sie öffnen es nicht.
Nine, Zee UHFF-*n'n ess nikht.*
No, you do not open it.

IMPORTANT NOTE: Once again we encounter case endings. This time it is the *accusative*. The only change to remember is that "the" (masculine) *der* becomes *den* when it is a direct object, *er* becomes *ihn*, while *die* and *das, sie* and *es* remain unchanged.

31	32	33
einunddreissig	**zweiunddreissig**	**dreiunddreissig**
INE-*oon-drigh-ssikh*	TSVIGH-*oont-drigh-ssikh*	DRIGH-*oont-drigh-ssikh*

34	35
vierunddreissig	**fünfunddreissig**
FEER-*oont-drigh-ssikh*	FEWNF-*oont-drigh-ssikh*

THINKING IN GERMAN
(Answers on page 252)

1. Was tut der Lehrer?
2. Nimmt der Lehrer das Buch?
3. Legt er das Buch hin?
4. Nimmt er die Schachtel?
5. Sitzt der Lehrer?

6. Schliesst der Lehrer das Fenster?
7. Was tut er?
8. Öffnet der Lehrer die Tür
   oder das Fenster?
9. Schliessen Sie die Tür?
10. Was tue ich?

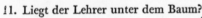

11. Liegt der Lehrer unter dem Baum?
12. Steht er oder sitzt er?
13. Sitzt er auf dem Baum?
14. Wer liegt unter dem Baum?
15. Wo sitzen Sie?
16. Ist der Baum gross?

ÜBUNG NR. 8

Ich zähle
Ikh TSAY-*leh*
I count

1	6	11	16
eins	**sechs**	**elf**	**sechzehn**
eye'nss	*zeks*	*elf*	ZEKH-*tsain*
2	7	12	17
zwei	**sieben**	**zwölf**	**siebzehn**
tsvigh	ZEE-*b'n*	*tsvuhlf*	ZEEP-*tsain*
3	8	13	18
drei	**acht**	**dreizehn**	**achtzehn**
drigh	*ahkht*	DRIGH-*tsain*	AHKHT-*tsain*
4	9	14	19
vier	**neun**	**vierzehn**	**neunzehn**
feer	*noin*	FEER-*tsain*	NOIN-*tsain*
5	10	15	20
fünf	**zehn**	**fünfzehn**	**zwanzig**
fewnf	*tsain*	FEWNF-*tsain*	TSVAHN-*tsikh*

21
einundzwanzig
INE-*oont-tsvahn-tsikh*

22
zweiundzwanzig
TSVIGH-*oont-tsvahn-tsikh*

30
dreissig
DRIGH-*ssikh*

31
einunddreissig
INE-*oont-drigh-ssikh*

32
zweiunddreissig
TSVIGH-*oont-drigh-ssikh*

40
vierzig
FEER-*tsikh*

41
einundvierzig
INE-*oont-feer-tsikh*

42
zweiundvierzig
TSVIGH-*oont-feer-tsikh*

50
fünfzig
FEWNF-*tsikh*

51
einundfünfzig
INE-*oont-fewnf-tsikh*

52
zweiundfünfzig
TSVIGH-*oont-fewnf-tsikh*

60
sechzig
ZEKH-*tsikh*

61
einundsechzig
INE-*oont-zekh-tsikh*

62
zweiundsechzig
TSVIGH-*oont-zekh-tsikh*

70
siebzig
ZEEP-*tsikh*

71
einundsiebzig
INE-*oont-zeep-tsikh*

72
zweiundsiebzig
TSVIGH-*oont-zeep-tsikh*

80
achtzig
AHKHT-*tsikh*

81
einundachtzig
INE-*oont-ahkht-tsikh*

82
zweiundachtzig
TSVIGH-*oont-ahkht-tsikh*

90
neunzig
NOIN-*tsikh*

91
einundneunzig
INE-*oont-noin-tsikk*

92
zweiundneunzig
TSVIGH-*oont-noin-tsikh*

100
hundert (einhundert)
HOON-*d'rt* (INE-*hoon-d'rt*)

1000
tausend (eintausend)
TAOU-*z'nt* (INE-*taou-z'nt*)

10,000
zehntausend
TSAIN-*taou-z'nt*

100,000
hunderttausend
HOON-*d'rt-taou-z'nt*

1950
Neunzehnhundertfünfzig
NOIN-*tsain-hoon-d'rt*-FEWNF-*tsikh*

Ich zähle.
Ikh TSAY-*leh.*
I count.

Bitte zählen Sie!
BIT-*teh* TSAY-*l'n Zee!*
Please, count!

Sie zählen.
Zee TSAY-*l'n.*
You count.

Zwanzig ist eine Zahl.
TSVAHN-*tsikh ist* EYE-*neh Tsahl.*
Twenty is a number.

Welche Zahl ist das: 88?
VEL-*kheh Tsahl ist dahs: 88?*
Which number is this: 88?

Das ist ein Bleistift.
Dahs ist ine BLIGH-*shtift.*
This is a pencil.

Das ist ein Hut.
Dahs ist ine Hoot.
This is a hat.

Das ist ein Stuhl.
Dahs ist ine Shtool.
This is a chair.

Das ist eine Feder.
Dahs ist EYE-*neh* FAY-*d'r.*
This is a pen.

Das ist eine Krawatte.
Dahs ist EYE-*neh Krah-*VAH-*teh.*
This is a tie.

Das ist eine Zahl.
Dahs ist EYE-*neh Tsahl.*
This is a number.

Das ist ein Buch.
Dahs ist ine Bookh.
This is a book.

Das ist ein Kleid.
Dahs ist ine Klight.
This is a dress.

Das ist ein Fenster.
Dahs ist ine FEN-*st'r.*
This is a window.

Ist das ein Buch oder eine Feder?
Ist dahs ine Bookh OH-*d'r* EYE-*neh* FAY-*d'r.*
Is this a book or a pen?

Ist das ein Schuh oder ein Hut?
Ist dahs ine Shoo OH-*d'r ine Hoot?*
Is this a shoe or a hat?

Das ist ein Bleistift und das ist ein Bleistift:
Dahs ist ine BLIGH-*shtift oont dahs ist ine* BLIGH-*shtift:*
This is a pencil, and this is a pencil:

Zwei Bleistifte.
Tsvigh BLIGH-*shtif-teh.*
Two pencils.

Zwei Stühle.
Tsvigh SHTEW-*leh.*
Two chairs.

Zwei Tische.
Tsvigh TISH-*eh.*
Two tables.

Zwei Schuhe.
Tsvigh SHOO·*heh.*
Two shoes.

Das ist eine Feder.
Dahs ist EYE-*neh* FAY-*d'r.*
This is a pen.

Zwei Federn.
Tsvigh FAY-*d'rn.*
Two pens.

Zwei Türen.
Tsvigh TEW-*r'n.*
Two doors.

Ist das ein Buch?
Ist dahs ine Bookh?
Is this a book?

Zwei Bücher.
Tsvigh BEW-*kh'r.*
Two books.

Zwei Kleider.
Tsvigh KLIGH-*d'r.*
Two dresses.

Zwei Taschentücher.
Tsvigh TAH-*shen-tew-kh'r.*
Two handkerchiefs.

Ein Herr.
Ine Herr.
A gentleman.

Zwei Herren.
Tsvigh HERR'*n.*
Two gentlemen.

Eine Dame
EYE-*neh* DAH-*meh*
A lady

Zwei Damen.
Tsvigh DAH-*m'n.*
Two ladies.

NOTE to Student: In German the plural is formed in a variety of ways, by the endings r—n—e and the use of the *Umlaut* but almost never by adding s as in English. Here you can see the origin of many of our irregular English plurals, such as "children", "mice", "oxen", "feet", "sheep", etc.

Auf dem Tisch ist ein Bleistift.
Aouf daim Tish ist ine BLIGH-*shtift.*
On the table (there) is a pencil.

Auf dem Tisch sind zwei Bleistifte.
Aouf daim Tish zint tsvigh BLIGH-*shtif-teh.*
On the table are two pencils.

Wieviele Bleistifte liegen auf dem Tisch?
*Vee-*FEE-*leh* BLIGH-*shtif-teh* LEE-*g'n aouf daim Tish?*
How many pencils are lying on the table?

Wieviele Bücher?
*Vee-*FEE-*leh* BEW-*kh'r?*
How many books?

Wieviele Federn sind auf dem Tisch?
*Vee-*FEE-*leh* FAY-*d'rn zint aouf daim Tish?*
How many pens are (there) on the table?

Wieviele Stühle sind hier?
*Vee-*FEE-*leh* SHTEW-*leh zint here?*
How many chairs are here?

Wieviele Herren sind hier?
*Vee-*FEE-*leh* HERR'*n zint here?*
How many gentlemen are here?

Wieviele Damen sind hier?
*Vee-*FEE-*leh* DAH-*m'n zint here?*
How many ladies are here?

Die Zeitung kostet zehn Pfennig.
Dee TSIGH-*toonk* KOSS-*tet tsain* PFEN-*nikh.*
The paper costs ten pennies.

Das Buch kostet zwanzig Mark.
Dahs Bookh KOSS-*tet* TSVAHN-*tsikh Mahrk.*
The book costs twenty marks.

Wieviel kostet der Hut?
*Vee-*FEEL KOSS-*tet dehr Hoot?*
How much does the hat cost?

Wieviel kostet ein Bleistift?
*Vee-*FEEL KOSS-*tet ine* BLIGH-*shtift?*
How much does a pencil cost?

Kostet die Zeitung zehn Pfennig?
KOSS-*tet dee* TSIGH-*toonk tsain* PFEN-*nikh?*
Does the paper cost ten pennies?

Kostet der Hut hundert Mark?
KOSS-*tet dehr* HOOT HOON-*d'rt Mahrk?*
Does the hat cost 100 marks?

Das ist eine Hand.
Dahs ist EYE-*neh Hahnt.*
This is a hand.

Das sind zwei Hände.
Dahs zint tsvigh HEN-*deh.*
These are two hands.

Beide Hände.
BY-*deh* HEN-*deh.*
Both hands.

Das ist ein Fuss.
Dahs ist ine Fooss.
This is a foot.

Das sind zwei Füsse.
Dahs zint tsvigh FEW-*sseh.*
These are two feet.

Die beiden Füsse.
Dee BY-d'n FEW-*sseh.*
Both feet.

Das ist der Kopf.
Dahs ist dehr Koppf.
This is the head.

Sind das zwei Köpfe?
Zint dahs tsvigh KUHP-*feh?*
Are these two heads?

Das ist ein Auge und das ist ein Ohr.
Dahs ist ine AOU-*ggeh oont dahs ist ine Ohr.*
This is an eye and this is an ear.

Das sind zwei Augen, das sind zwei Ohren.
Dahs zint tsvigh AOU-*g'n, dahs zint tsvigh* OH-*r'n.*
These are two eyes; these are two ears.

Was ist das, ein Auge oder ein Ohr?
Vahss ist dahs, ine AOU-*ggeh* OH-*d'r ine Ohr?*
What is this, an eye or an ear?

THINKING IN GERMAN
(Answers on page 252)

1. Zählen Sie von eins bis zehn! Was tun Sie?

2. Ich zähle: Zwanzig, einundzwanzig, zweiundzwanzig. Was tue ich?

3. Wieviele Stühle sind hier?

4. Was tut der Lehrer?

5. Ist hier ein Tisch?

6. Wieviele Bücher sind auf dem Tisch?

7. Ist eine Dame hier?

8. Wer sitzt hinter dem Tisch?

9. Wieviele Füsse zählen Sie?

10. Was kostet der Hut?

11. Ist das ein Rock?

12. Ist ein Taschentuch auf dem Tisch?

13. Wieviel ist zwei und zwei?

14. Wieviel kostet ein Berlitz-Buch?

ÜBUNG NR. 9

Was tun wir?
Vahss toon veer?
What are we doing?

Nehmen Sie ein Buch!
NAY-*m'n Zee ine Bookh!*
Take a book!

Was tun Sie?
Vahss toon Zee?
What are you doing?

Ich nehme ein Buch.
Ikh NAY-*meh ine Bookh.*
I am taking a book.

Ich habe ein Buch in der Hand.
Ikh HAH-*beh ine Bookh in dehr Hahnt.*
I have a book in (my) hand.

Sie haben ein Buch in der Hand.
Zee HAH-*b'n ine Bookh in dehr Hahnt.*
You have a book in (your) hand.

Ich habe zwei Bücher.
Ikh HAH-*beh tsvigh* BEW-*kher.*
I have two books.

Fräulein Gertrude hat einen Hut auf dem Kopf.
FROY-*line Gger-*TROO-*deh haht* EYE-*n'n Hoot aouf daim Koppf.*
Miss Gertrude has a hat on (her) head.

Ich habe keinen Hut auf dem Kopf.
Ikh HAH-*beh* KIGH-*n'n Hoot aouf daim Koppf.*
I have no hat on (my) head.

36

NOTE: In German, you can say that you have a hat on *the* head. Germans feel, with some logic, that you will not normally have a hat on some one else's head, and that the meaning is therefore clear, without the possessive pronoun "your". The same is true of a book in *the* hand, a shoe on *the* foot, etc.

Habe ich einen Hut auf dem Kopf?
HAH-beh ikh EYE-n'n Hoot aouf daim Koppf?
Have I a hat on (my) head?

Sie haben keinen Hut auf dem Kopf.
Zee HAH-b'n KIGH-n'n Hoot aouf daim Koppf.
You have no hat on (your) head.

REMEMBER: *Kein* is another way of expressing the negative. Ex.: "I have no book."—*Ich habe kein Buch.* Note that *kein* changes its endings according to gender and case in the same way as *ein,* as it is merely the negative form of *ein.* (*ein*—one; *kein*—not one—none).

Ich habe einen schwarzen Rock.
Ikh HAH-beh EYE-n'n SHVAHR-tsen Rokk.
I have a black coat.

Sie haben einen braunen.
Zee HAH-b'n EYE-n'n BRAOU-n'n.
You have a brown one.

Frau Berg hat ein blaues Kleid.
Fraou Bairk haht ine BLAOU-es Klight.
Mrs. Berg has a blue dress.

Das Fräulein hat kleine Schuhe.
Dahs FROY-line haht KLIGH-neh SHOO-heh.
The young lady has small shoes.

Ich habe grosse.
Ikh HAH-beh GROH-sseh.
I have large ones.

Haben Sie ein Buch in der Hand?
HAH-b'n Zee ine Bookh in dehr Hahnt?
Have you a book in (your) hand?

Hat Frau Berg ein blaues Kleid?
Haht Fraou Bairk ine BLAOU-es Klight?
Has Mrs. Berg a blue dress?

Hat das Fräulein kleine Schuhe?
Haht dahs FROY-line KLIGH-neh SHOO-heh?
Has the young lady small shoes?

Nehme ich ein Buch?
NAY-meh ikh ine Bookh?
Do I take a book?

Ja, Sie nehmen ein Buch.
Yah, Zee NAY-m'n ine Bookh.
Yes, you take a book.

Bitte, nehmen Sie ein Buch!
BIT-*teh*, NAY-*m'n Zee ine Bookh!*
Please, take a book!

Ich nehme ein Buch.
Ikh NAY-*meh ine Bookh.*
I take a book.

Was tun wir?
Vahss toon veer?
What are we doing?

Wir nehmen Bücher.
Veer NAY-*m'n* BEW-*kh'r.*
We take books.

Ich nehme zwei Bücher.
Ikh NAY-*meh tsvigh* BEW-*kh'r.*
I take two books.

Wir haben zwei Hände.
Veer HAH-*b'n tsvigh* HEN-*deh.*
We have two hands.

Wieviele Hände haben wir?
*Vee-*FEE-*leh* HEN-*deh* HAH-*b'n veer?*
How many hands do we have?

Ich habe zwei Augen und zwei Ohren.
Ikh HAH-*beh tsvigh* AOU-*g'n oont tsvigh* OH-*r'n.*
I have two eyes and two ears.

Wieviele Augen und Ohren haben Sie?
*Vee-*FEE-*leh* AOU-*g'n oont* OH-*r'n* HAH-*b'n Zee?*
How many eyes and ears have you?

Herr Berlitz nimmt ein Buch.
Herr BEHR-*lits nimt ine Bookh.*
Mr. Berlitz takes a book.

Was tut Herr Berlitz?
Vahss toot Herr BEHR-*lits?*
What is Mr. Berlitz doing?

Ich nehme einen Bleistift.
Ikh NAY-*meh* EYE-*n'n* BLIGH-*shtift.*
I take a pencil.

Was tue ich?
Vahss TOO-*eh ikh?*
What am I doing?

Sie nehmen einen Bleistift.
ZEE NAY-*m'n* EYE-*n'n* BLIGH-*shtift.*
You take a pencil.

Wir nehmen zwei Bücher.
Veer NAY-*m'n tsvigh* BEW-*kh'r.*
We take two books.

Was tun wir?
Vahss toon veer?
What are we doing?

Die Schüler nehmen Bleistifte.
Dee SHEW-*l'r* NAY-*m'n* BLIGH-*shtif-teh.*
The pupils take pencils.

Was tun die Schüler?
Vahss toon dee SHEW-*l'r?*
What are the pupils doing?

Sie nehmen Bleistifte.
Zee NAY-*m'n* BLIGH-*shtif-teh.*
They take pencils.

IMPORTANT NOTE: Verbs change their endings and spelling according to the person performing the action. For example *gehen*, "to go": *Ich gehe, er geht, wir gehen, Sie gehen* and *sie gehen* mean "I go, he goes, we go, you go and they go". By the way, German verb changes are not so numerous as those in Latin languages, a distinct point in their favor. Note also that whether you want to say "I am going" or "I go", in German you always say *ich gehe*. There is no "progressive" form.

Machen Sie das Buch auf!
MAH-kh'n Zee dahs Bookh aouf!
Open the book!

Ich mache das Buch auf.
Ikh MAH-kheh dahs Bookh aouf.
I open the book.

Was tue ich?
Vahss TOO-eh ikh?
What am I doing?

Was tun Sie?
Vahss toon Zee?
What are you doing?

Was tun wir?
Vahss toon veer?
What are we doing?

Sie machen das Buch auf.
Zee MAH-kh'n dahs Bookh aouf.
You open the book.

Wir machen die Bücher auf.
Veer MAH-kh'n dee BEW-kh'r aouf.
We open the books.

Sie machen das Buch auf.
Zee MAH-kh'n dahs Bookh aouf.
You are opening the book.

Ich mache das Buch auf.
Ikh MAH-kheh dahs Bookh aouf.
I am opening the book.

Wir machen die Bücher auf.
Veer MAH-kh'n dee BEW-kh'r aouf.
We are opening the books.

Der Lehrer macht das Buch auf,
Dehr LAY-r'r makht dahs Bookh aouf,
The teacher opens the book,

die Schüler machen die Bücher zu.
dee SHEW-l'r MAH-kh'n dee BEW-kh'r tsoo.
the pupils close the books.

Was macht der Lehrer?
Vahss makht dehr LAY-r'r?
What is the teacher doing?

Was machen die Schüler?
Vahss MAH-kh'n dee SHEW-l'r?
What are the pupils doing?

Sie haben einen Bleistift,
Zee HAH-b'n EYE-n'n BLIGH-shtift,
You have a pencil,

Er macht das Buch auf.
Air makht dahs Bookh aouf.
He is opening the book.

Sie machen die Bücher zu.
Zee MAH-kh'n dee BEW-kh'r tsoo.
They are closing the books.

ich habe einen Bleistift,
ikh HAH-beh EYE-n'n BLIGH-shtift,
I have a pencil,

wir haben zwei Bleistifte.
veer HAH-b'n tsvigh BLIGH-shtif-teh.
we have two pencils.

Was haben Sie?
Vahss HAH-b'n Zee?
What have you?

Sie haben einen Bleistift.
Zee HAH-b'n EYE-n'n BLIGH-shtift.
You have a pencil.

Ich habe einen Bleistift.
Ikh HAH-beh EYE-n'n BLIGH-shtift.
I have a pencil.

Habe ich einen Bleistift?
HAH-beh ikh EYE-n'n BLIGH-shtift?
Have I a pencil?

Wir haben zwei Bleistifte.
Veer HAH-*b'n tsvigh* BLIGH-*shtif-teh.*
We have two pencils.

Haben wir zwei Bleistifte?
HAH-*b'n veer tsvigh* BLIGH-*shtif-teh?*
Have we two pencils?

Wir machen das Fenster zu.
Veer MAH-*kh'n dahs* FEN-*st'r tsoo.*
We close the window.

Machen Sie das Fenster auf?
MAH-*kh'n Zee dahs* FEN-*st'r aouf?*
Do you open the window?

Nein, ich mache das Fenster zu.
Nine, ikh MAH-*kheh dahs* FEN-*st'r tsoo.*
No, I close the window.

Herr Berlitz nimmt ein Buch.
Herr BEHR-*lits nimt ine Bookh.*
Mr. Berlitz takes a book.

Was hat Herr Berlitz in der Hand?
Vahss haht Herr BEHR-*lits in dehr Hahnt?*
What has Mr. Berlitz in (his) hand?

Er hat ein Buch in der Hand.
Air haht ine Bookh in dehr Hahnt.
He has a book in his hand.

Fräulein Gertrude hat einen Hut auf dem Kopf.
FROY-*line Gger*-TROO-*deh haht* EYE-*n'n Hoot aouf daim Koppf.*
Miss Gertrude has a hat on her head.

Die Damen haben Hüte auf.
Dee DAH-*m'm* HAH-*b'n* HEW-*teh aouf.*
The ladies have hats on.

Hat der Lehrer einen Hut auf?
Haht dehr LAY-*r'r* EYE-*n'n Hoot aouf?*
Has the teacher a hat on?

Nein, er hat keinen Hut auf.
Nine, air haht KIGH-*n'n Hoot aouf.*
No, he has no hat on.

der Garten	der Park	das Theater
dehr GAHR-*t'n*	*dehr Pahrk*	*dahs Teh-*AH-*t'r*
the garden	the park	the theatre

das Kino	das Büro	die Schule
dahs KEE-*noh*	*dahs Bew-*ROH	*dee* SHOO-*leh*
the movie house	the office	the school

die Kirche	das Haus
dee KEER-*kheh*	*dahs Haous*
the church	the house

Ich gehe in den Garten.
Ikh GAY-*heh in dain* GAHR-*t'n.*
I go into the garden.

Gehen Sie in den Garten!
GAY-*h'n Zee in dain* GAHR-*t'n!*
Go into the garden!

Gehen wir in den Garten?
GAY-h'n veer in dain GAHR-t'n?
Are we going into the garden?

Ja, wir gehen in den Garten.
Yah, veer GAY-h'n in dain GAHR-t'n.
Yes, we are going into the garden.

Herr Herrnfeld kommt aus dem Park.
Herr HERRN-felt kommt aous daim Park.
Mr. Herrnfeld is coming out of the Park.

Herr Berlitz geht in den Park.
Herr BEHR-lits gait in dain Park.
Mr. Berlitz goes into the park.

Ich gehe ins Theater.
Ikh GAY-heh ince Teh-AH-t'r.
I am going to the theatre.

Gehen Sie ins Theater?
GAY-h'n Zee ince Teh-AH-t'r?
Are you going to the theatre?

Nein, ich gehe nicht ins Theater,
Nine, ikh GAY-heh nikht ince Teh-AH-t'r,
No, I am not going to the theatre,

ich gehe ins Kino.
ikh GAY-heh ince KEE-noh.
I am going to the movies.

Gehen Sie in die Schule!
GAY-h'n Zee in dee SHOO-leh!
Go to school!

Wir gehen in die Schule.
Veer GAY-h'n in dee SHOO-leh.
We are going to school.

Gehen Sie in die Kirche?
GAY-h'n Zee in dee KEER-kheh?
Are you going to church?

Ja, ich gehe in die Kirche.
Yah, ikh GAY-heh in dee KEER-kheh.
Yes, I am going to church.

Ich gehe nicht ins Kino,
Ikh GAY-heh nikht ince KEE-noh,
I am not going to the movies,

ich gehe ins Büro.
ikh GAY-heh ince Bew-ROH.
I am going to the office.

Der Schüler kommt in die Schule.
Dehr SHEW-l'r kommt in dee SHOO-leh.
The pupil is coming to school.

Der Schüler kommt aus der Schule.
Dehr SHEW-l'r kommt aous dehr SHOO-leh.
The pupil is coming out of school.

Gehe ich ins Haus?
GAY-heh ikh ince Haous?
Am I going into the house?

Sie gehen ins Haus.
Zee GAY-h'n ince Haous.
You are going into the house.

Wir kommen aus dem Haus.
Veer KOMM'n aous daim Haous.
We are coming out of the house.

NOTE to Student: Verbs denoting *motion towards* a specified objective, take the accusative case after these prepositions: *an, auf, hinter, in, neben, über, unter, vor* and *zwischen*. For instance: "I go to the theatre."—*Ich gehe in* DAS *Theater*. But: "I am in the theatre."—*Ich bin in* DEM *Theater* (dative case). Moreover, *in das, auf das, an das* can be contracted to *ins, aufs, ans* and *in dem, an dem* to *im* and *am* respectively.

Sitzen wir oder stehen wir?
ZITS'n veer OH-d'r SHTAY-h'n veer?
Are we sitting or are we standing?

Wir sitzen, wir stehen nicht.
Veer ZITS'n, veer SHTAY-h'n nikht.
We are sitting, we are not standing.

Sitzt der Lehrer oder steht er?
Zitst dehr LAY-r'r OH-d'r shtait air?
Is the teacher sitting or is he standing?

Der Lehrer steht.
Dehr LAY-r'r shtait.
The teacher is standing.

Sitzen wir Schüler oder stehen wir?
ZITS'n veer SHEW-l'r OH-d'r SHTAY-h'n veer?
Are we pupils sitting or standing?

Wir Schüler sitzen.
Veer SHEW-l'r ZITS'n.
We pupils are sitting.

Liegt das Buch auf dem Tisch?
Leegt dahs Bookh aouf daim Tish?
Is the book lying on the table?

Liegen Bücher auf dem Tisch?
LEE-g'n BEW-kh'r aouf daim Tish?
Are there books lying on the table?

Liegen Bleistifte auf dem Stuhl?
LEE-g'n BLIGH-shtif-teh aouf daim Shtool?
Are there pencils lying on the chair?

THINKING IN GERMAN
(Answers on page 252)

1. Gehen wir in die Berlitz-Schule?
2. Haben die Herren Hüte auf?
3. Gehen die Damen ins Kino?
4. Geht Herr Berlitz ins Büro?
5. Machen die Schüler die Augen zu?
6. Nehmen Sie einen Bleistift in die Schule?
7. Nehmen Sie Bücher in die Kirche?
8. Kommt Fräulein Gertrude aus dem Park?
9. Liegen Hüte auf dem Tisch?
10. Haben Sie drei Augen?
11. Kommen die Schüler aus der Schule?
12. Geht Herr Berlitz aus dem Haus in den Garten?
13. Gehen Sie in den Garten oder in die Kirche?
14. Haben Sie ein Haus?
15. Haben Sie einen Hut auf dem Kopf?

ÜBUNG NR. 10

Ich schreibe das A—B—C
Ikh SHRIGH-*beh dahs Ah—Bay—Tsay*
I am writing the Alphabet

Der Lehrer nimmt die Kreide.
Dehr LAY-*r'r nimt dee* KRIGH-*deh.*
The teacher takes the chalk.

Er schreibt das A—B—C.
Air shrighbt dahs Ah—Bay—Tsay.
He is writing the alphabet.

Er schreibt an die Tafel.
Air shrighbt ahn dee TAH-*f'l.*
He writes on the blackboar'

Was tut der Lehrer?
Vahss toot dehr LAY-*r'r?*
What is the teacher doing.

Wer schreibt an die Tafel?
Vair shrighbt ahn dee TAH-*f'l?*
Who is writing on the blackboard?

Was schreibt der Lehrer an die Tafel?
Vahss shrighbt dehr LAY-*r'r ahn dee* TAH-*f'l?*
What does the teacher write on the blackboard?

Nehmen Sie Bleistift und Papier!
NAY-*m'n Zee* BLIGH-*shtift oont Pah-*PEER!
Take pencil and paper!

Schreiben Sie auf das Papier!
SHRIGH-*b'n Zee aouf dahs Pah-*PEER!
Write on the paper!

44

Nehmen Sie das Heft oder das Papier?
NAY-*m'n Zee dahs Heft* OH-*d'r dahs Pah-*PEER?
Do you take the note-book or the paper?

Sie schreiben in das Heft.
Zee SHRIGH-*b'n in dahs Heft.*
You write in the note-book.

Der Lehrer schreibt nicht in das Heft,
Dehr LAY-*r'r shrighbt nikht in dahs Heft,*
The teacher does not write in the note-book,

er schreibt an die Tafel.
air shrighbt ahn dee TAH-*f'l.*
he writes on the blackboard.

Schreiben Sie auf das Papier?
SHRIGH-*b'n Zee aouf dahs Pah-*PEER?
Do you write on the paper?

Schreiben Sie das A—B—C!
SHRIGH-*b'n Zee dahs Ah—Bay—Tsay!*
Write the alphabet!

Schreiben Sie an die Wand?
SHRIGH-*b'n Zee ahn dee Vahnt?*
Do you write on the wall?

Nein, ich schreibe nicht an die Wand.
Nine, ikh SHRIGH-*beh nikht ahn dee Vahnt.*
No, I do not write on the wall.

Schreibe ich an die Tür?
SHRIGH-*beh ikh ahn dee Tewr?*
Do I write on the door?

Nein, Sie schreiben nicht an die Tür, Sie schreiben an die Tafel.
Nine, Zee SHRIGH-*b'n nikht ahn dee Tewr, Zee* SHRIGH-*b'n ahn dee* TAH-*f'l.*
No, you do not write on the door, you write on the blackboard.

REMEMBER: Writing on something involves *motion toward;* therefore *schreiben* takes the accusative case after the prepositions *an, in,* and *auf:* "I write on the wall."—*Ich schreibe an die Wand.* "I write on the paper."—*Ich schreibe auf das Papier.* "I write in the book."—*Ich schreibe in das Buch.*

Was schreiben wir?
Vahss SHRIGH-*b'n veer?*
What are we writing?

Wir schreiben Buchstaben.
Veer SHRIGH-*b'n* BOOKH-*shtah-b'n.*
We write letters (of the alphabet).

Schreiben Herr Bach und Herr Lang an die Tafel?
SHRIGH-*b'n Herr Bahkh oont Herr Lahnk ahn dee* TAH-*f'l?*
Are Mr. Bach and Mr. Lang writing on the blackboard?

Was schreiben Sie?
Vahss SHRIGH-*b'n Zee?*
What are they writing?

Die Herren schreiben Buchstaben.
Dee HERR-*'n* SHRIGH-*b'n* BOOKH-*shtah-b'n.*
The gentlemen are writing letters.

Der Lehrer nimmt das Buch;   **er macht es auf,**   **er liest.**
Dehr LAY-*r'r nimt dahs Bookh;*   *air mahkt ess aouf,*   *air leest.*
The teacher takes the book;   he opens it,   he reads.

Wer liest?
Vair leest?
Who is reading?

Der Lehrer liest.
Dehr LAY-r'r leest.
The teacher is reading.

Ich nehme mein Buch.
Ikh NAY-meh mine Bookh.
I take my book.

Ich lese in dem Buch.
Ikh LAY-zeh in daim Bookh.
1 am reading in the book.

Ich lese das deutsche A—B—C.
Ikh LAY-zeh dahs DOIT-sheh Ah—Bay—Tsay.
I am reading the German A—B—C.

Nehmen Sie Ihr Buch!
NAY-m'n Zee Eer Bookh!
Take your book!

Machen Sie Ihr Buch auf!
MAH-kh'n Zee Eer Bookh aouf!
Open your book!

Lesen Sie das deutsche A—B—C!
LAY-z'n Zee dahs DOIT-sheh Ah—Bay—Tsay!
Read the German alphabet!

Was tun Sie?
Vahss toon Zee?
What are you doing?

Ich lese das deutsche A—B—C.
Ikh LAY-zeh dahs DOIT-sheh Ah—Bay—Tsay.
I am reading the German alphabet.

Wir lesen.
Veer LAY-z'n.
We are reading.

Was lesen wir?
Vahss LAY-z'n veer?
What are we reading?

Auf welcher Seite lesen wir?
Aouf VEL-kh'r ZIGH-teh LAY-z'n veer?
On what page are we reading?

Wir lesen auf Seite 46.
Veer LAY-z'n aouf ZIGH-teh 46.
We are reading on page 46.

Lesen Sie auf Seite 46?
LAY-z'n Zee aouf ZIGH-teh 46?
Do you read on page 46?

Ja, ich lese das A—B—C auf Seite 46.
Yah, ikh LAY-zeh dahs Ah—Bay—Tsay aouf ZIGH-teh 46.
Yes, I read the alphabet on page 46.

A	**B**	**C**	**D**	**E**	**F**	**G**
Ah	*Bay*	*Tsay*	*Day*	*Ay*	*Eff*	*Gay*
H	**I**	**J**	**K**	**L**	**M**	**N**
Hah	*Ee*	*Yot*	*Kah*	*Ell*	*Emm*	*Enn*
O	**P**	**Q**	**R**	**S**	**T**	**U**
Oh	*Pay*	*Koo*	*Air*	*Ess*	*Tay*	*Oo*
V	**W**	**X**		**Y**		**Z**
Faou	*Vay*	*Eeks*		*EW-psee-lon*		*Tsett*

Das ist das A, das ist das B.
Dahs ist dahs Ah, dahs ist dahs Bay.
This is the A, this is the B.

Wie heisst dieser Buchstabe?
Vee highst DEEZ'r BOOKH-*shtah-beh?*
What is this letter called?

Dieser Buchstabe heisst C.
DEEZ'r BOOKH-*shtah-beh highst Tsay.*
This letter is called C.

Wie heisst dieser? X.
Vee highst DEEZ'r*? Eeks.*
What is this one called? X.

Und dieser? P.
Oont DEEZ'r*? Pay.*
And this one? P.

Ich schreibe Buchstaben.
Ikh SHRIGH-*beh* BOOKH-*shtah-b'n.*
I write letters.

Ich schreibe Wörter.
Ikh SHRIGH-*beh* VUHR-*t'r.*
I write words.

Sie lesen Wörter.
Zee LAY-z'n VUHR-*t'r.*
You read words.

Was tun Sie?
Vahss toon Zee?
What are you doing?

Ich lese Wörter.
Ikh LAY-zeh VUHR-*t'r.*
I read words.

Was schreibe ich?
Vahss SHRIGH-*beh ikh?*
What am I writing?

Sie schreiben Buchstaben.
Zee SHRIGH-b'n BOOKH-*shtah-b'n.*
You are writing letters.

Ich schreibe einen Satz: Der Lehrer geht.
Ikh SHRIGH-*beh* EYE-n'n *Zahts: Dehr* LAY-r'r *gait.*
I write a sentence: The teacher is going.

Ist das ein Satz?
Ist dahs ine Zahts?
Is this a sentence?

Ja, "Der Lehrer geht" ist ein Satz.
Yah, "Dehr LAY-r'r *gait" ist ine Zahts.*
Yes, "The teacher is going" is a sentence.

Ist "Tisch" ein Wort oder ein Buchstabe?
Ist "Tish" ine Vohrt OH-d'r *ine* BOOKH-*shtah-beh?*
Is "Tisch" a word or a letter?

"Tisch" ist ein Wort.
"Tish" ist ine Vohrt.
"Tisch" is a word.

Wieviele Buchstaben hat das Wort "Tisch"?
*Vee-*FEE-leh BOOKH-*shtah-b'n haht dahs Vohrt "Tish"?*
How many letters has the word "Tisch"?

Es hat 5 Buchstaben.
Ess haht fewnf BOOKH-*shtah-b'n.*
It has 5 letters.

Wieviele Wörter hat der Satz: "Der Lehrer liest"?
*Vee-*FEE-leh VUHR-*t'r haht dehr Zahts: "Dehr* LAY-r'r *leest"?*
How many words has the sentence: "The teacher reads"?

Er hat drei Wörter.
Air haht drigh VUHR-*t'r.*
It has 3 words.

Ist "Garten" ein Wort oder ein Satz? **"Garten" ist ein Wort.**
Ist "GAHR-t'n" ine Vohrt OH-d'r ine Zahts? *"GAHR-t'n" ist ine Vohrt.*
Is "garden" a word or a sentence? "Garden" is a word.

  Das Wort "Garten" hat zwei Silben: "Gar" und "ten".
  Dahs Vohrt "GAHR-t'n" haht tsvigh ZEEL-b'n: "GAHR" oont "ten".
  The word "Garten" has two syllables: "Gar" and "ten".

Wieviele Buchstaben hat das Wort "Theater"?
Vee-FEE-leh BOOKH-shtah-b'n haht dahs Vohrt "Teh-AH-t'r"?
How many letters has the word "Theatre"?

   Ist "Ich gehe ins Theater" ein Satz?
   Ist "Ikh GAY-heh ince Teh-AH-t'r" ine Zahts?
   Is "I go to the theatre" a sentence?

   Wieviele Wörter hat der Satz?
   Vee-FEE-leh VUHR-t'r haht dehr Zahts?
   How many words has the sentence?

Wieviele Silben hat das Wort "Theater"?
Vee-FEE-leh ZEEL-b'n haht dahs Vohrt "Teh-AH-t'r"?
How many syllables has the word "Theatre"?

   Das A—B—C beginnt mit A und endet mit Z.
   Dahs Ah—Bay—Tsay beh-GGINT mit Ah oont EN-dett mit Tsett.
   The alphabet begins with A and ends with Z.

   A ist der erste Buchstabe.
   Ah ist dehr AIR-steh BOOKH-shtah-beh.
   A is the first letter.

B ist der zweite, **C der dritte,** **D der vierte,**
Bay ist dehr TSVIGH-teh, *Tsay dehr DRIT-teh,* *Day dehr FEER-teh,*
B is the second, C the third, D the fourth,

   Z ist der letzte Buchstabe.
   Tsett ist dehr LETS-teh BOOKH-shtah-beh.
   Z is the last letter.

E der fünfte,   **F der sechste usw.**
Ay dehr FEWNF-teh, *Eff dehr SEKS-teh oont zoh VIGH-t'r.*
E the fifth,   F the sixth, etc.

NOTE: *usw.* stands for *und so weiter*—"and so forth". It is exactly equivalent to "etc".

THINKING IN GERMAN

(Answers on page 253)

1. Schreiben Sie den Buchstaben A auf das Papier! Was tun Sie?
2. Ich schreibe das Wort "Kino". Was tue ich?
3. Herr Strump schreibt das A—B—C an die Tafel. Wer schreibt das A—B—C?
4. Lesen Sie den Satz: "Ich bin der Schüler". Was tun Sie?
5. Wieviele Wörter hat der Satz: "Der Lehrer geht in die Kirche"?
6. Wieviele Silben hat er?
7. Was lesen Sie in dem Buch?
8. Ich lese: "A, b, c, d, e, f, usw." Was lese ich?
9. Ist "ich" ein Satz oder ein Wort?
10. Welches A—B—C lesen Sie?
11. Beginnt das A—B—C mit P?
12. Ist H der erste Buchstabe?
13. Schreiben Sie in Ihr Heft?
14. Nemen Sie mein Buch oder Ihr Buch?
15. Hat das Wort "Bleistift" vier Silben?
16. Welches ist der erste Buchstabe?
17. Was lesen Sie auf Seite 35?
18. Hat der Satz Wörter und Buchstaben?
19. Hat die Silbe Wörter?

ÜBUNG NR. 11

Sprechen Sie deutsch?
SPREH-*kh'n Zee doitsh?*
Do you speak German?

Wieviele Buchstaben hat das deutsche A—B—C?
Vee-FEE-leh BOOKH-*shtah-b'n haht dahs* DOIT-*sheh Ah—Bay—Tsay?*
How many letters has the German alphabet?

Es hat 26 Buchstaben.
Ess haht ZEKS-*oont-tsvahn-tsikh* BOOKH-*shtah-b'n.*
It has 26 letters.

D ist der vierte Buchstabe.
Day ist dehr FEER-*teh* BOOKH-*shtah-beh.*
D is the fourth letter.

Der wievielte Buchstabe ist D?
*Dehr vee-*FEEL*-teh* BOOKH-*shtah-beh ist Day?*
Which letter is D?

NOTE: *Der wievielte* which we translate by "which", **really** means "the how-many-eth".

Der wievielte Buchstabe ist B, der zweite oder dritte?
*Dehr vee-*FEEL*-teh* BOOKH-*shtabe ist Bay, dehr* TSVIGH-*teh* OH-*d'r* DRIT-*teh?*
Which letter is B, the second or third?

Mit welchem Buchstaben beginnt das deutsche A—B—C?
Mit VEL-*kh'm* BOOKH-*shtah-b'n beh-*GGINT *dahs* DOIT-*sheh Ah—Bay—Tsay?*
With which letter does the German alphabet begin?

Mit welchem Buchstaben endet es?   Es endet mit Z.
Mit VEL-*kh'm* BOOKH-*shtah-b'n* EN-*dett ess?*   *Ess* EN-*dett mit Tsett.*
With which letter does it end?   It ends with Z.

Mit welchem Wort beginnt dieser Satz?
Mit VEL-*kh'm Vohrt beh-*GGINT DEEZ'*r Zahts?*
With which word does this sentence begin?

Mit welchem Wort endet er?
Mit VEL-*kh'm Vohrt* EN-*dett air?*
With which word does it end?

Auf welcher Seite Ihres Buches endet die Übung Nr. 5?
Aouf VEL-*kher* ZIGH-*teh* EE-*res* BOO-*khes* EN-*dett dee* EW-*boonk* NOOM'*r fewnf?*
On which page of your book does Exercise No. 5 end?

Auf welcher Seite beginnt die Übung Nr. 11?
Aouf VEL-*kher* ZIGH-*teh beh-*GGINT *dee* EW-*boonk* NOOM'*r elf?*
On which page does Exercise No. 11 start?

Das A steht vor dem B;   das E steht nach dem D.
Dahs Ah shtait for daim Bay;   *dahs Ay shtait nahkh daim Day.*
A stands before B;   E stands after D.

Das H steht zwischen dem G und dem I.
Dahs Hah shtait TSVISH'*n daim Gay oont daim Ee.*
H stands between G and I.

Steht das S vor oder nach dem T?
Shtait dahs Ess fohr OH-*d'r nahkh daim Tay?*
Does S stand before or after T?

Das W kommt nach dem V.
Dahs Vay kommt nahkh daim Faou.
W comes after V.

Welcher Buchstabe steht vor dem Z?
VEL-*kher* BOOKH-*shtah-beh shtait fohr daim Tsett?*
Which letter stands before Z?

Welcher Buchstabe steht zwischen M und O?
VEL-*kher* BOOKH-*shtah-beh shtait* TSVISH*'n Emm oont Oh?*
Which letter stands between M and O?

Was kommt nach L?
Vahss kommt nahkh El?
What comes after L?

Dieses Wort ist deutsch: "Buch";	dieses ist englisch: "book".
DEEZ's *Vohrt ist doitsh: "Bookh";*	DEEZ's *ist* ENNG-*lish: "book".*
This word is German: "Buch";	this one is English: "book".

"Livre" ist französisch.	**"Buch" heisst "book" auf englisch.**
"LEEV'r" *ist frahn-*TSUH-*zish.*	*"Bookh" highst "book" aouf* ENNG-*lish.*
"Livre" is French.	"Buch" is called "book" in English.

Wie heisst dieser Buchstabe auf englisch: Y?	**Auf deutsch?**
Vee highst DEEZ'r BOOKH-*shtah-beh aouf* ENNG-*lish: Y?*	*Aouf doitsh?*
What is this letter called in English: Y?	In German?

Wie heisst "Tisch" auf englisch?
Vee highst "Tish" aouf ENNG-*lish?*
What is "Tisch" called in English?

Lesen Sie dieses Wort auf deutsch: Berlin!
LAY-*z'n Zee* DEEZ's *Vohrt aouf doitsh: Behr-*LEEN*!*
Read this word in German: Berlin!

Lesen Sie es auf englisch!
LAY-*z'n Zee ess aouf* ENNG-*lish!*
Read it in English!

Lesen Sie dieses Wort auf deutsch: Paris!
LAY-*z'n Zee* DEEZ's *Vohrt aouf doitsh: Pah-*REES*!*
Read this word in German: Paris!

Lesen Sie es auf Englisch!	**Ist das ein englisches Buch?**
LAY-*z'n Zee ess aouf* ENNG-*lish!*	*Ist dahs ine* ENNG-*lee-shess Bookh?*
Read it in English!	Is this an English book?

Was für ein Buch ist das?	**Und dieses?**
Vahss fewr ine Bookh ist dahs?	*Oont* DEEZ's*?*
What kind of a book is this?	And this one?

Lesen Sie deutsch?
LAY-z'n Zee doitsh?
Do you read German?

Schreiben Sie französisch?
SHRIGH-b'n Zee frahn-TSUH-zish?
Do you write French?

Sprechen Sie englisch?
SHPREH-kh'n Zee ENNG-lish?
Do you speak English?

Sprechen Sie französisch?
SHPREH-kh'n Zee frahn-TSUH-zish?
Do you speak French?

Ich lese, schreibe und spreche deutsch.
Ikh LAY-zeh, SHRIGH-beh oont SHPREH-kheh doitsh.
I read, write and speak German.

Sprechen Sie spanisch?
SHPREH-kh'n Zee SHPAH-nish?
Do you speak Spanish?

Nein, ich spreche es nicht, aber ich lese es.
Nine, ikh SHPREH-kheh ess nikht, AH-b'r ikh LAY-zeh- ess.
No, I don't speak it, but I read it.

In Paris spricht man französisch,
In Pah-REES shprikht mahn frahn-TSUH-zish,
In Paris they speak French,

in Berlin deutsch,
in Behr-LEEN doitsh,
in Berlin German,

in London englisch,
in LOHN-don ENNG-lish,
in London English,

in Buenos Aires spanisch
in BWAY-noss EYE-ress SHPAH-nish
in Buenos Aires Spanish

und in Rom italienisch.
oont in Rohm ee-tahl-YAY-nish.
and in Rome Italian.

REMEMBER: In German, when you wish to say: "they speak", "they do", etc. meaning all people generally at a certain place or time, you must use the impersonal form *man spricht, man tut*—"one speaks", "one does", etc.

Ich buchstabiere das Wort "Fenster": F-e-n-s-t-e-r.
Ikh bookh-shtah-BEE-reh dahs Vohrt "FEN-st'r": Eff, Ay, Enn, Ess, Tay, Ay, Air.
I spell the word "Fenster": F-e-n-s-t-e-r.

Was tue ich?
Vahss TOO-eh ikh?
What am I doing?

Sie buchstabieren.
Zee bookh-shtah-BEE-r'n.
You are spelling.

Welches Wort buchstabiere ich?
VEL-khes Vohrt bookh-shtah-BEE-reh ikh?
Which word am I spelling?

Buchstabieren Sie das Wort "Tisch"!
*Bookh-shtah-*BEE-*r'n Zee dahs Vohrt "Tish"!*
Spell the word "Tisch"!

Buchstabieren Sie: "Buch",   **"weiss",**   **"dreissig",**
*Bookh-shtah-*BEE-*r'n Zee: "Bookh",*   *"vice",*   *"*DRIGH-*ssikh",*
Spell: "book",   "white",   "thirty",

"nein",	**"deutsch",**	**"italienisch"**	**und**	**"Lehrer"!**
"nine",	*"doitsh",*	*"ee-tahl-*YAY-*nish"*	*oont*	*"*LAY-*r'r"!*
"no",	"German",	"Italian"	and	"teacher"!

Wie schreibt man "Notizbuch"?   **Wie schreibt man "Tasche"?**
*Vee skrighbt mahn "Noh-*TEETS-*bookh"?*   *Vee shrighbt mahn "*TAH-*sheh"?*
How do you write "note-book"?   How does one write "pocket"?

Buchstabieren Sie "Hände"!
*Bookh-shtah-*BEE-*r'n Zee "*HEN-*deh"!*
Spell "hands"!

Was steht nach dem H in diesem Wort?
Vahss shtait nahkh daim Hah in DEEZ'*m Vohrt?*
What stands after H in this word?

Nach dem "H" steht "ä".
Nahkh daim "Hah" shtait "eh".
After the "h" stands "ä".

 **NOTE** on the *Umlaut:* Certain nouns containing the vowels *A, O,* or *U* take the umlaut in their plural forms. Ex.

der Fuss	—	die Füsse
die Hand	—	die Hände
das Wort	—	die Wörter.

The same vowel change occurs in certain verb forms, as we shall see in subsequent lessons. **See the Note on Pronunciation** before Lesson 1 to refresh your memory on the pronunciation of vowels with the *Umlaut.*

Hier sind Sätze: **Was ist das?**   **Das ist ein Buch.**
Here zint ZET-*tseh:*   *Vahss ist dahs?*   *Dahs ist ine Bookh.*
Here are sentences: What is this?   This is a book.

"Was ist das?" ist die Frage,
"Vahss ist dahs?" ist dee FRAH-*ggeh,*
"What is this?" is the question,

"Das ist ein Buch" ist die Antwort.
"Dahs ist ine Bookh" ist dee AHNT-*vohrt.*
"This is a book" is the answer.

Ich frage: "Was tun Sie?"
Ikh FRAH-*ggeh: "Vahss toon Zee?"*
I ask: "What are you doing?"

Sie antworten: 'Ich lese."
Zee AHNT-*vohr-t'n: "Ikh* LAY-*zeh."*
You answer: "I am reading."

Sie fragen: "Wo ist das Buch?"
Zee FRAH-*g'n: "Voh ist dahs Bookh?"*
You ask: "Where is the book?"

Ich antworte: "Es ist in der Hand."
Ikh AHNT-*vohr-teh: "Ess ist in dehr Hahnt."*
I answer: "It is in (my) hand."

Ich frage: "Wer bin ich?"
Ikh FRAH-*ggeh: "Vair bin ikh?"*
I am asking: "Who am I?"

Bitte, antworten Sie!
BIT-*teh,* AHNT-*vohr-t'n Zee!*
Please, answer!

Fragen Sie mich, wo mein Hut ist!
FRAH-*g'n Zee mikh, voh mine Hoot ist!*
Ask me where my hat is!

Bitte, wo ist Ihr Hut?
BIT-*teh, voh ist Eer Hoot?*
Please, where is your hat?

Mein Name ist Berlitz.
Mine NAH-*meh ist* BEHR-*lits.*
My name is Berlitz.

Ich heisse Berlitz.
Ikh HIGH-*sseh* BEHR-*lits.*
I am called Berlitz.

Was ist mein Name?
Vahss ist mine NAH-*meh?*
What is my name?

Wie heisse ich?
Vee HIGH-*sseh ikh?*
What am I called?

Sie heissen Berlitz.
Zee HIGH-*ss'n* BEHR-*lits.*
You are called: Berlitz.

Ihr Name ist Berlitz.
Ihr NAH-*meh ist* BEHR-*lits.*
Your name is Berlitz.

Wie heisst der Präsident?
*Vee highsst dehr Preh-zee-*DENT?
What is the president called?

Wie heissen Sie?
Vee HIGH-*ss'n Zee?*
What are you called?

Fragen Sie mich, wieviele Bücher ich habe!
FRAH-*g'n Zee mikh, vee-*FEE-*leh* BEW-*kh'r ikh* HAH-*beh!*
Ask me how many books I have!

Was ist Ihr Name?
Vahss ist Eer NAH-*meh?*
What is your name?

Wo ist Ihr Buch?
Voh ist Eer Bookh?
Where is your book?

NOTE: "My" is *mein, meine, mein* and "your" is *Ihr, Ihre, Ihr.* These follow the same case changes as *ein* and *kein,* which we have already studied. See page 37.

THINKING IN GERMAN

(Answers on page 253)

1. Wieviele Buchstaben hat das deutsche A—B—C?
2. Steht das C vor dem P?
3. Endet das A—B—C mit W?
4. Wieviele Selbstlaute haben wir?
5. Ist K ein Selbstlaut?
6. Wieviele Umlaute haben wir?
7. Ist "Buch" englisch?
8. Was für ein Buch ist das?
9. Wie spricht man in Paris?
10. Spricht man in Berlin französisch?
11. Wie schreiben Sie "Hände"?
12. Ich frage: "Wer bin ich?" Antworten Sie bitte!
13. Antwortet der Lehrer?
14. Fragt der Schüler oder antwortet er?
15. Ist das mein Bleistift?
16. Wo ist Ihr Mantel?

ÜBUNG NR. 12

Was haben Sie?
Vahss HAH-*b'n Zee?*
What have you?

Ich habe einen Rock und Sie haben einen Rock.
Ikh HAH-*beh* EYE-*n'n Rokk oont Zee* HAH-*b'n* EYE-*n'n Rokk.*
I have a coat and you have a coat.

Mein Rock ist lang,
Mine Rokk ist lahnk,
My coat is long,

Ihr Rock ist kurz.
Eer Rokk ist koorts.
your coat is short.

Das ist Herr Karl.
Dahs ist Herr Kahrl.
This is Mr. Karl.

Herrn Karls Hut ist auf dem Kopf.
Herrn Kahrls Hoot ist aouf daim Koppf.
Mr. Karl's hat is on (his) head.

Das ist Herr Lang.
Dahs ist Herr Lahnk.
This is Mr. Lang.

Wo ist Herrn Langs Hut?
Voh ist Herrn Lahnks Hoot?
Where is Mr. Lang's hat?

Das ist Fräulein Berta.
Dahs ist FROY-line BEHR-tah.
This is Miss Bertha.

Wie ist Fräulein Bertas Kleid?
Vee ist FROY-line BEHR-tahs Klight?
What color is Miss Bertha's dress?

Ist Herrn Langs Kopf gross?
Ist Herrn Lahnks Koppf grohss?
Is Mr. Lang's head large?

Ja, sein Kopf ist gross.
Yah, zine Koppf ist grohss.
Yes, his head is large.

Was hat Fräulein Berta in der Hand?
Vahss haht FROY-line BEHR-tah in dehr Hahnt?
What has Miss Bertha in (her) hand?

Ist das Frau Langs Handtasche?
Ist dahs Fraou Lahnks HAHNT-tah-sheh?
Is this Mrs. Lang's handbag?

Ist Ihre Handtasche klein?
Ist EE-reh HAHNT-tah-sheh kline?
Is your handbag small?

Wo ist Herrn Langs Bleistift?
Voh ist Herrn Lahnks BLIGH-shtift?
Where is Mr. Lang's pencil?

Sein Bleistift ist in der Tasche.
Zine BLIGH-shtift ist in dehr TAH-sheh.
His pencil is in (his) pocket.

Ist die Hose des Herrn Berlitz lang?
Ist dee HOH-zeh dess Herrn BEHR-lits lahnk?
Are Mr. Berlitz's trousers long?

Wie ist sein Hut?
Vee ist zine Hoot?
What color is his hat?

Wie ist unser Zimmer, gross oder klein?
Vee ist OON-z'r TSIMM'r, grohss OH-d'r kline?
How is our room, large or small?

Wie sind Ihre Schuhe?
Vee zint EE-reh SHOO-heh?
What color are your shoes?

Wo sind unsere Bücher?
Voh zint oon-z'reh BEW-kh'r?
Where are our books?

Sind das Herrn Langs Bücher?
Zint dahs Herrn Lahnks BEW-kh'r?
Are these Mr. Lang's books?

Wer ist die Dame?
Vair ist dee DAH-meh?
Who is the lady?

Hat die Dame ein Kleid?
Haht dee DAH-meh ine Klight?
Has the lady a dress?

NOTE: *Wer,* pronounced *vair*—means "who". English speaking people often use it for "where" which can lead to some funny boners.

Wessen Kleid ist das?
VESS'n Klight ist dahs?
Whose dress is this?

Wessen Schuhe sind das?
VESS'n SHOO-heh zint dahs?
Whose shoes are these?

Der Hut des Herrn Berlitz ist auf dem Kopf.
Dehr Hoot dess Herrn BEHR-*lits ist aouf daim Koppf.*
Mr. Berlitz's hat is on (his) head.

Wessen Hut ist das?
VESS'*n Hoot ist dahs?*
Whose hat is this?

Ist Fräulein Berta die Schülerin des Herrn Berlitz?
Ist FROY-*line* BEHR-*tah dee* SHEW-*leh-rin dess Herrn* BEHR-*lits?*
Is Miss Bertha Mr. Berlitz's pupil?

Wessen Schüler ist Herr Lang?
VESS'*n* SHEW-*l'r ist Herr Lahnk?*
Whose pupil is Mr. Lang?

Wessen Rock ist schwarz?
VESS'*n Rokk ist shvahrtss?*
Whose coat is black?

Haben Sie Ihre Handschuhe?
HAH-*b'n Zee* EE-*reh* HAHNT-*shoo-heh?*
Have you your gloves?

Wessen Lehrer ist Herr Berlitz?
VESS'*n* LAY-*r'r ist Herr* BEHR-*lits?*
Whose teacher is Mr. Berlitz?

REMEMBER: "Whose"—*wessen* requires an answer in the possessive (genitive) case, which is the last new case we shall encounter. The possessive of *der* and *das* is *des;* the possessive of *die* is *der*. Also the possessive of *ein* is *eines,* and that of *eine* is *einer.* Sometimes the nouns themselves change, but we shall worry about that in a later lesson. Observe the following examples: "Mr. Mauser's money"—*Herrn Mausers Geld,* or "the money of Mr. Mauser"—*das Geld des Herrn Mauser.* As in English, either form is correct. Notice that there is no possessive apostrophe in German.

Herr Lang hat eine Zigarette.
Herr Lahnk haht EYE-*neh Tsee-gah-*RET-*teh.*
Mr. Lang has a cigarette.

Er hat kein Streichholz.
Air haht kine SHTRIGHKH-*hohlts.*
He has no match.

Herr Berlitz hat eine Schachtel Streichhölzer.
Herr BEHR-*lits haht* EYE-*neh* SHAHKH-*t'l* SHTRIGHKH-*huhll-ts'r.*
Mr. Berlitz has a box of matches.

NOTE to Student: In German no genitive of quantity is used. We say: *ein Glas Wasser*—"a glass water," *eine Schachtel Streichhölzer*—"a box matches," *eine Tasse Kaffee*—"a cup coffee," etc.

Wessen Streichhölzer sind das?
VESS'*n* SHTRIGHKH-*huhll-ts'r zint dahs?*
Whose matches are these?

Wessen Zigarette ist das?
VESS'*n Tsee-gah-*RET-*teh ist dahs?*
Whose cigarette is this?

Herr Berlitz nimmt zwei Streichhölzer.
Herr BEHR-*lits nimt tsvigh* SHTRIGHKH-*huhll-ts'r.*
Mr. Berlitz takes two matches.

Er nimmt sie aus der Schachtel.
Air nimt zee aous dehr SHAHKH-*t'l.*
He takes them out of the box.

Er hat zwei Streichhölzer in der Hand.
Air haht tsvigh SHTRIGHKH-*huhll-ts'r in dehr Hahnt.*
He has two matches in (his) hand.

Wieviele Streichhölzer hat Herr Lang?
*Vee-*FEE-*leh* SHTRIGHKH-*huhll-ts'r haht Herr Lahnk?*
How many matches has Mr. Lang?

Hat er soviele Streichhölzer wie Herr Berlitz?
*Haht air zoh-*FEE-*leh* SHTRIGHKH-*huhll-ts'r vee Herr* BEHR-*lits?*
Has he as many matches as Mr. Berlitz?

Haben Sie Streichhölzer?
HAH-*b'n Zee* SHTRIGHKH-*huhll-ts'r?*
Have you matches?

Wessen Streichhölzer sind das?
VESS'n SHTRIGHKH-*huhll-ts'r zint dahs?*
Whose matches are these?

Hat Herr Berlitz mehr als Sie?
Haht Herr BEHR-*lits mair ahls Zee?*
Has Mr. Berlitz more than you?

Hat Herr Lang weniger als Herr Berlitz?
Haht Herr Lahnk VAY-*nee-g'r ahls Herr* BEHR-*lits?*
Has Mr. Lang less than Mr. Berlitz?

Fräulein Berta hat zwei Handschuhe;
FROY-*line* BEHR-*tah haht tsvigh* HAHNT-*shoo-heh;*
Miss Bertha has two gloves;

Herr Lang hat einen Handschuh.
Herr Lahnk haht EYE-*n'n* HAHNT-*shoo.*
Mr. Lang has one glove.

Wer hat mehr Handschuhe?
Vair haht mair HAHNT-*shoo-heh?*
Who has more gloves?

Hat Herr Lang soviele Handschuhe wie Fräulein Berta?
*Haht Herr Lahnk zoh-*FEE-*leh* HAHNT-*shoo-heh vee* FROY-*line* BEHR-*tah?*
Has Mr. Lang as many gloves as Miss Bertha?

Sie haben drei Bleistifte,
Zee HAH-*b'n drigh* BLIGH-*shtif-teh,*
You have three pencils,

ich habe zwei.
ikh HAH-*beh tsvigh.*
I have two.

Habe ich soviele Bleistifte wie Sie?
HAH-*beh ikh zoh-*FEE-*leh* BLIGH-*shtif-teh vee Zee?*
Have I as many pencils as you?

Wer hat mehr Bleistifte, Sie oder ich?
Vair haht mair BLIGH-*shtif-teh, Zee* OH-*d'r ikh?*
Who has more pencils, you or I?

Wieviele Bleistifte haben wir zusammen?
Vee-FEE-leh BLIGH-*shtif-teh* HAH-*b'n veer tsoo-*ZAH-*m'n?*
How many pencils have we together?

Bitte, nehmen Sie meine Bleistifte!
BIT-*teh,* NAY-*m'n Zee* MIGH-*neh* BLIGH-*shtif-teh!*
Please, take my pencils!

Wieviele Bleistifte haben Sie?
*Vee-*FEE-*leh* BLIGH-*shtif-teh* HAH-*b'n Zee?*
How many pencils have you?

Habe ich mehr als Sie?
HAH-*beh ikh mair ahls Zee?*
Have I more than you?

Wieviele Krawatten haben Herr Lang und Herr Berlitz zusammen?
*Vee-*FEE-*leh Krah-*VAH-*t'n* HAH-*b'n Herr Lahnk oont Herr* BEHR-*lits tsoo-*
ZAH-*m'n?*
How many ties have Mr. Lang and Mr. Berlitz together?

Hat Herr Lang soviele Krawatten wie Herr Berlitz?
*Haht Herr Lahnk zoh-*FEE-*leh Krah-*VAH-*t'n vee Herr* BEHR-*lits?*
Has Mr. Lang as many ties as Mr. Berlitz?

Herrn Langs Rock hat viele Taschen,
Herrn Lahnks Rokk haht FEE-*leh* TAH-*sh'n,*
Mr. Lang's coat has many pockets,

der Rock des Herrn Berlitz hat wenige.
dehr Rokk dess Herrn BEHR-*lits haht* VAY-*nee-ggeh.*
Mr. Berlitz's coat has few.

Wessen Rock hat mehr Taschen?
VESS'*n Rokk haht mair* TAH-*sh'n?*
Whose coat has more pockets?

Wer hat mehr Taschen?
Vair haht mair TAH-*sh'n?*
Who has more pockets?

Dieses Buch hat viele Seiten, es ist dick;
DEEZ'*s Bookh haht* FEE-*leh* ZIGH-*t'n, ess ist dick;*
This book has many pages, it is thick;

dieses ist dünn, es hat wenige Seiten.
DEEZ'*s ist dewn, ess haht* VAY-*nee-ggeh* ZIGH-*ten.*
this one is thin, it has few pages.

Welches Buch hat weniger Seiten?
VEL-*khes Bookh haht* VAY-*nee-g'r* ZIGH-*ten?*
Which book has fewer pages?

In welchem Buch sind mehr Seiten?
In VEL-*khem Bookh zint mair* ZIGH-*ten?*
In which book are there more pages?

NOTE: The *Umlaut* is very often used to help form the plural. Ex. *Blatt—Blätter, Streichholz—Streichhölzer, Buch —Bücher. Hut—Hüte, Kopf—Köpfe*, etc.

Sind viele Seiten in dem dicken Buch?
Zint FEE-*leh* ZIGH-*t'n in daim* DIK-*k'n Bookh?*
Are there many pages in the thick book?

Sind viele Streichhölzer in der grossen Schachtel?
Zint FEE-*leh* SHTRIGHKH-*huhll-ts'r in dehr* GROH-*ss'n* SHAHKH-*t'l?*
Are there many matches in the big box?

Sind Herr Lang und Fräulein Berta die Schüler des Herrn Berlitz?
Zint Herr Lahnk oont FROY-*line* BEHR-*tah dee* SHEW-*l'r dess Herrn* BEHR-*lits'*
Are Mr. Lang and Miss Bertha the pupils of Mr. Berlitz?

Wieviele Schulen hat Herr Berlitz?
*Vee-*FEE-*leh* SHOO-*l'n haht Herr* BEHR-*lits?*
How many schools has Mr. Berlitz?

Er hat viele Schulen in allen Ländern.
Air haht FEE-*leh* SHOO-*l'n in* AHL-*len* LEND'*rn.*
He has many schools in all countries.

Ich habe tausend Mark in der Tasche; Sie haben hundert Mark.
Ikh HAH-*beh* TAOU-*z'nt Mark in dehr* TAH-*sheh; Zee* HAH-*b'n* HOON-*d'rt Mark.*
I have 1000 Marks in my pocket; you have 100 Marks.

> **Habe ich viel Geld?**
> HAH-*beh ikh feel Ggelt?*
> Have I much money?

> **Haben Sie weniger oder mehr Geld als ich?**
> HAH-*b'n Zee* VAY-*nee-g'r* OH-*d'r mair Ggelt ahls ikh?*
> Have you less or more money than I?

Hat Rockefeller viel Geld?   Hat er mehr Geld als wir zusammen?
Haht ROKK-*eh-fell'r feel Ggelt?   Haht air mair Ggelt ahls veer tsoo-*ZAH-*m'n?*
Has Rockefeller much money?   Has he more money than we together?

> **Herr Lang hat zwanzig Pfennige.**
> *Herr Lahnk haht* TSVAHN-*tsikh* PFEN-*nee-ggeh.*
> Mr. Lang has 20 pennies.

> **Hat er viel oder wenig Geld?**
> *Haht air feel* OH-*d'r* VAY-*neekh Ggelt?*
> Has he much or little money?

THINKING IN GERMAN

(Answers on page 254)

1. Wer hat mehr Geld, der Herr Lehrer oder Frau Huber?

2. Hat er so viel Geld wie Vanderbilt?

3. Wieviel Geld hat Liese?

4. Hat der Lehrer einen Bleistift hinter dem Ohr?

5. Hat er mehr Bleistifte als Liese?

6. Hat Liese weniger Bücher als der Herr Lehrer?

7. Hat Frau Huber viel Geld?

8. Wessen Hut hat Frau Huber auf dem Kopf?

9. Wessen Rock ist kurz, Lieses oder Frau Hubers Rock?

10. Haben Sie viel Geld?

11. Haben Sie mehr Geld als Bleistifte?

12. Sind viele Seiten in diesem Buch?

13. Wieviele Buchstaben sind in dem Wort "Streichholz"?

ÜBUNG NR. 13

Ich gebe Ihnen ein Buch
Ikh GAY-beh EE-n'n ine Bookh
I give you a book

Ich gebe Ihnen ein Buch.
Ikh GAY-beh EE-n'n ine Bookh.
I give you a book.

Sie geben mir ein Buch.
Zee GAY-b'n meer ine Bookh.
You give me a book.

Ich gebe Ihnen ein Buch.
Ikh GAY-beh EE-n'n ine Bookh.
I give you a book.

Wer gibt Ihnen das Buch?
Vair ggipt EE-n'n dahs Bookh?
Who gives you the book?

Was tue ich?
Vahss TOO-eh ikh?
What do I do?

Ich bekomme ein Buch von Ihnen.
Ikh beh-KOM-meh ine Bookh fonn EE-n'n.
I receive a book from you.

Sie bekommen ein Buch von mir.
Zee beh-KOMM'n ine Bookh fonn meer.
You receive a book from me.

Was gebe ich Ihnen?
Vahss GAY-beh ikh EE-n'n?
What do I give you?

Von wem bekommen Sie das Buch?
Fonn vaim beh-KOMM'n Zee dahs Bookh?
From whom do you get the book?

64

Bekommen Sie das Buch von mir?
*Beh-*KOMM*'n Zee dahs Bookh fonn meer?*
Do you get the book from me?

WATCH OUT! *Bekommen* means in German "to get", "to receive". Do not confound it with our "become" which is translated by *werden.* Ex. *Ich bekomme Geld*—"I receive money".

Sie geben mir Geld.
Zee GAY-*b'n meer Ggelt.*
You give me money.

Von wem bekomme ich das Geld?
*Fonn vaim beh-*KOM-*meh ikh dahs Ggelt?*
From whom do I get the money?

Wem geben Sie das Geld?
Vaim GAY-*b'n Zee dahs Ggelt?*
To whom do you give the money?

Wer bekommt das Geld?
*Vair beh-*KOMMT *dahs Ggelt?*
Who gets the money?

NOTE ON THE DATIVE: When you give something to someone or tell him something, the word representing the person who receives or is told something must be expressed in the dative. (This corresponds to the indirect object in English.) Ex. "You give me a check."—*Sie geben* MIR *einen Scheck.*

Geben Sie diesen Bleistift Herrn Lang!
GAY-*b'n Zee* DEEZ*'n* BLIGH-*shtift Herrn Lahnk!*
Give this pencil to Mr. Lang!

Was tun Sie?
Vahss toon Zee?
What are you doing?

Bekommt Herr Lang den Bleistift?
*Beh-*KOMMT *Herr Lahnk dain* BLIGH-*shtift?*
Does Mr. Lang get the pencil?

Von wem bekommt er den Bleistift?
*Fonn vaim beh-*KOMMT *air dain* BLIGH-*shtift?*
From whom does he get the pencil?

Bekommen Sie einen Bleistift von Herrn Berlitz?
*Beh-*KOMM*'n Zee* EYE-*n'n* BLIGH-*shtift fonn Herrn* BEHR-*lits?*
Do you get a pencil from Mr. Berlitz?

Wer bekommt ihn?
*Vair beh-*KOMMT *een?*
Who gets it?

Geben Sie Frau Huber ein Papier!
GAY-*b'n Zee Fraou* HOO-*b'r ine Pah-*PEER!
Give a (piece of) paper to Mrs. Huber!

Wer bekommt das Papier?
*Vair beh-*KOMMT *dahs Pah-*PEER?
Who gets the paper?

Wem geben Sie es?
Vaim GAY-b'n Zee ess?
To whom do you give it?

Bekommt sie das Papier von Ihnen?
Beh-KOMMT zee dahs Pah-PEER fonn EE-n'n?
Does she get the paper from you?

Ich gebe der Dame einen Stuhl.
Ikh GAY-beh dehr DAH-meh EYE-n'n Shtool.
I give the lady a chair.

Geben Sie den Damen Stühle!
GAY-b'n Zee dehn DAH-men SHTEW-leh!
Give the ladies chairs!

Geben Sie ihr einen Stuhl!
GAY-b'n Zee eer EYE-n'n Shtool!
Give her a chair!

Geben Sie ihnen Stühle!
GAY-b'n Zee EE-n'n SHTEW-leh!
Give them chairs!

Ist Herr Berlitz Ihr Lehrer?
Ist Herr BEHR-lits Eer LAY-r'r?
Is Mr. Berlitz your teacher?

Gibt er Ihnen Bücher?
Ggipt air EE-n'n BEW-kh'r?
Does he give you books?

Gibt er seinen Schülern Bücher?
Ggipt air ZIGH-n'n SHEW-l'rn BEW-kh'r?
Does he give his pupils books?

Ja, er gibt ihnen Bücher.
Yah, air ggipt EE-n'n BEW-kh'r.
Yes, he gives them books.

Geben Sie dem Lehrer Geld?
GAY-b'n Zee daim LAY-r'r Ggelt?
Do you give the teacher money?

Von wem bekommt er das Geld?
Fonn vaim beh-KOMMT air dahs Ggelt?
From whom does he get the money?

Was gibt Ihnen der Lehrer?
Vahss ggipt EE-n'n dehr LAY-r'r?
What does the teacher give you?

Bekommen Sie Geld von ihm?
Beh-KOMM'n Zee Ggelt fonn eem?
Do you get money from him?

Nein, der Lehrer gibt uns kein Geld; er gibt uns Stunden.
Nine, dehr LAY-r'r ggipt oons kine Ggelt; air ggipt oons SHTOON-d'n.
No, the teacher gives us no money; he gives us lessons.

Wer bekommt die Stunden?
Vair beh-KOMMT dee SHTOON-d'n?
Who gets the lessons?

Wir nehmen (bekommen) die Stunden.
Veer NAY-m'n (beh-KOMM'n) dee SHTOON-d'n.
We take (receive) the lessons.

Gibt der Lehrer dem Herrn Lang Stunden?
Ggipt dehr LAY-r'r daim Herrn Lahnk SHTOON-d'n?
Does the teacher give lessons to Mr. Lang?

Bekommen Sie von Herrn Berlitz deutsche Stunden?
Beh-KOMM'n Zee fonn Herrn BEHR-lits DOIT-sheh SHTOON-d'n?
Do you get German lessons from Mr. Berlitz?

Was bekommen Sie von ihm?
*Vahss beh-*KOMM*'n Zee fonn eem?*
What do you get from him?

Herr Berlitz spricht deutsch.
Herr BEHR-*lits shprikht doitsh.*
Mr. Berlitz speaks German.

Sprechen Sie deutsch?
SHPREH-*kh'n Zee doitsh?*
Do you speak German?

Sprechen Sie!
SHPREH-*kh'n Zee!*
Speak!

Spricht der Lehrer?
Shprikht dehr LAY-*r'r?*
Does the teacher speak?

Ja, der Lehrer spricht.
Yah, dehr LAY-*r'r shprikht.*
Yes, the teacher speaks.

Was sagt der Lehrer?
Vahss zahgt dehr LAY-*r'r?*
What does the teacher say?

Er sagt etwas.
Air zahgt ETT-*vahss.*
He says something.

Er sagt: "Die Tür ist offen."
Air zahgt: "Dee Tewr ist off'n."
He says: "The door is open."

Sagen Sie, dass die Tür offen ist!
ZAH-*g'n Zee, dahss dee Tewr off'n ist!*
Say that the door is open!

Was sagen Sie mir?
Vahss ZAH-*g'n Zee meer?*
What do you say to me?

NOTE on Word Order: The normal word order is: *Die Tür ist offen* and is used in independent clauses with the subject preceding the verb. In questions the order is inverted: *Ist die Tür offen?* as well as in clauses beginning with an adverb, a complement or a predicate adjective. Ex: *Jetzt ist die Tür offen*—"Now is the door open."

Sprechen Sie deutsch?
SHPREH-*kh'n Zee doitsh?*
Do you speak German?

Spricht Herr Lang deutsch?
Shprikht Herr Lahnk doitsh?
Does Mr. Lang speak German?

Sagen Sie mir, was Sie in der Hand haben!
ZAH-*g'n Zee meer, vahss Zee in dehr Hahnt* HAH-*b'n!*
Tell me, what you have in your hand!

Sprechen Sie!
SHPREH-*kh'n Zee!*
Speak!

Ist dieser Herr Herr Berlitz?
Ist DEEZ'r *Herr Herr* BEHR-*lits?*
Is this gentleman Mr. Berlitz?

Sagen Sie mir, wer jener Herr ist!
ZAH-*g'n Zee meer, vair* YEH-*n'r Herr ist!*
Tell me who that gentleman is!

NOTE on *Herr*: The word *Herr* has various meanings in German. It means "gentleman": *Wer ist der Herr?*—it means "Mister": *Das ist Herr Berlitz*—and it means "master": *er ist der Herr des Hauses*—"he is the master of the house". *Dieser Herr, Herr Berlitz, ist der Herr des Hauses.*—"This gentleman, Mr. Berlitz, is the master of the house".

Was sagen Sie?
Vahss ZAH-*g'n Zee?*
What do you say?

Spricht Fräulein Berta englisch?
Shprikht FROY-*line* BEHR-*tah* ENNG-*lish?*
Does Miss Bertha speak English?

Sagen Sie mir, bitte, wer dieser Herr ist!
ZAH-*g'n Zee meer,* BIT-*teh, vair* DEEZ'*r Herr ist!*
Tell me, please, who this gentleman is!

Das ist Herr Kurz.
Dahs ist Herr Koorts.
This is Mr. Kurz.

Kurz ist der Name des Herrn.
Koorts ist dehr NAH-*meh dess Herrn.*
Kurz is the gentleman's name.

Er heisst Kurz.
Air highst Koorts.
He is called Kurz.

Sagen Sie mir, wie Sie heissen!
ZAH-*g'n Zee meer, vee Zee* HIGH-*ss'n!*
Tell me what you are called!

Mein Name ist Kurz; ich heisse Kurz.
Mine NAH-*meh ist Koorts; ikh* HIGH-*sseh Koorts.*
My name is Kurz; I am called Kurz.

Sagen Sie mir Ihren Namen!
ZAH-*g'n Zee meer* EE-*r'n* NAH-*m'n!*
Tell me your name!

Mein Name ist Berlitz.
Mine NAH-*meh ist* BEHR-*lits.*
My name is Berlitz.

Was tun Sie?
Vahss toon Zee?
What are you doing?

Ich sage Ihnen, wie jener Herr heisst.
Ikh Zah-ggeh EE-*n'n, vee* YEH-*n'r Herr highst.*
I am telling you what that gentleman is called.

Sagen Sie mir Ihren Namen!
ZAH-*g'n Zee meer* EE-*r'n* NAH-*m'n!*
Tell me your name!

Mein Name ist Berlitz, ich bin Herr Berlitz.
Mine NAH-*meh ist* BEHR-*lits, ikh bin Herr* BEHR-*lits.*
My name is Berlitz, I am Mr. Berlitz.

Was sagt der Lehrer vor der Stunde?
Vahss zaght dehr LAY-*r'r fohr dehr* SHTOON-*deh?*
What does the teacher say before the lesson?

Er sagt: Guten Tag!
Air zahgt: GOO-*t'n Tahk!*
He says: Good day!

Was antworten ihm die Schüler?
Vahss AHNT-*vohr-t'n eem dee* SHEW-*l'r?*
What do the pupils answer?

Die Schüler antworten: Guten Tag!
Dee SHEW-*l'r* AHNT-*vohr-t'n:* GOO-*t'n Tahk!*
The pupils answer: Good day!

Nach der Stunde sagt er: Auf Wiedersehen!
Nahkh dehr SHTOON-*deh zahgt air: Aouf* VEE-*d'r-zehn!*
After the lesson he says: Till we meet again!

NOTE: You may greet an acquaintance in German with *Guten Tag!*—"Good day!" or *Guten Abend!*—"Good evening!". There is no corresponding form for "Good afternoon". When leaving someone late at night or prior to retiring, say *Gute Nacht!*—"Good night!". Of course, you can use *Auf Wiedersehen!*—"Till we meet again!" at any time.

Was sagen die Schüler nach der Stunde?
Vahss ZAH-*g'n dee* SHEW-*l'r nahkh dehr* SHTOON-*deh?*
What do the pupils say after the lesson?

Auf dem Tisch liegt das Buch.
Aouf daim Tish leekt dahs Bookh.
The book is lying on the table.

Liegt etwas auf dem Stuhl?
Leekt ETT-*vahss aouf daim Shtool?*
Is there something lying on the chair?

Nein, auf dem Stuhl liegt nichts.
Nine, aouf daim Shtool leekt nikhts.
No, there is nothing lying on the chair.

Was liegt auf diesem Stuhl?
Vahss leekt aouf DEEZ'*m Shtool?*
What is lying on this chair?

Auf diesem Tisch liegt etwas.
Aouf DEEZ'*m Tish leekt* ETT-*vahss.*
There is something lying on this table.

Was ist es? **Es ist ein Buch.**
Vahss ist ess? *Ess ist ine Bookh.*
What is it? It is a book.

Liegt etwas auf jenem Tisch?
Leekt ETT-*vahss aouf* YEH-*n'm Tish?*
Is there something lying on that table?

Nein, auf jenem Tisch liegt nichts.
Nine, aouf YEH-*n'm Tish leekt nikhts.*
No, there is nothing lying on that table.

Was liegt unter dem Tisch?
Vahss leekt OON-*t'r daim Tish?*
What is lying under the table?

Was liegt hinter der Tür?
Vahss leekt HINT-*r dehr Tewr.*
What is lying behind the door?

Auf diesem Buch liegt ein Bleistift.
Aouf DEEZ'*m Bookh leekt ine* BLIGH-*shtift.*
On this book lies a pencil.

Auf diesem Buch liegt etwas.
Aouf DEEZ'*m Bookh leekt* ETT-*vahss.*
Something is lying on this book.

Was liegt auf dem Buch?
Vahss leekt aouf daim Bookh?
What is lying on the book?

Auf diesem Stuhl sitzt Herr Viktor.
Aouf DEEZ'*m Shtool zitst Herr* VIK-*tohr.*
Mr. Victor is sitting on this chair.

Sitzt jemand auf diesem Stuhl?
Zitst YEH-*mahnt aouf* DEEZ'*m Shtool?*
Is someone sitting on this chair?

Ja, Herr Viktor sitzt auf diesem Stuhl.
Yah, Herr VIK-*tohr zitst aouf* DEEZ'*m Shtool.*
Yes, Mr. Victor is sitting on this chair.

Auf jenem Stuhl sitzt niemand.
Aouf YEH-*n'm Shtool zitst* NEE-*mahnt.*
No one is sitting on that chair.

Sitzt jemand auf dem andern Stuhl?
Zitst YEH-*mahnt aouf daim* AHN-*d'rn Shtool?*
Is someone sitting on the other chair?

Niemand sitzt auf dem andern Stuhl.
NEE-*mahnt zitst aouf daim* AHN-*d'rn Shtool.*
No one is sitting on the other chair.

Steht der Schüler vor dem Lehrer?
Shtait dehr SHEW-*l'r fohr daim* LAY-*r'r?*
Does the pupil stand in front of the teacher?

Steht jemand vor dem Lehrer?
Shtait YEH-*mahnt fohr daim* LAY-*r'r?*
Is somebody standing in front of the teacher?

Wer sitzt hinter dem Tisch?
Vair zitst HINT'*r daim Tish?*
Who is sitting behind the table?

Niemand sitzt hinter dem Tisch.
NEE-*mahnt zitst* HINT'*r daim Tish.*
Nobody is sitting behind the table.

Steht jemand auf dem Tisch?
Shtait YEH-*mahnt aouf daim Tish?*
Is somebody standing on the table?

Nein, niemand steht auf dem Tisch.
Nine, NEE-*mahnt shtait aouf daim Tish.*
No, nobody is standing on the table.

Auf Wiedersehen, Liese!
Aouf VEE-*d'r-zehn,* LEE-*zeh!*
Till we meet again, Liese!

Danke, Herr Berlitz!
DAHN-*keh, Herr* BEHR-*lits!*
Thank you, Mr. Berlitz!

THINKING IN GERMAN

(Answers on page 254)

1. Gibt der Lehrer der Frau Huber ein Buch?

2. Was gibt der Lehrer der Liese?

3. Was sagt Frau Huber?

4. Bekommt der Lehrer einen Hut von Frau Huber?

5. Wer gibt Liese Geld?

6. Wie heisst die Dame?

7. Wer sitzt vor Frau Huber?

8. Sagt Schnucki etwas?

9. Bekommt der Hund etwas?

10. Sitzt jemand auf dem Stuhl?

11. Hat der Lehrer etwas in der Hand?

12. Sagen Sie mir, wer auf dem Stuhl sitzt!

13. Was sagen Sie mir?

14. Wem gibt der Lehrer eine deutsche Stunde?

15. Spricht der Hund englisch?

ÜBUNG NR. 14

Was ist auf dem Ofen?
Vahss ist aouf daim OH-*f'n?*
What's cooking?

Was ist das?
Vahss ist dahs?
What is this?

Das ist der Ofen.
Dahs ist dehr OH-*f'n.*
This is the stove.

Wer geht an den Ofen?
Vair gait ahn dain OH-*f'n?*
Who goes to the stove?

Der Koch geht an den Ofen.
Dehr Kohkh gait ahn dain OH-*f'n.*
The cook goes to the stove.

Wohin geht der Koch?
*Voh-*HIN *gait dehr Kohkh?*
Where is the cook going?

Er geht an den Ofen.
Air gait ahn dain OH-*f'n.*
He is going to the stove.

Hat er etwas in der Hand?
Haht air ETT-*vahss in dehr Hahnt?*
Has he something in his hand?

Ja, er hat einen Topf in der Hand.
Yah, air haht EYE-*n'n Toppf in dehr Hahnt.*
Yes, he has a pot in his hand.

Er kommt von dem Tisch.
Air kommt fonn daim Tish.
He is coming from the table.

Woher kommt er?
*Voh-*HAIR *kommt air?*
Where is he coming from?

NOTE: *Wohin—woher* correspond to "whither" and "whence" which are no longer very much used in English. In German—however—they are essential. When you mean "where to"—use *wohin;* when you mean "where from"—use *woher.*

Was ist auf dem Tisch?
Vahss ist aouf daim Tish?
What is there on the table?

Auf dem Tisch liegt ein Löffel.
Aouf daim Tish leegt ine LUHFF'*l.*
There is a spoon lying on the table.

Liegt der Löffel unter dem Tisch?
Leegt dehr LUHFF'*l* OON-*t'r daim Tish?*
Is the spoon lying under the table?

Wer sitzt auf dem Stuhl?
Vair zitst aouf daim Shtool?
Who is sitting on the chair?

Der Hund Schnucki sitzt auf dem Stuhl.
Dehr Hoont SHNOO-*kee zitst aouf daim Shtool.*
Schnucki the dog is sitting on the chair.

Wo steht der Stuhl, am Ofen oder am Tisch?
Voh shtait dehr Shtool, ahm OH-*f'n* OH-*d'r ahm Tish?*
Where does the chair stand, by the stove or by the table?

Sitzt jemand auf dem Stuhl?
Zitst YEH-*mahnt aouf daim Shtool?*
Is there somebody sitting on the chair?

Was steht auf dem Ofen?
Vahss shtait aouf daim OH-*f'n?*
What is standing on the stove?

Was ist in dem Topf auf dem Ofen?
Vahss ist in daim Toppf aouf daim OH-*f'n?*
What is in the pot on the stove?

Der Pudding ist in dem Topf.
Dehr POO-*dink ist in daim Toppf.*
The pudding is in the pot.

Was stellt der Koch in den Ofen?
Vahss shtellt dehr Kohkh in dain OH-*f'n?*
What does the cook put in the stove?

Er stellt den Braten in den Ofen.
Air shtellt dain BRAH-*t'n in dain* OH-*f'n.*
He puts the roast in the stove.

Wohin stellt er ihn?
*Voh-*HIN *shtellt air een?*
Where does he put it?

Wo ist der Braten?
Voh ist dehr BRAH-*t'n?*
Where is the roast?

Steht jemand hinter dem Tisch?
Shtait YEH-*mahnt* HINT'*r daim Tish?*
Is there someone standing behind the table?

Woher kommt der Junge?
*Voh-*HAIR *kommt dehr* YOON-*ggeh?*
Where does the boy come from?

Er kommt vom Bäcker.
Air kommt fom BECK'*r.*
He comes from the baker's.

Der Junge bringt den Kuchen.
Dehr YOON-*ggeh brinkt dain* KOO-*kh'n.*
The boy brings the cake.

Der Koch sagt: Bitte, kommen Sie nicht an den Ofen!
Dehr Kohkh zahgt: BIT-*teh,* KOMM'*n Zee nikht ahn dain* OH-*f'n!*
The cook says: Please, do not come near the stove!

Stellen Sie den Kuchen auf den Tisch!
SHTELL'*n Zee dain* KOO-*kh'n aouf dain Tish!*
Put the cake on the table!

Wohin lege ich den Löffel vom Tisch? fragt der Junge.
*Voh-*HIN LEH-*ggeh ikh dain* LUHFF'*l fom Tish? frahgt dehr* YOON-*ggeh.*
Where do I put the spoon from the table? the boy asks.

Der Koch antwortet: Bringen Sie mir den Löffel, ich nehme ihn!
Dehr Kohkh AHNT-*vohr-tett:* BRING'*n Zee meer dain* LUHFF'*l, ikh* NAY-*meh
    een!*
The cook answers: Bring me the spoon, I (shall) take it!

Sie sind neu!
Zee zint noy!
You are new!

Wie heissen Sie?
Vee HIGH-*ss'n Zee?*
What is your name?

Mein Name ist Franz.
Mine NAH-*meh ist Frahnts.*
My name is Francis.

Gehen Sie an den Schrank!
GAY-*h'n Zee ahn dain Shrahnk!*
Go to the cabinet!

Danke, Franz!
DAHN-*keh, Frahnts!*
Thank you, Francis!

Öffnen Sie ihn!
UHFF-*n'n Zee een!*
Open it!

In dem Schrank liegt ein Schilling.
In daim Shrahnk leegt ine SHILL-*ink.*
In the cabinet is a shilling.

Nehmen Sie ihn!
NAY-*m'n Zee een!*
Take it!

IMPORTANT NOTE: The prepositions *an*—"at" or "near", *auf*—"on", *hinter*—"behind", *vor*—"before", "in front of", *in*—"in", *neben*—"beside", *über*—"over", *unter*—"under", *zwischen*—"between" take the accusative (direct object case) if used in connection with a verb indicating motion in a certain direction or change of position. The same prepositions take the dative (indirect object case) when the verb merely indicates a position. *Ich gehe in das Zimmer,*—"I go into the room", *ich bin in dem Zimmer*—"I am in the room."

Hoppla!
HOPP-lah!
Oops!

Der Schilling liegt unter dem Schrank auf dem Fussboden.
Dehr SHILL-ink leegt OON-t'r daim Shrahnk aouf daim FOOSS-boh-d'n.
The shilling lies under the cabinet on the floor.

Auf Wiedersehen!
Aouf VEE-d'r-zehn!
Goodbye!

Ich habe den Braten im Ofen und den Pudding auf dem Ofen!
Ikh HAH-beh dain BRAH-t'n im OH-f'n oont dain POO-dink aouf daim OH-f'n.
I have the roast in the oven and the pudding on the stove!

Wer steht an dem Ofen?
Vair shtait ahn daim OH-f'n?
Who is standing at the stove?

Was ist auf dem Tisch?
Vahss ist aouf daim Tish?
What is on the table?

Wo liegt der Schilling?
Voh leegt dehr SHILL-ink?
Where is the shilling?

Der Schilling liegt auf dem Boden.
Dehr SHILL-ink leegt aouf daim BOH-d'n.
The shilling lies on the floor.

Woher kommt der Junge?
Voh-HAIR kommt dehr YOON-ggeh?
Where does the boy come from?

Wo sitzt Schnucki?
Voh zitst SHNOO-kee?
Where is Schnucki sitting?

Er sitzt auf dem Stuhl.
Air zitst aouf daim Shtool.
He is sitting on the chair.

Was liegt im Schrank?
Vahss leegt im Shrahnk?
What is lying in the cabinet?

Wohin geht der Junge?
Voh-HIN gait dehr YOON-ggeh?
Where does the boy go?

NOTE to Student: *All nouns* used in this lesson are masculine, so that you may master the masculine case endings. Notice that they vary according to whether or not *motion toward* is indicated. Do not worry too much about this: you will gradually get it by practice, just as the Germans do.

Stellt der Koch den Braten in den Ofen?
Shtellt dehr Kohkh dain BRAH-*t'n in dain* OH-*f'n?*
Does the cook put the roast in the oven?

Wo sitzt der Hund, auf oder unter dem Stuhl?
Voh zitst dehr Hoont, aouf OH-*d'r* OON-*t'r daim Shtool?*
Where is the dog sitting, on or under the chair?

Der Koch hat einen weissen Mantel.
Dehr Kohkh haht EYE-*n'n* VIGH-*ss'n* MAHN-*t'l.*
The cook has a white coat.

Der Mantel hängt im Schrank.
Dehr MAHN-*t'l henkt im Shrahnk.*
The coat hangs in the cabinet.

Wir hängen den Mantel in den Schrank.
Veer HEN-*g'n dain* MAHN-*t'l in dain Shrahnk.*
We hang the coat in the closet.

Woher nimmt er ihn?　　　**Der Koch nimmt ihn aus dem Schrank.**
*Voh-*HAIR *nimt air een?*　　*Dehr Kohkh nimt een aous daim Shrahnk.*
Where does he take it from?　The cook takes it out of the cabinet.

THINKING IN GERMAN

(Answers on page 254)

1. Wo sitzt der Koch?
2. Ist der Braten in dem Ofen?
3. Sitzt der Hund an dem Tisch?
4. Wo liegt der Braten?
5. Woher kommt er?
6. Ist der Mantel im Schrank?
7. Wer geht von dem Ofen zum Stuhl?
8. Was liegt auf dem Tisch?
9. Steht der Koch an dem Ofen?
10. Wer kommt von dem Schrank?
11. Liegt etwas auf dem Tisch?
12. Woher kommt der Kuchen?
13. Wer bringt den Kuchen?
14. Ist der Junge unter dem Tisch?
15. Sitzt jemand auf dem Ofen?

ÜBUNG NR. 15

Fräulein Klara bekommt Besuch.
FROY-*line* KLAH-*rah beh*-KOMMT *Beh*-ZOOKH
Miss Clara receives a visit

Wir gehen in Fräulein Klaras Wohnzimmer.
Veer GAY-*h'n in* FROY-*line* KLAH-*rahs* VOHN-*tsimm'r.*
We go into Miss Clara's living room.

Wo ist Fräulein Klara?
Voh ist FROY-*line* KLAH-*rah?*
Where is Miss Clara?

Fräulein Klara sitzt auf dem Sofa.
FROY-*line* KLAH-*rah zitst aouf daim* ZOH-*fah.*
Miss Clara is sitting on the sofa.

Steht sie nicht an dem Fenster?
Shtait zee nikht ahn daim FEN-*st'r?*
Is she not standing at the window?

Nein, sie kommt von dem Fenster und setzt sich auf das Sofa.
Nine, zee kommt fonn daim FEN-*st'r oont zetst zeekh aouf dahs* ZOH-*fah.*
No, she comes from the window and sits down on the sofa.

REMEMBER: The prepositions *von*—"from", *aus*—"out of", *bei*—"at", *mit*—"with", *zu*—"to" always take the dative case (indirect object case). *Von dem Fenster*—"from the window", *aus dem Zimmer*—"out of the room", *mit dem Schüler*—"with the student".

Auf dem Sofa liegt ein Buch.
Aouf daim ZOH-*fah leekt ine Bookh.*
On the sofa there lies a book.

Wo liegt Klaras Buch?
Voh leekt KLAH-*rahs Bookh?*
Where is Clara's book lying?

Sie nimmt das Buch von dem Sofa.
Zee nimt dahs Bookh fonn daim ZOH-*fah.*
She takes the book from the sofa.

Sie macht es auf.
Zee mahkht ess aouf.
She opens it.

Sie liest in dem Buch.
Zee leest in daim Bookh.
She reads in the book.

Was liest sie?
Vahss leest zee?
What does she read?

Sie legt das Taschentuch auf das Piano.
Zee laigt dahs TAH-*shen-tookh aouf dahs* p'YAH-*noh.*
She puts the handkerchief down on the piano.

Wohin legt sie es?
*Voh-*HIN *laigt zee ess?*
Where does she put it?

Was steht auf dem Tischchen?
Vahss shtait aouf daim TISH-*kh'n?*
What is on the little table?

NOTE to Student: The suffixes *-chen* and *-lein* indicate the diminutive. No matter what the gender of a word, it becomes neuter when turned into a diminutive by adding either of these suffixes. Ex. *Der Tisch, das Tischchen* or *das Tischlein.* Many such diminutives take an *Umlaut*, Ex. *das Haus, das Häuschen.*

Das Radio steht auf dem Tischchen.
Dahs RAHD-*yoh shtait aouf daim* TISH-*kh'n.*
The radio stands on the little table.

Das Konzert kommt aus dem Radio.
*Dahs Kohn-*TSAIRT *kommt aous daim* RAHD-*yoh.*
The concert comes over the radio.

Das Kätzchen liegt vor dem Sofa.
Dahs KETSS-*kh'n leekt fohr daim* ZOH-*fah.*
The kitten is lying in front of the sofa.

Jemand steht vor der Tür.
YEH-mahnt shtait fohr dehr Tewr.
Somebody is standing before the door.

Das Fräulein geht von dem Sofa an die Tür.
Dahs FROY-line gait fonn daim ZOH-fah ahn dee Tewr.
The young lady goes from the sofa to the door.

Das Fräulein öffnet die Tür.	**Herr Vollmer steht vor der Tür.**
Dahs FROY-line UHFF-net dee Tewr.	*Herr FOLL-m'r shtait fohr dehr Tewr.*
The young lady opens the door.	Mr. Vollmer stands outside the door.

Guten Tag, Fräulein Klara!	**Ich bin es!**
GOO-t'n Tahk, FROY-line KLAH-rah!	*Ikh bin ess!*
Good day, Miss Clara!	It is I!

EXPRESSION to Remember: *Ich bin es!*—"It is I" means literally "I am it". Similarly *Er ist es*—"It is he", *Wir sind es*—"It is we", *Sie sind es*—"It is you".

Guten Tag, Herr Vollmer! Komen Sie, bitte, in das Zimmer herein!
GOO-t'n Tahk, Herr FOLL-m'r! KOMM'n Zee, BIT-teh, in dahs TSIMM'r hair-INE!
Good day, Mr. Vollmer! Come into the room, please!

Sie gehen zusammen in das Zimmer, Herr Vollmer hinter dem Fräulein.
Zee GAY-h'n tsoo-ZAHM'n in dahs TSIMM'r, Herr FOLL-m'r HINT-r daim FROY-line.
They go together into the room, Mr. Vollmer after the young lady.

Wo sitzen Sie, Fräulein Klara?	**Auf dem Sofa.**
Voh ZIT-s'n Zee, FROY-line KLAH-rah?	*Aouf daim ZOH-fah.*
Where are you sitting, Miss Clara?	On the sofa.

Herr Vollmer sagt: Ich stelle mich an das Fenster.
Herr FOLL-m'r zahgt: Ikh SHTELL-eh mikh ahn dahs FEN-st'r.
Mr. Vollmer says: I'll stand at the window.

Fräulein Klara antwortet: Setzen Sie sich auf das Sofa
FROY-line KLAH-rah AHNT-vohr-tet: ZET-s'n Zee zikh aouf dahs ZOH-fah
Miss Clara answers: Sit down on the sofa

oder an das Klavier.
OH-d'r ahn dahs Klah-VEER.
or at the piano.

Woher kommen Sie?
*Voh-*HAIR *KOMM'n Zee?*
Where are you coming from?

Ich komme aus dem Konzert.
Ikh KOM-*meh aous daim Kohn-*TSAIRT.
I am coming from the concert.

Wohin lege ich meinen Hut?
*Voh-*HIN LAY-*ggeh ikh* MIGH-*n'n Hoot?*
Where do I put my hat?

Legen Sie ihn auf das Fensterbrett oder in den Schrank!
LAY-*g'n Zee een aouf dahs* FEN-*st'r-brett* OH-*d'r in dehn Shrahnk!*
Put it on the window-board or in the closet!

NOTE to Student: In this lesson we observe the modification of articles used with neuter nouns after certain prepositions. It will be helpful to remember that the dative article forms (*dem* and *einem*) with neuter nouns are exactly the same as the masculine forms; the accusative form is *das* in the neuter, and *den* in the masculine.

Herr Vollmer legt seinen Hut auf das Sofa.
Herr FOLL-*m'r laigt* ZIGH-*n'n Hoot aouf dahs* ZOH-*fah.*
Mr. Vollmer puts his hat on the sofa.

Wo liegt der Hut?
Voh leekt dehr Hoot?
Where is the hat?

Wohin legt er ihn?
*Voh-*HIN *laigt air een?*
Where does he put it?

Woher kommt er?
*Voh-*HAIR *kommt air?*
Where is he coming from?

THINKING IN GERMAN
(Answers on page 255)

1. Wo sitzt Herr Vollmer?
2. Liest Fräulein Klara in dem Buch?
3. Wo sitzt das Kätzchen?
4. Sind Herr Vollmer und Fräulein Klara in dem Zimmer?
5. Steht das Glas auf dem Klavier?
6. Sitzt jemand an dem Fenster?
7. Ist das Fenster hinter dem Sofa?
8. Wo steht das Radio?
9. Woher kommt Herr Vollmer?
10. Liegt Fräulein Klara auf dem Sofa?
11. Sitzt das Kätzchen auf dem Klavier?
12. Ist etwas in dem Glas?
13. Wer sitzt an dem Klavier?
14. Liest Herr Vollmer in dem Buch?
15. Woher kommt das Konzert?

ÜBUNG NR. 16

DAMEN · MODEN

Die Bluse in der Auslage
Dee BLOO-*zeh in dehr* AOUS-*lah-ggeh*
The blouse in the display

Geben Sie mir diese rote Bluse aus der Auslage!
GAY-*b'n Zee meer* DEE-*zeh* ROH-*teh* BLOO-*zeh aous deh1* AOUS-*lah-ggeh!*
Give me this red blouse out of the display!

Welche?	**Die Bluse hinter der schwarzen Handtasche!**
VEL-*kheh?*	*Dee* BLOO-*zeh* HINT'*r dehr* SHVAHRTS'*n* HAHNT-*tah-sheh!*
Which one?	The blouse behind the black handbag!

Diese Bluse auf der Stange?
DEE-*zeh* BLOO-*zeh aouf dehr* SHTAHN-*ggeh?*
This blouse on the rod?

Ja, diese unter der Lampe.
Yah, DEE-*zeh* OON-*t'r dehr* LAHM-*peh.*
Yes, this one under the lamp.

Nein, bitte, nehmen Sie die Bluse nicht in die Hand!
Nine, BIT-teh, NAY-m'n Zee dee BLOO-zeh nikht in dee Hahnt!
No, please, do not take the blouse in your hand!

Kommen Sie an die Tür!   **Stehen Sie nicht auf der Strasse!**
KOMM'n Zee ahn dee Tewr!   *SHTAY-h'n Zee nikht aouf dehr SHTRAH-sseh!*
Come to the door!   Do not stand in the street!

Wir gehen von der Strasse an die Tür.
Veer GAY-h'n fonn dehr SHTRAH-sseh ahn dee Tewr.
We go from the street to the door.

Haben Sie Geld in der Tasche?
HAH-b'n Zee Ggelt in dehr TAH-sheh?
Have you money in your pocket?

Ja, ich nehme es aus der Tasche und lege es in Ihre Hand.
Yah, ikh NAY-meh ess aous dehr TAH-sheh oont LEH-ggeh ess in EE-reh Hahnt.
Yes, I take it out of my pocket and put it in your hand.

Wo ist Liese?   **Liese ist in der Warenausgabe.**
Voh ist LEE-zeh?   *LEE-zeh ist in dehr VAH-r'n-aous-gah-beh.*
Where is Liese?   Liese is at the wrapping-counter.

Was tut sie dort?   **Sie nimmt die Puppe in die Hand.**
Vahss toot zee dohrt?   *Zee nimt dee POO-peh in dee Hahnt.*
What is she doing there?   She is taking the doll in her hand.

Die Verkäuferin geht in die Warenausgabe.
Dee Fair-KOY-feh-rin gait in dee VAH-r'n-aous-gah-beh.
The salesgirl goes behind the wrapping-counter.

Sie nimmt die Puppe aus Lieses Hand.
Zee nimt dee POO-peh aous LEE-zehs Hahnt.
She takes the doll out of Liese's hand.

Sie legt die Puppe auf die Bluse.
Zee laigt dee POO-peh aouf dee BLOO-zeh.
She puts the doll on top of the blouse.

Liese, nehmen Sie Ihr Taschentuch aus der Tasche!
LEE-zeh, NAY-m'n Zee Eer TAH-shen-tookh aous dehr TAH-sheh!
Liese, take your handkerchief out of your pocket!

REMEMBER: the imperative form. The indicative *Sie nehmen*—"you take" is inverted: *Nehmen Sie!*—"Take!"

Legen Sie die Bluse in die Handtasche?
LAY-g'n ZEE dee BLOO-zeh in dee HAHNT-tah-sheh?
Do you put the blouse in the handbag?

Ist die Bluse unter der Puppe?
Ist dee BLOO-zeh OON-t'r dehr POO-peh?
Is the blouse under the doll?

Wo ist der Professor, vor oder in der Auslage?
Voh ist dehr Proh-FESS-or, fohr OH-d'r in dehr AOUS-lah-ggeh?
Where is the professor, in front of or in the show-window?

Weinen Sie nicht!
VIGH-n'n zee nikht!
Don't cry!

Sie bekommen ein schönes Geschenk zu Weihnachten!
Zee beh-KOH-m'n ine SHUH-nes geh-SHENK tsoo VIGH-nakh-t'n.
You are getting a beautiful present for Christmas.

CASE ENDINGS FOR ADJECTIVES: When ein, kein
or the possessives mein, sein, ihr etc. precede an adjective,
it takes the endings -er for a masculine noun, -e for a
feminine and -es for a neuter one. Examples:

Ein brauner Hut. Eine blaue Blume. Ein grosses Buch.
"A brown hat". "A blue flower". "A big book".
This applies only to the nominative case.
In the other cases the adjective is modified according to whether it is pre-
ceded by any article or possessive or by none at all.
If preceded by any form of der-die-das or ein etc., the adjective ends in -en,
with the exception of the feminine and neuter singular accusative forms
which remain unchanged. Examples:

**Wir besuchen unsere alte Schule. Er gibt dem faulen Kellner ein kleines
Trinkgeld.**
"We are visiting our old school". "He gives the lazy waiter a small tip".
When the adjective is *not* so preceded it takes the endings that the article
would normally take with the exception of the masculine and neuter
genitive singular which end in -en. Examples:

Die Wichtigkeit kleiner Sachen.—"The importance of small things".

Die Beispiele grosser Männer.—"The examples of great men".

THINKING IN GERMAN

(Answers on page 255)

1. Ist die Bluse in der Auslage?
2. In wessen Hand ist die Puppe?
3. Wo steht die Verkäuferin?
4. Steht der Professor vor der Auslage?
5. Ist eine Handtasche in der Auslage?
6. Von wem bekommt die Verkäuferin das Geld?
7. Woher nimmt Frau Huber das Geld?
8. Wer steht vor der Tür?
9. Was trägt der Hund?
10. Ist Geld in der Handtasche?
11. Wo ist Ihr Taschentuch?
12. Wohin gehen die Schüler?
13. Sitzen Sie vor der Tür?
14. Was habe ich in der Hand?
15. Hat der Lehrer eine Puppe in der Hand?

ÜBUNG NR. 17

Womit gehen wir?
*Voh-*MIT GAY-*h'n veer?*
With what do we walk?

Wir schreiben mit dem Bleistift auf das Papier.
Veer SHRIGH-*b'n mit daim* BLIGH-*shtift aouf dahs Pah-*PEER.
We write with the pencil on the paper.

Sie schreiben mit der Kreide an die Tafel.
Zee SHRIGH-*b'n mit dehr* KRIGH-*deh ahn dee* TAH-*f'l.*
You write with the chalk on the blackboard.

HELPFUL REMINDER: It may be helpful to state that you use *ich schreibe an die Tafel*—"I write on the blackboard", because the blackboard is in a vertical (upright) position. *Ich schreibe an die Wand*—"I write on the wall" yet when you write on something which is in a horizontal position like the paper, you say *Ich schreibe auf das Papier*—"I write on the paper". If the object you are writing on can be closed like a notebook, you say *Ich schreibe in das Notizbuch*—"I write in the notebook". Now write this in your memory—*schreiben Sie das in Ihr Gedächtnis* and don't forget it!

Das ist das Messer.
Dahs ist dahs MESS-*'r.*
This is the knife.

Wir schneiden mit dem Messer.
Veer SHNIGH-*d'n mit daim* MESS*'r.*
We cut with the knife.

Das sind die Hände.
Dahs zint dee HEN-*deh.*
These are the hands.

Wir halten mit den Händen.
Veer HAHL-*t'n mit dain* HEN-*d'n.*
We hold (things) with our hands.

Was tun wir mit der Feder?
Vahss toon veer mit der FAY-*d'r?*
What do we do with the pen?

REMEMBER: *Mit* is one of the prepositions which AL-WAYS take the dative. Other useful ones to remember are *nach*—"after", *zu*—"to", *aus*—"out of", *ausser*—"except", *seit* —"since" and *bei*. This last word has a variety of meanings depending on the phrase you use it in. Ex. *bei mir*—"in my opinion", "at my house"; *bei New York*—"near New York"; *bei der Kirche* —"next to the church"; *bei Berlitz*—"at Berlitz", etc.

Womit schneiden wir?
*Voh-*MIT SHNIGH-*d'n veer?*
With what do we cut?

Womit gehen wir?
*Voh-*MIT GAY-*h'n veer?*
With what do we walk?

Das ist der Fuss.
Dahs ist dehr Fooss.
This is the foot.

Wir gehen mit den Füssen.
Veer GAY-*h'n mit dain* FEW-ss*'n.*
We walk with our feet.

Das ist das Auge.
Dahs ist dahs AOU-*ggeh.*
This is the eye.

Wir sehen mit den Augen.
Veer ZAY-*h'n mit dain* AOU-*g'n.*
We see with our eyes.

Das ist das Ohr.
Dahs ist dahs Ohr.
This is the ear.

Wir hören mit den Ohren.
Veer HUH-*r'n mit dain* OH-*r'n.*
We hear with our ears.

Was tun wir mit den Augen?
Vahss toon veer mit dain AOU-*g'n?*
What are we doing with our eyes?

Was sehen Sie in diesem Zimmer?
Vahss ZAY-*h'n Zee in* DEEZ*'m* TSIMM*'r?*
What do you see in this room?

Sehen Sie jemand hinter dem Stuhl?
ZAY-*h'n Zee* YEH-*mahnt* HINT*'r daim Shtool?*
Do you see anybody behind the chair?

Ich stehe hinter der Tür, sehen Sie mich?
Ikh SHTAY-*heh* HINT'*r dehr Tewr,* ZAY-*h'n Zee mikh?*
I am standing behind the door, do you see me?

Womit sieht man?
*Voh-*MIT *zeet mahn?*
With what does one see?

Sieht man mit geschlossenen Augen?
*Zeet mahn mit ggeh-*SHLOSS-*eh-n'n* AOU-*g'n?*
Do we see with (our) eyes shut?

Ich klopfe.
Ikh KLOPP-*feh.*
I am knocking.

Hören Sie etwas?
HUH-*r'n Zee* ETT-*vahss?*
Do you hear anything?

Hören Sie mich gehen?
HUH-*r'n Zee mikh* GAY-*h'n?*
Do you hear me go?

Ja, ich höre Sie gehen.
Yah, ikh HUH-*reh Zee* GAY-*h'n.*
Yes, I hear you go.

Was tue ich?
Vahss TOO-*eh ikh?*
What am I doing?

Sie klopfen.
Zee KLOPPF'*n.*
You are knocking.

Die Rose, die Nelke, die Tulpe, das Veilchen, das Stiefmütterchen
Dee ROH-*zeh, dee* NELL-*keh, dee* TOOL-*peh, dahs* FILE-*khen, dahs* SHTEEF-*mew-t'r-khen*
The rose, the carnation, the tulip, the violet, the pansy

und das Gänseblümchen sind Blumen.
oont dahs GGEN-*zeh-blewm-kh'n zint* BLOO-*m'n.*
and the daisy are flowers.

Wir riechen mit der Nase.
Veer REE-*kh'n mit dehr* NAH-*zeh.*
We smell with our nose.

Die Rose riecht gut.
Dee ROH-*zeh reekht goot.*
The rose smells good.

Das Gas riecht schlecht.
Dahs Gahs reekht shlekht.
Gas smells bad.

Das Veilchen riecht gut.
Dahs FILE-*khen reekht goot.*
The violet smells good.

Die Tinte riecht schlecht.
Dee TIN-*teh reekht shlekht.*
Ink smells bad.

Wie riecht diese Blume, gut oder schlecht?
Vee reekht DEE-*zeh* BLOO-*meh, goot* OH-*d'r shlekht?*
How does this flower smell, good or bad?

Wie riecht das Veilchen?
Vee reekht dahs FILE-*kh'n?*
How does the violet smell?

Wie riecht das Gas?
Vee reekht dahs Gahs?
How does gas smell?

Wir sprechen mit dem Mund.
Veer SHPREH-*kh'n mit daim Moont.*
We speak with our mouth.

Sprechen wir hier englisch oder deutsch?
SHPREH-*kh'n veer here* ENNG-*lish* OH-*d'r doitsh?*
Do we speak English or German here?

Sprechen Sie französisch so gut wie deutsch?
SHPREH-*kh'n Zee frahn-*TSUH-*zish zoh goot vee doitsh?*
Do you speak French as well as German?

Mit dem Mund essen und trinken wir.
Mit daim Moont ESS'*n oont* TRINK'*n veer.*
We eat and drink with our mouth.

Sagen Sie mir bitte die Namen mehrerer Getränke!
ZAH-*g'n Zee meer* BIT-*teh dee* NAH-*m'n* MAY-*reh-r'r Ggeh-*TREN-*keh!*
Tell me please the names of several beverages!

Ist Limonade ein Getränk?
*Ist Lee-moh-*NAH-*deh ine Ggeh-*TRENK?
Is lemonade a beverage?

Limonade macht man aus Zitronen, Wasser und Zucker.
*Leemoh-*NAH-*deh mahkt mahn aous Tsee-*TROH-*n'n,* VAH-*ss'r oont* TSOO-*k'r.*
We make lemonade from lemons, water and sugar.

Sagen Sie mir, woraus man den Wein macht!   **(aus Weintrauben)**
ZAH-*g'n Zee meer, voh-*RAOUS *mahn dain Vine mahkht!*   (*aous* VINE-*traoub'n*)
Tell me of what we make wine!   (out of grapes)

NOTE to Student: There are some compound words with *wo*—"where" you must keep in your mind. *Wohin*—"where to", "whither", *woher*—"where from", "whence", *womit*—"with what", *woraus*—"out of what", *worin*—"in what", etc.

Und woraus macht man den Apfelwein?   **(aus Äpfeln)**
*Oont voh-*RAOUS *mahkht mahn dain* APF'*l-vine?*   (*aous* EP-*f'ln*)
And of what does one make cider?   (out of apples)

Trinken Sie Apfelwein?   **Äpfel und Birnen sind Früchte;**
TRIN-*k'n Zee* APF'*l-vine?*   EPF'*l oont* BEER-*n'n zint* FREWKH-*teh;*
Do you drink cider?   Apples and pears are fruits;

Bohnen, Erbsen, Kartoffeln und Kohl sind Gemüse.
BOH-*n'n,* AIRP-*s'n, Kahr-*TOFF-'*ln oont Kohl zint Ggeh-*MEW-*zeh.*
beans, peas, potatoes and cabbage are vegetables.

Essen Sie viel Gemüse?
ESS'*n Zee feel Ggeh-*MEW-*zeh?*
Do you eat many vegetables?

Bitte, nennen Sie mir die Namen verschiedener Gemüse!
BIT-*teh,* NENN-*en Zee meer dee* NAH-*m'n fehr-*SHEE-*deh-n'r Ggeh-*MEW-*zeh!*
Please, tell me the names of various vegetables!

Wir essen Brot, Fleisch, Gemüse und Früchte.
Veer ESS'*n Broht, Flighsh, Ggeh-*MEW-*zeh oont* FREWKH-*teh.*
We eat bread, meat, vegetables and fruits.

Wir trinken Wasser, Wein, Bier, Kaffee und Tee.
Veer TRIN-*k'n* VAH-*ss'r, Vine, Beer, Kah-*FEH *oont Teh.*
We drink water, wine, beer, coffee and tea.

NOTE: You have heard of pineapple-upside-down cake. The Germans have a habit of turning their verbs upside down. Notice the following sentence: *Mit dem Mund essen wir*—"With the mouth eat we."

Here is how you decide when to turn your verb around. If you start a sentence with an adverbial phrase like "with the mouth" above, or if you start it with any adverb or adverb clause, you put the subject of the sentence after the verb. Other examples: *Oft gehe ich ins Kino.*—"Often go I to the movies." *Wenn wir studieren, werden wir klug,* —"If we study, become we bright."

Essen Sie Äpfel?
ESS'*n Zee* EPF-'*l?*
Do you eat apples?

Essen Sie Brot zum Fleisch?
ESS'*n Zee Broht tsoom Flighsh?*
Do you eat bread with your meat?

Trinken Sie Kaffee?
TRIN-*k'n Zee Kah-*FEH?
Do you drink coffee?

Was nehmen Sie zum Kaffee?
Vahss NAY-*m'n Zee tsoom Kah-*FEH?
What do you take with your coffee?

Nehmen Sie Milch und Zucker zu Ihrem Tee?
NAY-*m'n Zee Milkh oont* TSOO-*k'r tsoo* EE-*r'm Teh?*
Do you take milk and sugar with your tea?

NOTE: Did you notice the use of *zu* in the foregoing sentences? This is a very good example of the *little words* you must master to get the feel of German.

Welche Farbe hat Kaffee ohne Milch?
VEL-*kheh* FAHR-*beh haht Kah*-FEH OH-*neh Milkh?*
What color has coffee without milk?

Trinken Sie Milch?
TRIN-*k'n Zee Milkh?*
Do you drink milk?

Alles, was man isst, nennt man Speise;
AHL-*less, vahss mahn isst, nent mahn* SHPIGH-*zeh;*
Everything we eat is called food;

> **alles, was man trinkt, nennt man Getränk.**
> AHL-*less vahss mahn trinkt, nent mahn Ggeh*-TRENK.
> everything we drink is called beverage.

> **Nennen Sie mehrere Gemüse!**
> NENN-*en Zee* MAY-*r'reh Ggeh*-MEW-*zeh!*
> Name several vegetables!

 REMEMBER: *Viel* means "much", *einige*—"a few", *mehrere*—"several", *ein paar*—"a few", but *ein Paar* means "a pair" or "a couple". Watch for the capital P in the latter case.

Wir essen Schweinefleisch, Rindfleisch, Hammelfleisch, Kalbfleisch und Geflügel.
Veer ESS'*n* SHVIGH-*neh-flighsh,* RINT-*flighsh,* HAHM'*l-flighsh,* KAHLP-*flighsh oont Ggeh*-FLEW-*g'l.*
We eat pork, beef, mutton, veal and fowl.

THINKING IN GERMAN

(Answers on page 255)

1. Riecht die Rose gut?
2. Riecht der Käse gut?
3. Schmeckt Kaffee mit Zucker gut?
4. Nehmen Sie Milch zum Kaffee?
5. Essen Sie gern Blumenkohl mit Butter?
6. Trinken Sie gern Limonade ohne Zucker?
7. Nennen Sie mir, bitte, einige Getränke!
8. Welche Speisen kennen Sie?
9. Trinken Sie gern Wein?
10. Sprechen Sie gern deutsch?
11. Ist die französische Sprache schön?
12. Haben Sie eine schöne Handschrift?
13. Essen Sie Brot zum Fleisch?
14. Womit essen Sie?
15. Womit gehen wir?
16. Sehen Sie mit geschlossenen Augen?
17. Welche Gemüse kennen Sie?
18. Was sehen Sie in diesem Zimmer?

ÜBUNG NR. 18

Wie schmeckt es?
Vee shmekkt ess?
How does it taste?

Vor dem Essen setzen wir uns an den Tisch.
Fohr daim ESS'n ZETZ'n veer oons ahn dain Tish.
Before the meal we sit down at the table.

Man legt ein weisses Tischtuch auf den Tisch.
Mahn laigt ine VIGH-sess TISH-tookh aouf dain Tish.
We put a white tablecloth on the table.

Vor jeder Person stehen Teller.
Fohr YEH-d'r Pair-ZOHN SHTAY-h'n TELL'r.
Before each person are plates.

Wir legen die Speisen auf die Teller.
Veer LAY-g'n dee SHPIGH-z'n aouf dee TELL'r.
We put the food on the plates.

Der Teller ist rund.
Dehr TELL'r ist roont.
The plate is round.

Dieser Tisch ist viereckig.
DEEZ'r Tish ist FEER-eck-ikh.
This table is square.

94

Welche Form hat der Teller?
VEL-kheh Form haht dehr TELL'r?
What is the shape of the plate?

Die Speisen trägt man in Schüsseln auf den Tisch.
Dee SHPIGH-z'n traigt mahn in SHEW-ss'ln aouf dain Tish.
Food is brought to the table on dishes.

Wir nehmen sie von den Schüsseln und legen sie auf unsere Teller.
Veer NAY-m'n zee fonn dain SHEW-ss'ln oont LAY-g'n zee aouf OON-z'reh TELL'r.
We take them from the dishes and put them on our plates.

 NOTE on china: We eat from "plates"—*Teller,* yet the soup is served from a "soup tureen"—*Suppenschüssel.* Meat is served on a "platter"— *Fleischschüssel.* A vegetable is served from a "dish"—*Gemüseschüssel.*

Wir essen Suppe mit dem Löffel, Fleisch mit der Gabel.
Veer ESS'n ZOO-peh mit daim LUHFF'l, Flighsh mit dehr GAH-b'l.
We eat soup with a spoon, meat with a fork.

Wir trinken Wasser aus dem Glas und Kaffee aus der Tasse.
Veer TRIN-k'n VAH-ss'r aous daim Glahs oont Kah-FEH aous dehr TAH-sseh.
We drink water from the glass and coffee from the cup.

Der Teller, die Schüssel, die Tasse, das Glas, die Flasche,
Dehr TELL'r, dee SHEW-ss'l, dee TAH-sseh, dahs Glahs, dee FLAH-sheh,
The plate, the dish, the cup, the glass, the bottle,

der Löffel, die Gabel, das Messer.
dehr LUHFF'l, dee GAH-b'l, dahs MESS'r.
the spoon, the fork, the knife.

Womit schneiden wir das Fleisch?
Voh-MIT SHNIGH-d'n veer dahs Flighsh?
With what do we cut the meat?

Womit essen wir Fleisch?
Voh-MIT ESS'n veer Flighsh?
With what do we eat meat?

Womit essen wir Suppe?
Voh-MIT ESS'n veer ZOO-peh?
With what do we eat soup?

Worin bringt man die Suppe auf den Tisch?
Voh-RIN bringt mahn dee ZOO-peh aouf dain Tish?
In what do we bring the soup onto the table?

Woraus (wovon) essen wir?
Voh-RAOUS (voh-FONN) ESS'n veer?
Out of what (from what) do we eat?

Worin (worauf) ist das Gemüse?
*Voh-*RIN *(voh-*RAOUF*) ist dahs Ggeh-*MEW*-zeh?*
In what (on what) are the vegetables?

Worauf liegt das Fleisch, wenn man es auf den Tisch trägt?
*Voh-*RAOUF *leekt dahs Flighsh, venn mahn ess aouf dain Tish traigt?*
On what is the meat, when we bring it to the table?

Woraus trinken wir Wein?
*Voh-*RAOUS TRIN*-k'n veer Vine?*
Out of what do we drink wine?

Trinken Sie aus der Flasche?
TRIN*-k'n Zee aous dehr* FLAH*-sheh?*
Do you drink from the bottle?

Nein, ich giesse den Wein aus der Flasche in das Glas.
Nine, ikh GGEE*-sseh dain Vine aous dehr* FLAH*-sheh in dahs Glahs.*
No, I pour the wine from the bottle into the glass.

Woraus trinkt man Kaffee?
*Voh-*RAOUS *trinkt mahn Kah-*FEH*?*
From what do we drink coffee?

Wir nehmen Zucker zum Kaffee.
Veer NAY*-m'n* TSOO*-k'r tsoom Kah-*FEH*.*
We take sugar with coffee.

Tee ohne Zucker schmeckt nicht gut.
Teh OH*-neh* TSOO*-k'r shmekkt nikht goot.*
Tea without sugar does not taste good.

Womit schmecken wir?
*Voh-*MIT SHMEKK*'n veer?*
With what do we taste?

Wir schmecken mit der Zunge.
Veer SHMEKK*'n mit dehr* TSOON*-ggeh.*
We taste with the tongue.

Wie schmeckt Kaffee ohne Zucker?
*Vee shmekkt Kah-*FEH OH*-neh* TSOO*-k'r?*
How does coffee taste without sugar?

Er schmeckt bitter.
Air shmekkt BITT*'r.*
It tastes bitter.

Und wie schmeckt Zucker?
Oont vee shmekkt TSOO*-k'r?*
And how does sugar taste?

Er schmeckt süss.
Air shmekkt sewss.
It tastes sweet.

Was für einen Geschmack hat die Zitrone?
Vahss fewr EYE*-n'n Ggeh-*SHMAHK *haht dee Tsee-*TROH*-neh?*
What taste has the lemon?

Sie schmeckt sauer.
Zee shmekkt ZAOU*'r.*
It tastes sour.

Wie schmeckt die Erdbeere?
Vee shmekkt dee EHRT*-bay-reh?*
How does the strawberry taste?

Wie riecht sie?
Vee reekht zee?
How does it smell?

Sie schmeckt sehr gut und riecht auch gut;
Zee shmekkt zair goot oont reekht aoukh goot;
It tastes very good and smells good too;

ihr Geschmack und ihr Geruch sind angenehm.
*eer Ggeh-*SHMAHK *oont eer Ggeh-*ROOKH *zint* AHN-*ggeh-naim.*
its taste and smell are pleasant.

Hat das Gas einen angenehmen Geruch?
Haht dahs Gahs EYE-*n'n* AHN-*ggeh-nay-m'n Ggeh-*ROOKH?
Has gas a pleasant smell?

Nein, es riecht sehr schlecht; es hat einen sehr unangenehmen Geruch.
Nine, ess reekht zair shlekht; ess haht EYE-*n'n zair* OON-*ahn-ggeh-nay-m'n*
*Ggeh-*ROOKH.
No, it smells bad, it has a very unpleasant smell.

REMEMBER: The use of the adverb *gern* with a verb, meaning "to like". Note the following: *Ich habe die Berlitz Methode gern.—*"I like the Berlitz Method." *Er trinkt Bier gern.—*"He likes to drink beer." However, *mögen,* a verb, also means "to like". *Wir mögen Sauerkraut nicht.—*"We do not like sauerkraut."

Alles, was angenehme Formen und angenehme Farben hat, ist schön.
AHL-*less, vahss* AHN-*ggeh-nay-meh* FOR-*m'n oont* AHN-*ggeh-nay-meh* FAHR-*b'n*
haht, ist shuhn.
Everything which has pleasant forms and colors is beautiful.

Was schön ist, sehen wir gern.
Vahss shuhn ist, ZAY-*h'n veer gairn.*
What is beautiful we like to see.

Was nicht schön ist, sehen wir nicht gern; es ist hässlich.
Vahss nikht shuhn ist, ZAY-*h'n veer nikht gairn; ess ist* HESS-*likh.*
What is not beautiful we do not like to see; it is ugly.

Der Kölner Dom ist schön.   **Die Venus von Milo ist schön.**
Dehr KUHL-*ner Dohm ist shuhn.*   *Dee* VAY-*noos fonn* MEE-*loh ist shuhn.*
The Cologne cathedral is beautiful.   The Venus of Milo is beautiful.

Das Krokodil ist hässlich.   **Der Affe ist hässlich.**
*Dahs Kroh-koh-*DEEL *ist* HESS-*likh.*   *Dehr* AHF-*feh ist* HESS-*likh.*
The crocodile is ugly.   The monkey is ugly.

Ist das Pferd schöner als das Kamel?
Ist dahs Pfairt SHUH-*n'r ahls dahs Kah-*MAIL?
Is the horse more beautiful than the camel?

REMEMBER: *So schön wie* and *schöner als!* Examples: *Sie ist so schön wie die Venus!—*"She is as beautiful as Venus!" *Herr Berlitz spricht ein schöneres Deutsch als ich.—*"Mr. Berlitz speaks a more beautiful German than I."

Ist die Rose eine schöne Blume?
Ist dee ROH-*zeh* EYE-*neh* SHUH-*neh* BLOO-*meh?*
Is the rose a beautiful flower?

Ist der Kölner Dom schön?
Ist dehr KUHL-*ner Dohm shuhn?*
Is the Cologne cathedral beautiful?

Ist die Venus von Milo eine schöne Statue?
Ist dee VAY-*noos fonn* MEE-*loh* EYE-*neh* SHUH-*neh* SHTAH-*too-eh?*
Is Venus of Milo a beautiful statue?

Ist der Pfau schön?
Ist dehr Pfaou shuhn?
Is the peacock beautiful?

Hat er schöne Füsse?
Haht air SHUH-*neh* FEW-*sseh?*
Has it beautiful feet?

Ist die Eule schön?
Ist dee OY-*leh shuhn?*
Is the owl beautiful?

Ist das Schwein so schön wie das Pferd?
Ist dahs Shvine zoh shuhn vee dahs Pfairt?
Is the pig as beautiful as the horse?

THINKING IN GERMAN

(Answers on page 256)

1. Was legt man vor dem Essen auf den Tisch?
2. Wie sind die Teller?
3. Worin trägt man die Speisen auf den Tisch?
4. Womit essen wir die Suppe?
5. Woraus trinken Sie Kaffee und Wasser?
6. Schneiden Sie das Fleisch mit der Gabel?
7. Worauf liegt das Fleisch?
8. Womit schmecken Sie?
9. Was für einen Geschmack hat die Zitrone?
10. Sehen Sie gern, was schön ist?
11. Ist das Pferd schöner als das Krokodil?
12. Ist die Venus von Milo schön?
13. Wie schmeckt Tee ohne Zucker?

ÜBUNG NR. 19

Ich kann nicht sehen
Ikh kahn nikht ZAY-*h'n*
I cannot see

Ich gehe hinaus.	Ich komme herein.	Was tue ich?
Ikh GAY-*heh hin-*AOUS.	*Ikh* KOM-*meh hair-*INE.	*Vahss* TOO-*eh ikh?*
I go out.	I come in.	What am I doing?

Ich mache die Tür zu, die Tür ist zu; ich kann nicht hinausgehen.
Ikh MAH-*kheh dee Tewr tsoo, dee Tewr ist tsoo; ikh kahn nikht hin-*AOUS-*gay-h'n.*
I close the door, the door is closed; I cannot go out.

Ich mache die Tür auf, die Tür ist offen, ich kann hinausgehen.
Ikh MAH-*kheh dee Tewr aouf, dee Tewr ist* OFF'*n, ikh kahn hin-*AOUS-*gay-h'n.*
I open the door, the door is open; I can go out.

Ich habe einen Bleistift, ich kann schreiben;
Ikh HAH-*beh* EYE-*n'n* BLIGH-*shtift, ikh kahn* SHRIGH-*b'n;*
I have a pencil, I can write;

100

Sie haben keinen Bleistift, Sie können nicht schreiben.
Zee HAH-*b'n* KIGH-*n'n* BLIGH-*shtift, Zee* KUH-*n'n nikht* SHRIGH-*b'n.*
you have no pencil, you cannot write.

Karl hat ein Messer, er kann das Papier zerschneiden;
Kahrl haht ine MESS'*r air kahn dahs Pah-*PEER *tsair-*SHNIGH-*d'n;*
Karl has a knife, he can cut the paper;

ich habe kein Messer, ich kann das Papier nicht zerschneiden.
ikh HAH-*beh kine* MESS'*r, ikh kahn dahs Pah-*PEER *nikht tsair-*SHNIGH-*d'n.*
I have no knife, I cannot cut the paper.

Ich berühre die Wand.
*Ikh beh-*REW-*reh dee Vahnt.*
I touch the wall.

Was tue ich?
Vahss TOO-*eh ikh?*
What am I doing?

Die Decke ist hoch, wir können sie nicht berühren;
Dee DEK-*keh ist hohkh, veer* KUH-*n'n zee nikht beh-*REW-*r'n;*
The ceiling is high, we cannot touch it;

die Lampe ist niedrig, wir können sie berühren.
dee LAHM-*peh ist* NEE-*drikh, veer* KUH-*n'n zee beh-*REW-*r'n.*
the lamp is low, we can touch it.

Ich mache die Augen zu; ich kann nicht sehen.
Ikh MAH-*kheh dee* AOU-*g'n tsoo; ikh kahn nikht* ZAY-*h'n.*
I close my eyes; I cannot see.

Herr Berlitz hat eine Brille.
Herr BEHR-*lits haht* EYE-*neh* BRILL-*eh.*
Mr. Berlitz has (a pair of) glasses.

Mit einer Brille kann er gut sehen, ohne Brille kann er nicht gut sehen.
Mit EYE-*n'r* BRILL-*eh kahn air goot* ZAY-*h'n,* OH-*neh* BRILL-*eh kahn air nikht goot* ZAY-*h'n.*
With glasses he can see well, without glasses he cannot see well.

IMPORTANT Note: *Können* means "can" or "to be able" and combines directly with the infinitive form of the verb. The infinitive form of the verbs we have encountered up to now are *stellen, legen, gehen, geben, sagen, schliessen, öffnen, sprechen, fragen,* etc. The infinitive form of the verb "to be" is exceptional: *sein.*

Kann ich die Decke berühren?
Kahn ikh dee DEK-*keh beh-*REW-*r'n?*
Can I touch the ceiling?

Kann ich die Lampe berühren?
Kahn ikh dee LAHM-*peh beh-*REW-*r'n?*
Can I touch the lamp?

Können Sie meine Haare zählen?
KUH-*n'n Zee* MIGH-*neh* HAH-*reh* TSAY-*l'n?*
Can you count my hair?

Können Sie meine Bücher zählen?
KUH-*n'n* Zee MIGH-*neh* BEW-*kh'r* TSAY-*l'n?*
Can you count my books?

Kann Herr Berlitz ohne Brille gut sehen?
Kahn Herr BEHR-*lits* OH-*neh* BRILL-*eh goot* ZAY-*h'n?*
Can Mr. Berlitz see well without glasses?

IMPORTANT Note on *ich kann: Ich kann deutsch* means "I know how to speak German." *Ich kann lesen* means "I know how to read", *ich kann schwimmen*—"I know how to swim."

Können wir Suppe mit einer Gabel essen?
KUH-*n'n* veer ZOO-*peh* mit EYE-*n'r* GAH-*b'l* ESS'*n?*
Can we eat soup with a fork?

Können die Schüler ihre Bücher in ihre Taschen stecken?
KUH-*n'n* dee SHEW-*l'r* EE-*reh* BEW-*kh'r* in EE-*reh* TAH-*sh'n* SHTEK'*n?*
Can the pupils put their books in their pockets?

Ich habe kein Messer; ich kann das Papier nicht zerschneiden.
Ikh HAH-*beh kine* MESS'*r; ikh kahn dahs Pah-*PEER *nikht tsair-*SHNIGH-*d'n.*
I have no knife; I cannot cut the paper.

Warum kann ich das Papier nicht zerschneiden?
*Vah-*ROOM *kahn ikh dahs Pah-*PEER *nikht tsair-*SHNIGH-*d'n?*
Why can I not cut the paper?

Weil ich kein Messer habe.
Vile ikh kine MESS'*r* HAH-*beh.*
Because I have no knife.

NOTE: Observe the inverted word order after *weil.* This construction is ALWAYS necessary in clauses which cannot stand alone, and which are only PARTS of sentences. We shall highlight this matter further in succeeding lessons. Ex. *Weil die Tür zu ist, können Sie nicht hinausgehen*—literally: "Because the door closed is, can you not go out."

Warum können Sie nicht hinausgehen?   **Weil die Tür zu ist.**
*Vah-*ROOM KUH-*n'n* Zee nikht hin-*AOUS-*gay-*h'n? Vile dee Tewr zu ist.*
Why can't you go out?   Because the door is closed.

Das Buch ist gross, die Tasche ist klein.
Dahs Bookh ist grohss, dee TAH-*sheh ist kline.*
The book is large, the pocket is small.

Warum kann ich das Buch nicht in die Tasche stecken?
*Vah-*ROOM *kahn ikh dahs Bookh nikht in dee* TAH-*sheh* SHTEK*'n?*
Why can't I put the book in my pocket?

Weil das Buch gross und die Tasche klein ist.
Vile dahs Bookh grohss oont dee TAH-*sheh kline ist.*
Because the book is large and the pocket is small.

Herr Schultz ist nicht hier.
Herr Shults ist nikht here.
Mr. Schultz is not here.

Warum können wir Herrn Schultz nicht sehen?
*Vah-*ROOM KUH-*n'n veer Herrn Shults nikht* ZAY-*h'n?*
Why can't we see Mr. Schultz?

Weil er nicht hier ist.   **Herr Müller hat keinen Schlüssel.**
Vile air nikht here ist.   *Herr* MEW-*l'r haht* KIGH-*n'n* SHLEW-*ss'l.*
Because he is not here.   Mr. Müller has no key.

Kann er die Tür ohne Schlüssel öffnen?
Kahn air dee Tewr OH-*neh* SHLEW-*ss'l* UHFF-*n'n?*
Can he open the door without a key?

THINKING IN GERMAN
(Answers on page 256)

1. Könen Sie ohne Brille sehen?

2. Die Tür ist offen; können Sie hinausgehen?

3. Kann man ohne Bleistift oder Feder schreiben?

4. Er hat kein Messer; kann er das Fleisch schneiden?

5. Können Sie den Himmel berühren?

6. Können Sie deutsch sprechen?

7. Warum können Sie das Buch nicht in die Tasche stecken?

8. Herr Schultz ist nicht hier; kann man ihn sehen?

9. Können Sie ohne Mund essen?

10. Sie haben keinen Schlüssel; können Sie die Tür öffnen?

11. Können Sie Ihre Haare zählen?

12. Der Stuhl ist niedrig; können Sie ihn berühren?

ÜBUNG NR. 20

Ich will nicht
Ikh vill nikht
I don't want to

Ich kann das Papier zerreissen.
Ikh kahn dahs Pah-PEER tsair-RIGH-ss'n.
I can tear the paper.

Warum zerreisse ich es nicht?
Vah-ROOM tsair-RIGH-sseh ikh ess nikht?
Why don't I tear it?

Weil ich nicht will.
Vile ikh nikht vill.
Because I do not want to.

Sie können Ihre Brille zerbrechen.
Zee KUH-n'n EE-reh BRILL-eh tsair-BREH-kh'n.
You can break your glasses.

Warum zerbrechen Sie sie nicht?
Vah-ROOM tsair-BREH-kh'n Zee zee nikht?
Why don't you break them?

Weil ich nicht will.
Vile ikh nikht vill.
Because I do not want to.

Wollen Sie die Lampe zerbrechen?
VOLL'n Zee dee LAHM-peh tsair-BREH-kh'n?
Do you want to break the lamp?

105

Ich will sie nicht zerbrechen.
*Ikh vill zee nikht tsair-*BREH-*kh'n.*
I do not want to break it.

Will sie den Hut zerschneiden?	**Sie will ihn nicht zerschneiden.**
*Vill zee dain Hoot tsair-*SHNIGH-*d'n?*	*Zee vill een nikht tsair-*SHNIGH-*d'n.*
Does she want to cut up the hat?	She does not want to cut it up.

Will der Hund den Braten haben?
Vill dehr Hoont dain BRAH-*t'n* HAH-*b'n?*
Does the dog want to have the roast?

Ja, er will den Braten haben.
Yah, air vill dain BRAH-*t'n* HAH-*b'n.*
Yes, he wants to have the roast.

Wollen wir deutsch sprechen?	**Ja, wir wollen deutsch sprechen.**
VOLL*'n veer doitsh* SHPREH-*kh'n?*	*Yah, veer* VOLL*'n doitsh* SHPREH-*kh'n*
Do we want to speak German?	Yes, we want to speak German.

Wollen Frau Huber und Liese eine Bluse kaufen?
VOLL*'n Fraou* HOO-*b'r oont* LEE-*zeh* EYE-*neh* BLOO-*zeh* KAOU-*f'n?*
Do Mrs. Huber and Liese want to buy a blouse?

Wollen Sie eine Bluse kaufen?
VOLL*'n Zee* EYE-*neh* BLOO-*zeh* KAOU-*f'n?*
Do you want to buy a blouse?

Wollen Sie die Zeitung lesen?
VOLL*'n Zee dee* TSIGH-*toonk* LAY-*z'n?*
Do you want to read the paper?

Wollen Sie etwas trinken?
VOLL*'n Zee* ETT-*vahss* TRIN-*k'n?*
Do you want to drink something?

Nein, danke, ich will nichts trinken, ich will etwas essen.
Nine, DAHN-*keh, ikh vill nikhts* TRIN-*k'n, ikh vill* ETT-*vahss* ESS*'n.*
No, thanks, I do not want to drink anything, I want to eat something.

NOTE to Student: *Wollen* means "to wish" or "to want" and is used in combination with the infinitive as *können* was in the preceding lesson. It can be used as an invitation, as in: *Wollen Sie mit mir in das Theater gehen?*—"Do you wish to go to the theatre with me?" or as a polite imperative, as in: *Wollen Sie, bitte, den Satz wiederholen!*—"Please repeat the sentence!" Note carefully that *will* expresses a wish, and is not to be confused with "will" in English as used to form the simple or emphatic future.

Wollen Sie, dass ich das Fenster öffne?
VOLL'*n Zee, dahss ikh dahs* FEN-*st'r* UHFF-*neh?*
Do you want me to open the window?

Ich will, dass Sie die Tür schliessen.
Ikh vill, dahss Zee dee Tewr SHLEE-*ss'n.*
I want you to close the door.

Wenn die Tür zu ist, können wir nicht hinausgehen.
Venn dee Tewr tsoo ist, KUH-*n'n veer nikht hin-*AOUS-*gay-h'n.*
If the door is closed, we cannot go out.

Wenn ich die Augen zumache, kann ich nicht sehen.
Venn ikh dee AOU-*g'n* TSOO-*mah-kheh, kahn ikh nikht* ZAY-*h'n.*
If I close my eyes, I cannot see.

Können Sie schreiben, wenn Sie keinen Bleistift oder keine Feder haben?
KUH-*n'n Zee* SHRIGH-*b'n, venn Zee* KIGH-*n'n* BLIGH-*shtift* OH-*d'r* KIGH-*neh*
FAY-*d'r* HAH-*b'n?*
Can you write, if you have no pencil or no pen?

Kann der Koch den Braten schneiden, wenn er kein Messer hat?
Kahn dehr Kohkh dain BRAH-*t'n* SHNIGH-*d'n, venn air kine* MESS'*r haht?*
Can the cook cut up the roast if he has no knife?

LOOK OUT! Do not confuse this *wenn* which means "if" with *wann* meaning "when" which you will encounter in the next lesson. Almost everyone learning German does this; perhaps you will be an exception.

Wenn ich das Buch nicht öffne, kann ich nicht lesen.
Venn ikh dahs Bookh nikht UHFF-*neh, kahn ikh nikht* LAY-*z'n.*
If I do not open the book, I cannot read.

Wenn ich die Tür nicht aufmache, kann ich nicht hinausgehen;
Venn ikh dee Tewr nikht AOUF-*mah-kheh, kahn ikh nikht hin-*AOUS-*gay-h'n;*
If I do not open the door, I cannot go out;

ich muss die Tür aufmachen, wenn ich hinausgehen will.
ikh mooss dee Tewr AOUF-*mah-kh'n, venn ikh hin-*AOUS-*gay-h'n vill.*
I must open the door, if I want to go out.

Was muss ich aufmachen, um hinauszugehen?
Vahss mooss ikh AOUF-*mah-kh'n, oom hin-*AOUS-*tsoo-gay-h'n?*
What must I open to go out?

Was muss der Lehrer haben, um an die Tafel zu schreiben?
Vahss mooss dehr LAY-r'r HAH-*b'n, oom ahn dee* TAH-*f'l tsoo* SHRIGH-*b'n?*
What must the teacher have, to write on the blackboard?

Was müssen Sie tun, um zu sehen?
Vahss MEW-*ss'n Zee toon, oom tsoo* ZAY-*h'n?*
What must you do in order to see?

> **Ich muss die Augen öffnen, um zu sehen.**
> *Ikh mooss dee* AOU-*g'n* UHFF-*n'n oom tsoo* ZAY-*h'n.*
> I must open my eyes to see.

> **Was müssen wir tun, um hinauszugehen?**
> *Vahss* MEW-*ss'n veer toon, oom hin-*AOUS-*tsoo-gay-h'n?*
> What must we do to go out?

Wir müssen die Tür öffnen.
Veer MEW-*ss'n dee Tewr* UHFF-*n'n.*
We must open the door.

Wir müssen eine Eintrittskarte kaufen,
Veer MEW-*ss'n* EYE-*neh* INE-*tritts-kahr-teh* KAOU-*f'n,*
We must buy a ticket,

> **wenn wir in das Theater gehen wollen.**
> *venn veer in dahs Teh-*AH-*t'r* GAY-*h'n* VOLL*'n.*
> if we want to go to the theatre.

Können wir ohne Karte in das Theater gehen?
KUH-*n'n veer* OH-*neh* KAHR-*teh in dahs Teh-*AH-*t'r* GAY-*h'n?*
Can we go to the theatre without a ticket?

Wieviel müssen wir für die Karte bezahlen?
*Vee-*FEEL MEW-*ss'n veer fewr dee* KAHR-*teh beh-*TSAH-*l'n?*
How much must we pay for the ticket?

 NOTE: *Um zu* with the infinitive means "in order to".
Ex: *Wir essen um zu leben.*—"We eat in order to live."

THINKING IN GERMAN
(Answers on page 256)

1. Kann der Lehrer hinausgehen?
2. Was muss er tun, um hinauszugehen?
3. Kann er den Schirm halten, wenn seine Hände nicht frei sind?
4. Sein Schlüssel ist in der Tasche; muss er die Tasche öffnen, um ihn herauszunehmen?
5. Können Sie sitzen, ohne einen Stuhl zu haben?
6. Brauchen Sie eine Brille, um zu sehen?
7. Was muss der Koch haben, um einen Braten zu machen?
8. Was muss Frau Huber haben, um eine Bluse zu kaufen?
9. Was müssen Sie haben, um in das Theater zu gehen?
10. Wo gehen Sie hin, um deutsch zu lernen?
11. Muss man die Augen öffnen, um zu sprechen?
12. Leben wir, um zu essen oder essen wir, um zu leben?
13. Können Sie das Fenster zerbrechen?
14. Warum tun Sie es nicht?
15. Warum trinken Sie keine Tinte?

ÜBUNG NR. 21

Guten Appetit!
GOO-*t'n Ah-peh*-TEET!
Good appetite!

Wenn man hungrig ist, muss man essen.
Venn mahn HOON-*greekh ist, mooss mahn* ESS'*n.*
If one is hungry, one must eat.

Sie können zuhause essen oder in einem Restaurant.
Zee KUH-*n'n tsoo*-HAOU-*zeh* ESS'*n* OH-*d'r in* EYE-*n'm Reh-staou*-RAHNT.
You can eat at home or in a restaurant.

Sie gehen in den Speisesaal.
Zee GAY-*h'n in dain* SHPIGH-*zeh-zahl.*
You go into the dining room.

Sie rufen den Kellner: Herr Ober, bringen Sie mir die Speisekarte!
Zee ROO-*f'n dain* KELL-*n'r: Herr* OH-*b'r,* BRIN-*g'n Zee meer dee* SHPIGH-*zeh-*
kahr-teh!
You call the waiter: Waiter, bring me the menu!

NOTE on the use of *Kellner* and *Ober. Kellner* means
"waiter". *Ober* is a contraction of *Oberkellner*—"headwaiter", but you flatter all waiters in Germany by calling
them *Ober.* (A waitress is called *Fräulein.*)

110

Es gibt verschiedene Arten von Speisen:
Ess ggipt fehr-SHEE-deh-neh ART'n fonn SHPIGH-z'n:
There are different kinds of food:

Suppe,
zoo-*peh,*
Soup,

Vorspeisen,	**Eierspeisen,**	**Geflügel,**
FOHR-*shpigh-z'n,*	EYE'r-*shpigh-z'n,*	*Ggeh-*FLEW-*g'l,*
appetizers,	egg-dishes,	fowl,

Fische,
FISH-*eh,*
fish,

Fleischspeisen,	**Nachspeisen,**
FLIGHSH-*shpigh-z'n,*	NAHKH-*shpigh-z'n,*
meat dishes,	desserts,

Mehlspeisen.
MAIL-*shpigh-z'n.*
pastries.

Womit isst man die Suppe?
*Voh-*MIT *isst mahn dee zoo-peh?*
With what do you eat soup?

Mit dem Löffel.
Mit daim LUHFF'*l.*
With the spoon.

Das Fleisch schneidet man mit dem Messer und isst es mit der Gabel.
Dahs Flighsh SHNIGH-*dett mahn mit daim* MESS'*r oont isst ess mit dehr*
GAH-*b'l.*
We cut meat with the knife and eat it with the fork.

Messer, Gabel und Löffel bilden das Besteck.
MESS'*r,* GAH-*b'l oont* LUHFF'*l* BILL-*d'n dahs Beh-*SHTEKK.
Knife, fork and spoon form the place-setting.

Auf dem Tisch stehen Teller.
Aouf daim Tish SHTAY-*h'n* TELL'*r.*
On the table are plates.

NOTE ON SWEETS: After the main dish, Europeans take a *Mehlspeise,* which can be a cake, a pastry or a pie. You know the *Strudel,* which is also a *Mehlspeise,* made of *Mehl,* (flour). These homemade pastries are delicious. After the *Mehlspeise* you eat your dessert, *die Nachspeise,* and then you take your coffee, usually black.

Essen Sie Brot oder Brötchen zum Fleisch?
ESS'*n Zee Broht* OH-*d'r* BRUHT-*kh'n tsoom Flighsh?*
Do you eat bread or rolls with your meat?

Essen Sie gern Braten?
ESS'*n Zee gairn* BRAH-*t'n?*
Do you like to eat roasts?

Es gibt Kalbs-, Rinder-, Lamms- und Schweinebraten.
Ess ggipt KAHLPS-, REEN-*d'r-,* LAHMSS- *oont* SHVIGH-*neh-brah-t'n.*
There are roasts of veal, beef, lamb and pork.

Hühner, Gänse, Enten und Truthähne sind Geflügel.
HEW-*n'r,* GGEHN-*zeh,* ENT*'n oont* TROOT-*heh-neh zint* Ggeh-FLEW-*g'l.*
Chicken, geese, ducks and turkeys are fowl.

Karpfen, Forellen, Hechte und Makrelen sind Fische.
KAHR-*pf'n, Fohr-*ELL*'n,* HAIKH-*teh oont Mah-*KREH-*l'n zint* FISH-*eh.*
Carp, trout, pike and mackerel are fish.

Es gibt Rühreier, Spiegeleier, weiche und harte Eier.
Ess ggipt REWR-*eye-'r,* SHPEE-*g'l-eye-'r,* VIGH-*kheh oont* HAHR-*teh* EYE-*'r.*
There are scrambled, fried, soft- and hard-boiled eggs.

Obst isst man in Europa als Nachspeise.
*Ohpst isst mahn in Oy-*ROH-*pah ahls* NAHKH-*shpigh-zeh.*
One eats fruits as dessert in Europe.

Man trinkt Wasser, Wein oder Bier zur Mahlzeit.
Mahn trinkt VAH-*ss'r, Vine* OH-*d'r Beer tsoor* MAHL-*tsight.*
We drink water, wine or beer with our meal.

> **Schmeckt Ihnen das Essen?**
> *Shmekkt* EE-*n'n dahs* ESS*'n?*
> Do you like your food?

Was für Gemüse kennen Sie?
*Vahss fewr Ggeh-*MEW-*zeh* KEN-*nen Zee?*
Which vegetables do you know?

Essen Sie gern Spinat?
ESS*'n Zee gairn Shpee-*NAHT?
Do you like to eat spinach?

Kartoffeln kann man zu jeder Fleischspeise nehmen.
*Kahr-*TOFF*'ln kahn mahn tsoo* YEH-*d'r* FLIGHSH-*shpigh-zeh* NAY-*m'n.*
You can take potatoes with any meat dish.

In Bayern macht man gute Klösse.
In BIGH-*'rn mahkt mahn* GOO-*teh* KLUH-*sseh.*
In Bavaria, they make good dumplings.

 EXPRESSIONS TO REMEMBER: *Zuhause*—"at home",
ich esse gern—"I like to eat". You call the waiter in
German-speaking countries *Herr Ober,* which means Mr.
Headwaiter.

Als Nachspeise kann man Gebäck oder eine Mehlspeise nehmen.
Ahls NAHKH-*shpigh-zeh kahn mahn Ggeh-*BECK OH-*d'r* EYE-*neh* MAIL-*shpigh-
zeh* NAY-*m'n.*
For dessert you can take cake or pastry.

Nach dem Essen trinkt man Kaffee.
Nahkh daim ESS'n trinkt mahn Kah-FEH.
After the meal you drink coffee.

In Europa trinkt man den Kaffee oft schwarz oder mit sehr wenig Milch.
In Oy-ROH-pah trinkt mahn dain Kah-FEH offt shvartss OH-d'r mit zair VAIN-ikh Milkh.
In Europe they often drink coffee black, or with very little milk.

Wie trinken Sie Kaffee?
Vee TRIN-k'n Zee Kah-FEH?
How do you drink your coffee?

Käse ist ein beliebter Nachtisch.
KEH-zeh ist ine beh-LEEP-t'r NAHKH-tish.
Cheese is a favorite dessert.

Kennen Sie Schweizer Käse?
KEN-nen Zee SHVIGH-ts'r KEH-zeh?
Do you know Swiss cheese?

Nach dem Essen verlangen Sie die Rechnung.
Nahkh daim ESS'n fehr-LAHN-g'n Zee dee REKH-noonk.
After the meal you ask for the check.

Sie sagen: Herr Ober, zahlen!
Zee ZAH-g'n: Herr OH-b'r, TSAH-l'n!
You say: Waiter, my check!

Sie geben dem Oberkellner ein Trinkgeld.
Zee GAY-b'n daim OH-b'r-kell-n'r ine TRINK-ggelt.
You give the headwaiter a tip.

THINKING IN GERMAN

(Answers on page 257)

1. Wann essen Sie gewöhnlich?
2. Was für Vorspeisen nehmen Sie?
3. Wie wollen Sie die Eier haben?
4. Womit essen Sie die Suppe?
5. Gibt es kalte Suppen?
6. Woraus besteht ein Besteck?
7. Was finden Sie auf der Speisekarte?
8. Wer bedient Sie im Speisesaal?
9. Was verlangen Sie vom Kellner?
10. Was trinken Sie zu Ihrer Mahlzeit?
11. Nehmen Sie Zucker und Milch zum Kaffee?
12. Was für Gemüse kennen Sie?
13. Nehmen Sie Obst als Nachspeise?
14. Was verlangen Sie nach dem Essen?
15. Was geben Sie dem Ober?
16. Isst man in Amerika mehr Gänsebraten oder Entenbraten?
17. Essen Sie gern Fisch?
18. Wann isst man Forellen?
19. Haben wir alle den gleichen Geschmack?
20. Hat jedes Hotel einen Speisesaal?

ÜBUNG NR. 22

Die Uhr
Dee Oor
The Clock

Hier ist eine Taschenuhr.
Here ist EYE-*neh* TAH-*sh'n-oor.*
Here is a pocket-watch.

Dort ist eine Wanduhr.
Dohrt ist EYE-*neh* VAHNT-*oor.*
There is a wall-clock.

Auf dem Tisch steht die Tischuhr.
Aouf daim Tish shtait dee TISH-*oor.*
The table-clock is on the table.

Die Wanduhr hängt an der Wand.
Dee VAHNT-*oor henkt ahn dehr Vahnt.*
The wall-clock hangs on the wall.

Die Standuhr steht an der Wand.
Dee SHTAHNT-*oor shtait ahn dehr Vahnt.*
The standing clock stands against the wall.

Die Dame hat keine Taschenuhr, sie hat eine Armbanduhr.
Dee DAH-*meh haht* KIGH-*neh* TAH-*sh'n-oor, zee haht* EYE-*neh* ARM-*bahnt-oor.*
The lady has no pocket-watch, she has a wrist-watch.

Tragen Herren auch Armbanduhren?
TRAH-*g'n Herr'n aoukh* ARM-*bahnt-oo-r'n?*
Do gentlemen carry also wrist-watches?

Wo ist meine Taschenuhr?
Voh ist MIGH-*neh* TAH-*sh'n-oor?*
Where is my pocket-watch?

115

Sie ist in der Tasche.
Zee ist in dehr TAH-sheh.
It is in your pocket.

Was für Uhren gibt es?
Vahss fewr OO-r'n ggipt ess?
What (kind of) time-pieces are there?

Es gibt Taschenuhren, Armbanduhren, Wanduhren, Kuckucksuhren,
Ess ggipt TAH-sh'n-oo-r'n, ARM-bahnt-oo-r'n, VAHNT-oo-r'n, KOO-kooks-oo-r'n,
There are pocket-watches, wrist-watches, wall-clocks, cuckoo-clocks,

Kaminuhren, Tischuhren, Standuhren und Turmuhren.
Kah-MEEN-oo-r'n, TISH-oo-r'n, SHTAHNT-oo-r'n oont Toorm-oo-r'n.
mantel-clocks, table-clocks, floor-clocks and tower-clocks.

Eine Wanduhr ist aus Holz, eine Tischuhr ist aus feinen Hölzern.
EYE-neh VAHNT-oor ist aous Hohlts, EYE-neh TISH-oor ist aous FIGH-n'n
HUHLL-tsairn.
A wall-clock is made of wood, a table-clock is made of fine woods.

Es gibt auch Tischuhren aus Marmor oder Porzellan.
Ess ggipt aoukh TISH-oo-r'n aous MAHR-mohr OH-d'r Pohr-tseh-LAHN.
There are also table-clocks made of marble or china.

Eine Taschenuhr ist aus Metall.
EYE-neh TAH-sh'n-oor ist aous Meh-TAHLL.
A pocket-watch is made of metal.

Sie ist aus Gold oder aus Silber.
Zee ist aous Golt OH-d'r aous ZEEL-b'r.
It is made of gold or of silver.

NOTE to Student: You say: *Die Uhr ist aus Gold*—"The watch is (made) of gold", *Der Tisch ist aus Holz*—"The table is (made) of wood".

Haben Sie eine goldene Taschenuhr?
HAH-b'n Zee EYE-neh GOL-deh-neh TAH-sh'n-oor?
Have you a gold pocket-watch?

Nein, ich habe eine silberne.
Nine, ikh HAH-beh EYE-neh ZEEL-b'r-neh.
No, I have a silver one.

Diese Armbanduhr ist aus Stahl.
DEE-zeh ARM-bahnt-oor ist aous Shtahl.
This wrist-watch is made of steel.

Dort hängt eine hölzerne Wanduhr.
Dohrt henkt EYE-neh HUHLL-ts'r-neh VAHNT-oor.
There hangs a wooden wall-clock.

Woraus ist diese Kaminuhr?
*Voh-*RAOUS *ist* DEE-*zeh Kah-*MEEN-*oor?*
Of what is this mantel-clock made?

Sie ist aus feinem Porzellan.
Zee ist aous FIGH-*n'm Pohr-tseh-*LAHN.
It is made of fine china.

Eine Uhr hat zwei Zeiger, einen grossen und einen kleinen.
EYE-*neh Oor haht tsvigh* TSIGH-*g'r,* EYE-*n'n* GROH-*ss'n oont* EYE-*n'n* KLIGH-*n'n.*
A clock has two hands, a big one and a small one.

Der grosse Zeiger zeigt die Minuten, der kleine die Stunden.
Dehr GROH-*sseh* TSIGH-*g'r tsighkt dee Mee-*NOO-*t'n, dehr* KLIGH-*neh dee*
SHTOON-*d'n.*
The big hand shows the minutes, the small one the hours.

> **Welches ist der Minutenzeiger?**
> VEL-*khes ist dehr Mee-*NOO-*t'n-tsigh-g'r?*
> Which one is the big hand?

> **Welcher Zeiger zeigt die Stunden?**
> VEL-*kh'r* TSIGH-*g'r tsighkt dee* SHTOON-*d'n?*
> Which hand shows the hours?

> **Der kleine zeigt die Stunden.**
> *Dehr* KLIGH-*neh tsighkt dee* SHTOON-*d'n.*
> The little one shows the hours.

> **Eine Stunde hat 60 Minuten.**
> EYE-*neh* SHTOON-*deh haht* ZEKH-*tsikh Mee-*NOO-*t'n.*
> One hour has 60 minutes.

> **Eine Minute enthält 60 Sekunden.**
> EYE-*neh Mee-*NOO-*teh ent-*HELT SEKH-*tsikh Seh-*KOON-*d'n.*
> One minute contains 60 seconds.

> **Wieviele Sekunden hat eine Stunde?**
> *Vee-*FEE-*leh Seh-*KOON-*d'n haht* EYE-*neh* SHTOON-*deh?*
> How many seconds has one hour?

> **Vierundzwanzig Stunden sind ein Tag.**
> FEER-*oont-tsvahn-tsikh* SHTOON-*d'n zint ine Tahk.*
> 24 hours are a day.

> **Wieviele Stunden enthält ein Tag?**
> *Vee-*FEE-*leh* SHTOON-*d'n ent-*HELT *ine Tahk?*
> How many hours does a day contain?

Auf dieser Uhr ist es ein Uhr;
Aouf DEEZ'*r Oor ist ess ine Oor;*
On this clock it is one o'clock;

auf dieser ist es vier Uhr.
aouf DEEZ'*r ist ess feer Oor.*
on this one it is four o'clock.

Wie spät ist es auf Ihrer Uhr?
Vee shpait ist ess aouf EE-*r'r Oor?*
How late is it on your clock?

Wieviel Uhr ist es?
*Vee-*FEEL *Oor ist ess?*
What time is it?

Es ist zwölf Uhr.
Ess ist tsvuhlf Oor.
It is 12 o'clock.

Sechzig Minuten sind eine Stunde;
ZEKH-*tsikh Mee-*NOO-*t'n zint* EYE-*neh* SHTOON-*deh;*
60 minutes are one hour;

dreissig Minuten sind eine halbe Stunde
DRIGH-*ssikh Mee-*NOO-*t'n zint* EYE-*neh* HAHL-*beh* SHTOON-*deh*
30 minutes are a half-hour

und fünfzehn Minuten eine Viertelstunde.
oont FEWNF-*tsain Mee-*NOO-*t'n* EYE-*neh* FEER-*t'l-*SHTOON-*deh.*
and 15 minutes a quarter-hour.

Es ist fünfzehn Minuten nach drei Uhr
Ess ist FEWNF-*tsain Mee-*NOO-*t'n nahkh drigh Oor.*
It is 15 minutes after 3 o'clock

oder es ist drei Uhr fünfzehn.
OH-*d'r ess ist drigh Oor* FEWNF-*tsain.*
or it is 3:15.

Es ist einviertel nach drei Uhr.
Ess ist INE-*feer-t'l nahkh drigh Oor.*
It is a quarter after 3.

Es ist drei Uhr dreissig
Ess ist drigh Oor DRIGH-*ssikh*
It is 3:30

oder es ist halb vier.
OH-*d'r ess ist hahlp feer.*
or it is half of the fourth hour.

Ist es dreiviertel vier?
Ist ess DRIGH-*feer-t'l feer?*
Is it three quarters of the 4th hour?

Ja, es ist drei Uhr fünfundvierzig.
Yah, ess ist drigh Oor FEWNF-*oont-feer-tsikh.*
Yes, it is 3:45.

Es ist einviertel vor vier.
Ess ist INE-*feer-t'l fohr feer.*
It is a quarter before four.

Es ist fünf Minuten nach sechs
*Ess ist fewnf Mee-*NOO-*t'n nahkh zeks*
It is five minutes after 6

oder es ist sechs Uhr fünf.
OH-*d'r ess ist zeks Oor fewnf.*
or it is six five.

Est ist fünf Minuten vor halb sechs
*Ess ist fewnf Mee-*NOO-*t'n fohr hahlp zeks*
It is five minutes before half past five.

oder es ist fünf Uhr fünfundzwanzig.
OH-*d'r ess ist fewnf Oor* FEWNF-*oont-tsvahn-tsikh.*
or it is 5:25.

NOTE to Student: The Germans have a very unusual way to ask and to tell time. They ask: *Wie spät ist es?* which means literally translated "How late is it?" or *Wieviel Uhr ist es?*—"How much clock is it?" Even more unusual is the way of telling the time. For instance if they say *viertel fünf* —"quarter-five" they really mean "the first quarter of the fifth hour"—in other words "a quarter past four". This applies to half and three quarter hours also. *Dreiviertel vier* means "a quarter to four".

Ich stehe um halb sechs auf.
Ikh SHTAY-*heh oom hahlp zeks aouf.*
I get up at half past five.

Um wieviel Uhr stehen Sie auf?
*Oom vee-*FEEL *Oor* SHTAY'n *Zee aouf?*
At what time do you get up?

Wann frühstücken Sie?
Vahn FREW-*shtew-k'n Zee?*
When do you take breakfast?

Ich frühstücke um sieben Uhr.
Ikh FREW-*shtew-keh oom* ZEE-*b'n Oor.*
I take breakfast at 7 o'clock.

Sie essen um ein Uhr.
Zee ESS'n *oom ine Oor.*
You eat at one o'clock.

Essen Sie um eins?
ESS'n *Zee oom ine'ss?*
Do you eat at one?

Sie kommen um elf Uhr hierher.
ZEE KOMM'n *oom elf Oor here-*HAIR.
You come here at 11 o'clock.

Um wieviel Uhr kommen Sie hierher?
*Oom vee-*FEEL *Oor* KOMM'n *Zee here-*HAIR?
At what time do you come here?

Sie gehen um 12 Uhr fort.
Zee GAY-*h'n oom tsvuhlf Oor fohrt.*
You leave at 12 o'clock.

Wann gehen Sie fort?
Vahn GAY-*h'n Zee fohrt?*
When do you leave?

HITHER AND THITHER: These two words are not common in English any more, but their equivalents in German are very much so. Note that our English word "here", therefore is translated *hier* when you mean "in this place" and *hierher* when you mean "to this place" (hither). Likewise, "there" is *dort* and "to there" (thither) is *dorthin*.

Die Weckuhr geht nicht, sie steht.
Dee VEKK-*oor gait nikht, zee shtait.*
The alarm clock does not run, it is stopped.

Man muss sie aufziehen.
Mahn mooss zee AOUF-*tsee-h'n.*
We must wind it.

Wollen Sie sie aufziehen?
VOLL'*n Zee zee* AOUF-*tsee-h'n?*
Do you wish to wind it?

Stellen Sie die Uhr!
SHTELL'*n Zee dee Oor!*
Set the clock!

Auf dieser Uhr ist es zehn Uhr.
Aouf DEEZ'*r Oor ist ess tsain Oor.*
On this clock it is 10 o'clock.

Wie spät ist es wirklich?
Vee shpait ist ess VEERK-*likh?*
How late is it really?

Es ist genau halb zehn, stellen Sie die Uhr zurück!
*Ess ist ggeh-*NAOU *hahlp tsain,* SHTELL'*n Zee dee Oor tsoo-*REWK!
It is exactly half past nine; set the clock back!

> **Die Uhr geht vor.**
> *Dee Oor gait fohr.*
> The clock is fast.

Wenn die Uhr vorgeht, stellt man sie zurück.
Venn dee Oor FOHR-*gait, shtellt mahn zee tsoo-*REWK.
If the clock is fast, one sets it back.

Meine Uhr geht nach, ich muss sie vorstellen.
MIGH-*neh Oor gait nahhh, ikh mooss zee* FOHR-*shtell'n.*
My watch is slow; I must set it ahead.

Diese Kuckucksuhr geht weder nach noch vor, sie geht richtig.
DEE-*zeh* KOO-*kooks-oor gait* VAY-*d'r nahkh nokh fohr, zee gait* REEKH-*tikh.*
This cuckoo-clock is neither slow nor fast: it is right.

Wie geht Ihre Uhr?
Vee gait EE-*reh Oor?*
How does your watch run?

Sie geht gar nicht, sie steht.
Zee gait gahr nikht, zee shtait.
It does not run at all: it is stopped.

Eine Wanduhr ist grösser als eine Taschenuhr.
EYE-*neh* VAHNT-*oor ist* GRUH-*ss'r ahls* EYE-*neh* TAH-*sh'n-oor.*
A wall clock is larger than a pocket-watch.

Eine Taschenuhr ist kleiner als eine Wanduhr.
EYE-*neh* TAH-*sh'n-oor ist* KLIGH-*n'r ahls* EYE-*neh* VAHNT-*oor.*
A pocket-watch is smaller than a wall clock.

Der Minutenzeiger ist länger als der Stundenzeiger.
*Dehr Mee-*NOO-*t'n-tsigh-g'r ist* LENG'*r ahls dehr* SHTOON-*d'n-tsigh-g'r.*
The minute hand is longer than the hour hand.

Der Sekundenzeiger ist kürzer als der Stundenzeiger.
*Dehr Seh-*KOON-*d'n-tsigh-g'r ist* KEWR-*ts'r ahls dehr* SHTOON-*d'n-tsigh-g'r.*
The second hand is shorter than the hour hand.

> **Die Weste ist kürzer als der Rock.**
> *Dee* VES-*teh ist* KEWR-*ts'r ahls dehr Rokk.*
> The vest is shorter than the coat.

Der Tisch ist breiter als die Tischuhr.
Dehr Tish ist BRIGH-*t'r ahls dee* TISH-*oor.*
The table is wider than the table clock.

Mein Buch ist schmaler als Ihr Buch.
Mine Bookh ist SHMAH-*l'r ahls Eer Bookh.*
My book is narrower than your book.

Dieser Hut ist nicht so breit wie jener.
DEEZ'*r Hoot ist nikht zoh bright vee* YEH-*n'r.*
This hat is not so wide as that one.

Jener ist breiter, dieser ist schmaler.
YEH-*n'r ist* BRIGH-*t'r,* DEEZ'*r ist* SHMAH-*l'r.*
That one is wider, this one is narrower.

EXPRESSIONS TO REMEMBER: *Hierher* and its opposite *dorthin* mean "here to this place" and "there to that place" respectively.

Ist mein Rock so lang wie meine Weste?
Ist mine Rokk zoh lahnk vee MIGH-*neh* VES-*teh?*
Is my coat as long as my vest?

Ist die Weste kürzer als der Rock?
Ist dee VES-*teh* KEWR-*ts'r ahls dehr Rokh?*
Is the vest shorter than the coat?

Ist mein Buch so breit wie meine Tasche?
Ist mine Bookh zoh bright vee MIGH-*neh* TAH-*sheh?*
Is my book as wide as my pocket?

Ist die Tasche schmaler?
Ist dee TAH-*sheh* SHMAH-*l'r?*
Is the pocket narrower?

Was ist kürzer, eine Stunde oder sechzig Minuten?
Vahss ist KEWR-*ts'r,* EYE-*neh* SHTOON-*deh* OH-*d'r* ZEKH-*tsikh Mee-*NOO-*t'n?*
What is shorter, an hour or 60 minutes?

Sechzig Minuten sind so lang wie eine Stunde.
ZEKH-*tsikh Mee-*NOO-*t'n zint zoh lahnk vee* EYE-*neh* SHTOON-*deh.*
Sixty minutes are as long as an hour.

Schmeckt schwarzer Kaffee gut?
Shmekkt SHVAHR-*ts'r Kah-*FEH *goot?*
Does black coffee taste good?

Schmeckt Kaffee mit Milch besser?
*Schmekkt Kah-*FEE *mit Milkh* BESS'*r?*
Does coffee with milk taste better?

Sprechen Sie besser deutsch als englisch?
SHPREH-kh'n Zee BESS'r doitsh ahls ENNG-lish?
Do you speak German better than English?

Sprechen Sie englisch so gut wie deutsch?
SHPREH-kh'n Zee ENNG-lish zoh goot vee doitsh?
Do you speak English as well as German?

Welche Sprache sprechen Sie am besten?
VEL-kheh SHPRAH-kheh SHPREH-kh'n Zee ahm BEST'n?
Which language do you speak best?

Was ist am kürzesten, der Tag, die Stunde, die Minute oder die Sekunde?
Vahss ist ahm KEWR-tseh-st'n, dehr Tahk, dee SHTOON-deh, dee Mee-NOO-teh OH-d'r dee Seh-KOON-deh?
What is the shortest, the day, the hour, the minute or the second?

Welches Tier ist am grössten, der Hund, die Katze oder die Maus?
VEL-khes Teer ist ahm GRUH-st'n, dehr Hoont, dee KAH-tseh OH-d'r dee Maous?
What animal is the largest, the dog, the cat or the mouse?

Die Rose riecht besser als die Tulpe.
Dee ROH-zeh reekht BESS'r ahls dee TOOL-peh.
The rose smells better than the tulip.

Riecht Gas gut?
Reekht gahs goot?
Does gas smell good?

NOTE on comparison of adjectives: The comparison of adjectives is formed somewhat as in English. However, many one-syllable adjectives use an umlaut in the comparative and superlative. Ex: "Long, longer, longest"—*lang, länger, der längste.* Ex: *angenehm, angenehmer, der angenehmste*—"pleasant", "more pleasant", "the most pleasant." When used as a predicate to the verb or as an adverb the superlative is preceded by *am* and takes the ending *en.* Ex: *am längsten*—"the longest". Of course, there are exceptions like *gut, besser, am besten*—"good, better, best"; *hoch, höher, am höchsten*—"high, higher, highest": *nah, näher, am nächsten*—"near, nearer, nearest"; *viel, mehr, am meisten*—"much or many, more, most".

THINKING IN GERMAN

(Answers on page 257)

1. Ist eine Wanduhr in diesem Zimmer?
2. Wo befindet sie sich?
3. Haben Sie eine Armbanduhr?
4. Wie spät haben Sie?
5. Was hat der Uhrmacher in der Hand?
6. Geht die Uhr des Professors?
7. Wieviele Zeiger hat eine Taschenuhr?
8. Zeigt Ihre Uhr die Sekunden?
9. Wann fängt das Kino an?
10. Wann ist es zu Ende?
11. Wieviel Uhr zeigt die Wanduhr?

12. Wann essen Sie zu Mittag?

13. Wieviele Stunden hat ein Tag?

14. Wieviele Sekunden enthält eine Minute?

15. Geht Ihre Uhr richtig?

16. Ihre Uhr geht vor; was müssen Sie tun?

17. Wann ziehen Sie Ihre Weckuhr auf?

18. Ist eine Kuckucksuhr grösser als eine Taschenuhr?

19. Sehen Sie eine Kirchenuhr?

20. Geht die Schuluhr richtig?

21. Ist das Fenster breiter als der Stuhl?

22. Haben die Damen längere Haare als die Herren?

23. Sind Damenhüte höher als Herrenhüte?

24. Ist Wein besser als Wasser?

25. Sprechen Sie so gut deutsch wie englisch?

26. Können Sie mit einer Brille besser sehen als ohne Brille?

27. Hat Rockefeller mehr Geld als Sie?

28. Ist New York grösser als Berlin?

29. Ist es in Mexico wärmer als in Canada?

ÜBUNG NR. 23

Das Jahr
Dahs Yahr
The year

Vierundzwanzig Stunden sind ein Tag.
FEER-*oont-tsvahn-tsikh* SHTOON-*d'n zint ine Tahk.*
Twenty-four hours are a day.

Sieben Tage sind eine Woche.
ZEE-*b'n* TAH-*ggeh zint* EYE-*neh* VOH-*kheh.*
Seven days are a week.

Die sieben Tage der Woche heissen:
Dee ZEE-*b'n* TAH-*ggeh dehr* VOH-*kheh* HIGH-*ss'n:*
The seven days of the week are called:

Sonntag	**Montag**	**Dienstag**	**Mittwoch**
ZONN-*tahk*	MOHN-*tahk*	DEENS-*tahk*	MITT-*vohkh*
Sunday	Monday	Tuesday	Wednesday

Donnerstag	**Freitag**	**Sonnabend**	**(Samstag)**
DONN-*'rs-tahk*	FRIGH-*tahk*	ZONN-*ah-b'nd*	(ZAHMS-*tahk*)
Thursday	Friday	Saturday	(Saturday)

(either form correct)

Wie heissen die sieben Tage der Woche?
Vee HIGH-*ss'n dee* ZEE-*b'n* TAH-*ggeh dehr* VOH-*kheh?*
What are the seven days of the week called?

Wieviele Tage hat eine Woche?
*Vee-*FEE-*leh* TAH-*ggeh haht* EYE-*neh* VOH-*kheh?*
How many days has a week?

Dreissig oder einunddreissig Tage sind ein Monat.
DRIGH-*ssikh* OH-*d'r* INE-*oont-drigh-ssikh* TAH-*ggeh zint ine* MOH-*naht.*
Thirty or thirty-one days are a month.

Dreihundertfünfundsechzig Tage sind ein Jahr.
DRIGH-*hoon-d'rt-fewnf-oont-sekh-tsikh* TAH-*ggeh zint ine Yahr.*
Three hundred and sixty-five days are a year.

Ein Jahr hat 12 Monate,	**52 Wochen,**
Ine Yahr haht tsvuhlf MOH-*nah-teh,*	TSVIGH-*oont-fewnf-tsikh* VOH-*kh'n,*
A year has 12 months,	52 weeks,

365 Tage.
DRIGH-*hoon-d'rt-fewnf-oont-zekh-tsikh* TAH-*ggeh.*
365 days.

Die Monate heissen:
Dee MOH-*nah-teh* HIGH-*ss'n:*
The months are called:

Januar,	**Februar,**		
YAH-*noo-ahr,*	FEH-*broo-ahr,*		
January,	February,		
März,	**April,**	**Mai,**	**Juni,**
Mairts,	*Ah-*PREEL,	*Migh,*	YOO-*nee,*
March,	April,	May,	June,
Juli,	**August,**	**September,**	**Oktober,**
YOO-*lee,*	*Aou-*GOOST,	*Sepp-*TEHM-*b'r,*	*Ohk-*TOH-*b'r,*
July,	August,	September,	October,
November,	**Dezember.**		
*Noh-*VEHM-*b'r,*	*Deh-*TSEHM-*b'r.*		
November,	December.		

Wir sind jetzt im Monat August.
Veer zint yetst eem MOH-*naht Aou-*GOOST.
We are now in the month of August.

In welchem Monat sind wir?
In VEL-*khem* MOH-*naht zint veer?*
In what month are we?

Heute ist der dreizehnte August.
HOY-*teh ist dehr* DRIGH-*tsain-teh Aou-*GOOST.
Today is the 13th of August.

Mein Geburtstag ist am vierzehnten Januar.
*Mine Ggeh-*BOORTS-*tahk ist ahm* FEER-*tsain-t'n* YAH-*noo-ahr.*
My birthday is on the 14th of January.

Der wievielte ist heute?
Dehr vee-FEEL-teh ist HOY-*teh?*
The "how manieth" is today?

Der wievielte ist morgen?
Dehr vee-FEEL-teh ist MORG'*n?*
The "how manieth" is tomorrow?

NOTE to Student: See how *der fünfzehnte* or *der sechste* resembles our construction "the fifteenth" or "the sixth". But to say "on the fifteenth", use *am fünfzehnten. Der wievielte* is "the how manieth" an expression we do not use, but which is very much to the point when asking for a particular date.

Heute ist Donnerstag.
HOY-*teh ist* DONN-'*rs-tahk.*
Today is Thursday.

Welcher Tag ist morgen?
VEL-*kh'r Tahk ist* MORG'*n?*
What day is tomorrow?

CAUTION: *morgen* means "tomorrow", *am Morgen* and *morgens* mean "in the morning"; *drei Uhr morgens* is "at three o'clock in the morning".

Wir haben jetzt den Monat August;
Veer HAH-*b'n yetst dain* MOH-*naht Aou-*GOOST;
We are now in the month of August;

der vorige Monat war Juli;
dehr FOH-*ree-ggeh* MOH-*naht vahr* YOO-*lee;*
last month was July;

der nächste ist September.
dehr NAIK-*steh ist Sepp-*TEHM-*b'r.*
next month is September.

Heute ist der dreizehnte;
HOY-*teh ist dehr* DRIGH-*tsain-teh;*
Today is the thirteenth;

gestern war der zwölfte;
GGEST-'*rn vahr dehr* TSVUHLF-*teh;*
yesterday was the twelfth;

morgen ist der vierzehnte.
MORG'*n ist dehr* FEER-*tsain-teh.*
tomorrow is the 14th.

Der wievielte war gestern?
*Dehr vee-*FEEL-*teh vahr* GGEST-'*rn?*
What date was yesterday?

ATTENTION: Did you notice that we slipped in the past tense in *gestern war der zwölfte*—"yesterday *was* the twelfth." You will encounter the past of all verbs after 3 more lessons.

Sechs Tage in der Woche arbeiten wir;
Zeks TAH-*ggeh in dehr* VOH-*kheh* AHR-*bigh-t'n veer;*
Six days a week we work;

am Sonntag arbeiten wir nicht.
ahm ZONN-*tahk* AHR-*bigh-t'n veer nikht.*
on Sunday we don't work.

Wir ruhen am Sonntag, Sonntag ist ein Ruhetag.
Veer ROO-*h'n ahm* ZONN-*tahk,* ZONN-*tahk ist ine* ROO-*heh-tahk.*
We rest on Sunday: Sunday is a day of rest.

Montag und Dienstag sind Arbeitstage.
MOHN-*tahk oont* DEENS-*tahk zint* AHR-*bights-tah-ggeh.*
Monday and Tuesday are work-days.

Ist Mittwoch ein Ruhetag?
Ist MITT-*vohkh ine* ROO-*heh-tahk?*
Is Wednesday a day of rest?

Weihnachten und Ostern arbeiten wir nicht.
VIGH-*nahkh-t'n oont* OH-*st'rn* AHR-*bigh-t'n veer nikht.*
On Christmas and Easter we do not work.

Es sind Feiertage.
Ess zint FIRE-*tah-ggeh.*
They are holidays.

Weihnachten ist am fünfundzwanzigsten Dezember,
VIGH-*nahkh-t'n ist ahm* FEWNF-*oont-tsvahn-tsik-st'n Deh-*TSEHM-*b'r,*
Christmas is on December 25th,

Ostern ist im Frühling.
OH-*st'rn ist im* FREW-*link.*
Easter is in spring.

Ist Washingtons Geburtstag ein Feiertag?
Ist VAH-*shink-tonss Ggeh-*BOORTS-*tahk ine* FIRE-*tahk?*
Is Washington's Birthday a holiday?

Der Februar hat achtundzwanzig Tage.
Dehr FEH-*broo-ahr haht* AHKHT-*oont-tsvahn-tsikh* TAH-*ggeh.*
February has 28 days.

Alle 4 Jahre hat er neunundzwanzig Tage.
AHL-*leh feer* YAH-*reh haht air* NOIN-*oont-tsvahn-tsikh* TAH-*ggeh.*
Every four years it has 29 days.

Der neunundzwanzigste Februar ist ein Schalttag.
Dehr NOIN-*oont-tsvahn-tsik-steh* FEH-*broo-ahr ist ine* SHAHLT-*tahk.*
The 29th of February is leap year day.

Im Schaltjahr hat der Februar 29 Tage.
Im SHAHLT-*yahr haht dehr* FEH-*broo-ahr* NOIN-*oont-tsvahn-tsikh* TAH-*ggeh.*
In leap year February has 29 days.

Wieviel Tage hat ein Schaltjahr?
*Vee-*FEEL TAH-*ggeh haht ine* SHAHLT-*yahr?*
How many days has leap year?

Ein Schaltjahr hat dreihundertsechsundsechzig Tage.
Ine SHAHLT-*yahr haht* DRIGH-*hoon-d'rt-zeks-oont-zekh-tsikh* TAH-*ggeh.*
A leap year has 366 days.

 **NOTE to Student:** Don't become exasperated by the length of German words. If you take a good look at them and break them down syllable by syllable you will quite often find that they are composed of short words you already know.

Das Jahr hat vier Jahreszeiten:			**Frühling,**	**Sommer,**
Dahs Yahr haht feer YAH-*ress-tsigh-t'n:*			FREW-*link.*	ZOMM'*r,*
The year has 4 seasons:			spring,	summer,
	Herbst	**und**	**Winter.**	
	Hairpst	*oont*	VINT'*r.*	
	fall	and	winter.	

März, April und Mai sind die Frühlingsmonate;
*Mairts, Ah-*PREEL *oont Migh zint dee* FREW-*links-moh-nah-teh;*
March, April and May are the spring months;

Juni, Juli und August sind die Sommermonate;
YOO-*nee,* YOO-*lee oont Aou-*GOOST *zint dee* ZOMM'*r-moh-nah-teh;*
June, July and August are the summer months;

der Herbst umfasst die Monate September, Oktober und November
*dehr Hairpst oom-*FAHST *dee* MOH-*nah-teh Sepp-*TEHM-*b'r, Ohk-*TOH-*b'r oont*
    *Noh-*VEHM-*b'r*
the fall comprises the months of September, October and November

**und während der Monate Dezember, Januar und Februar haben wir
    Winter.**
oont VAY-*r'nd dehr* MOH-*nah-teh Deh-*TSEHM-*b'r,* YAH-*noo-ahr oont* FEH-*broo-ahr* HAH-*b'n veer* VINT'*r.*
and during the months of December, January and February we have
    winter.

Diese Jahreszeit dauert bis zum einundzwanzigsten März,
DEE-*zeh* YAH-*ress-tsight* DAOU-*'rt biss tsoom* INE-*oont-tsvahn-tsik-st'n Mairts,*
This season lasts till the 21st of March,

dann beginnt der Frühling.
*dahn beh-*GGINT *dehr* FREW-*link.*
then spring begins.

Nach dem Frühling kommt der Sommer.
Nahkk daim FREW-*link kommt dehr* ZOMM*'r.*
After spring comes summer.

Auf den Sommer folgt der Herbst.   **Was folgt auf den Herbst?**
Aouf dain ZOMM*'r fohlkt dehr Hairpst.*   *Vahss fohlkt aouf dain Hairpst?*
Fall follows summer.   What follows fall?

Im Kalender sind die Sonntage und Feiertage rot,
*Im Kah-*LEND*'r zint dee* ZOON-*tah-ggeh oont* FIRE-*tah-ggeh roht,*
On the calendar Sundays and holidays are red;

die Wochentage sind schwarz.
dee VOH-*kh'n-tah-ggeh zint shvahrtss.*
weekdays are black.

Hier ist ein Kalender!   **Sehen Sie her!**
*Here ist ine Kah-*LEND*'r!*   ZAY-*h'n Zee hair!*
Here is a calendar!   Look here!

Im vorigen Jahr war der erste Januar ein Mittwoch,
Im FOH-*ree-g'n Yahr vahr dehr* AIR-*steh* YAH-*noo-ahr ine* MITT-*vohkh,*
Last year the first of January was a Wednesday,

dieses Jahr fällt er auf einen Freitag.
DEE-*z's Yahr fellt air aouf* EYE-*n'n* FRIGH-*tahk.*
this year it falls on a Friday.

Neujahr fällt also auf einen Freitag.
NOY-*yahr fellt* AHL-*zoh aouf* EYE-*n'n* FRIGH-*tahk.*
New Year's Day thus falls on a Friday.

Auf welches Datum fällt Ostern dieses Jahr?
Aouf VEL-*khess* DAH-*toom fellt* OH-*st'rn* DEEZ*'s Yahr?*
On what day does Easter fall this year?

Und Weihnachten?
Oont VIGH-*nahkh-t'n?*
And Christmas?

THINKING IN GERMAN
(Answers on page 258)

1. Wieviele Tage sind in einem Jahr?
2. Wieviele Wochen und Monate hat ein Jahr?
3. Wann fängt das Jahr an?
4. Wann ist es zu Ende?
5. Welches ist der erste Monat des Jahres? Der achte? Der letzte?
6. Wieviele Tage hat der Februar?
7. Wieviele Tage hat ein Schaltjahr?
8. Der wievielte Monat ist März?
9. Der wievielte Tag der Woche ist Donnerstag?
10. Wie heissen die sieben Tage der Woche?
11. Wie heissen die Frühlingsmonate?
12. Wie lange dauert der Monat August?
13. War letzten Sonnabend der siebenundzwanzigste?
14. Ist das Jahr morgen zu Ende?
15. In welcher Jahreszeit sind wir jetzt?
16. Welche Jahreszeit kommt nach dem Winter?
17. Ist Weihnachten ein gewöhnlicher Wochentag?
18. Arbeiten Sie zu Ostern?
19. Wie heisst der Tag vor dem Sonntag?
20. Wie spät ist es jetzt?
21. Auf welchen Tag fällt dieses Jahr der einunddreissigste Dezember?
22. Haben Sie einen Kalender?
23. Welches ist der letzte Herbstmonat?

ÜBUNG NR. 24

Tag und Nacht
Tahk oont Nahkht.
Day and night

Wieviele Stunden hat der Tag?
Vee-FEE-leh SHTOON-*d'n haht dehr Tahk?*
How many hours has the day?

Er hat vierundzwanzig Stunden.
Air haht FEER-*oont-tsvahn-tsikh* SHTOON-*d'n.*
It has 24 hours.

Wir teilen die vierundzwanzig Stunden in zwei Teile:
Veer TIGH-*l'n dee* FEER-*oont-tsvahn-tsikh* SHTOON-*d'n in tsvigh* TIGH-*leh:*
We divide the 24 hours into two parts:

In Tag	**und Nacht.**
In Tahk	*oont Nahkht.*
Into day	and night.

Während des Tages ist die Sonne am Himmel;
VAY-*r'nt dess* TAH-*g's ist dee* ZON-*neh ahm* HIMM'*l;*
During the day the sun is in the sky;

es ist hell; wir können sehen.
ess ist hell; veer KUH-*n'n* ZAY-*h'n.*
it is light; we can see.

NOTE on *Hell*: Don't get excited, we are not swearing at you! We only want to point out to you that *hell* means "bright" or "light" in German. *Es ist hell* means "it is bright", *es ist heller Tag* means "it is broad daylight".

Das Tageslicht kommt von der Sonne.
Dahs TAH-*g's-likht kommt fonn dehr* ZON-*neh.*
The daylight comes from the sun.

Wann scheint die Sonne?
Vahn shighnt dee ZON-*neh?*
When does the sun shine?

Scheint die Sonne während der Nacht?
Shighnt dee ZON-*neh* VAY-*r'nd dehr Nahkht?*
Does the sun shine during the night?

Nein, sie scheint nicht.
Nine, zee shighnt nikht.
No, it does not shine.

Es ist dunkel.
Ess ist DOON-*k'l.*
It is dark.

NOTE: *Die Sonne ist am Himmel.*—"The sun is in the sky." But: *Gott ist im Himmel.*—"God is in heaven."

Sehen wir, wenn es dunkel ist?
ZAY-*h'n veer, venn ess* DOON-*k'l ist?*
Do we see when it is dark?

Nein, wir sehen nicht, wir müssen Licht machen, wenn wir sehen wollen.
Nine, veer ZAY-*h'n nikht, veer* MEW-*ss'n Likht* MAH-*kh'n, venn veer* ZAY-*h'n* VOLL'*n.*
No, we do not see; we must put on the light if we want to see.

Schalten Sie, bitte, das Licht ein, es ist dunkel. Danke.
SHAHL-*t'n Zee,* BIT-*teh, dahs Likht ine, ess ist* DOON-*k'l.* DAHN-*keh.*
Switch on the light, please, it is dark. Thanks.

Jetzt brennt Licht, es ist hell genug hier, wir können gut sehen.
*Yetst brent Likht, ess ist hell ggeh-*NOOK *here, veer* KUH-*n'n goot* ZAY-*h'n.*
The light now burns; it is light enough here; we can see well.

NOTE to Student: *Das Licht brennt*—"the light is burning", *wir zünden das Licht an*—"we light the light" goes back to the times of the kerosene lamps; yet you may still use these expressions even though you are referring to an electric light.

Wann machen wir Licht,
Vahn MAH-*kh'n veer Likht,*
When do we put on the light,

am Tage oder in der Nacht?
ahm TAH-*ggeh* OH-*d'r in dehr Nahkht?*
during the day or at night?

Man schaltet das elektrische Licht ein,
Mahn SHAHL-*t't dahs eh-*LEK-*trish-'eh Likht ine,*
We switch the electric light on,

man schaltet es aus,
mahn SHAHL-*t't ess aous,*
we switch it off,

man zündet das Licht an,
mahn TSEWN-*d't dahs Likht ahn,*
we light the light,

man löscht es aus.
mahn luhsht ess aous.
we extinguish it.

Wenn man das Zimmer betritt, schaltet man das Licht ein;
Venn mahn dahs TSIMM'*r beh-*TRITT, SHAHL-*t't mahn dahs Likht ine;*
If you enter the room you switch on the light;

man schaltet es aus, wenn man das Zimmer verlässt.
mahn SHAHL-*t't ess aous, venn mahn dahs* TSIMM'*r fair-*LESST.
you switch it off, if you leave the room.

Sie haben eine Zigarette,
Zee HAH-*b'n* EYE-*neh Tsee-gah-*RET-*teh,*
You have a cigarette,

sie brennt nicht.
zee brent nikht.
it does not burn.

Haben Sie ein Streichholz?
HAH-*b'n Zee ine* SHTRIGHKH-*hohlts?*
Have you a match?

Hier ist ein Streichholz!
Here ist ine SHTRIGHKH-*hohlts!*
Here is a match!

Bitte, zünden Sie die Zigarette an!
BIT-*teh,* TSEWN-*d'n Zee dee Tsee-gah-*RET-*teh ahn!*
Please, light the cigarette!

Danke, sie brennt schon.
DAHN-*keh, zee brent shohn.*
Thanks, it is already lit.

Zünden Sie während des Tages das Licht an?
TSEWN-*d'n Zee* VAY-*r'nd dess* TAH-*g's dahs Likht ahn?*
Do you light the light during the day?

Schlafen Sie während der Nacht?
SHLAH-*f'n Zee* VAY-*r'nd dehr Nahkht?*
Do you sleep during the night?

IMPORTANT NOTE: Pronouns, articles and nouns forming the object of the preposition *während*—"during" are always in the genitive; this applies equally to *wegen*—"because of", *anstatt*—"instead of", *innerhalb*—"within", *ausserhalb*—"without", etc. Observe: *Während des Tages*—"during the day". Here the noun itself has assumed a genitive form. However, feminine nouns do not change: *während der Nacht*—"during the night".

Während des Tages kann man die Sonne am Himmel sehen,
VAY-r'nd dess TAH-g's kahn mahn dee ZON-neh ahm HIMM'l ZAY-h'n,
During the day we can see the sun in the sky,

sie ist sichtbar.
zee ist ZIKHT-bahr.
it is visible.

Während der Nacht ist sie nicht sichtbar.
VAY-r'nd dehr Nahkht ist zee nikht ZIKHT-bahr.
During the night it is not visible.

Was sehen wir in der Nacht?
Vahss ZAY-h'n veer in dehr Nahkht?
What do we see at night?

Wir sehen den Mond und die Sterne.
Veer ZAY-h'n dain Mohnt oont dee SHTAIR-neh.
We see the moon and the stars.

Es gibt sehr viele Sterne; sie sind zahlreich.
Ess ggipt zair FEE-leh SHTAIR-neh; zee zint TSAHL-righkh.
There are many stars, they are numerous.

Können Sie die Sterne zählen?
KUH-n'n Zee dee SHTAIR-neh TSAY-l'n?
Can you count the stars?

Nein, sie sind unzählbar.
Nine, zee zint OON-tsayl-bahr.
No, they are innumerable.

Der Anfang des Tages heisst Morgen,
Dehr AHN-fahnk dess TAH-g's highst MOHR-g'n,
The beginning of the day is called morning;

das Ende heisst Abend.
dahs EN-deh highst AH-b'nt.
the end is called evening.

Wie heisst der Anfang der Nacht?
Vee highst dehr AHN-fahnk dehr Nahkht?
What is the beginning of the night called?

Wie heisst das Ende?
Vee highst dahs EN-deh?
What is the end called?

Am Morgen geht die Sonne im Osten auf,
Ahm MOHR-g'n gait dee ZON-neh im OST'n aouf,
In the morning the sun rises in the east,

am Abend geht sie im Westen unter.
ahm AH-b'nt gait zee im VEST'n OON-t'r.
in the evening it sets in the west.

Der Mond und die Sterne gehen in der Nacht auf.
Dehr Mohnt oont dee SHTAIR-neh GAY-h'n in dehr Nahkht aouf.
The moon and the stars rise at night.

Am Mittag steht die Sonne im Süden.
Ahm MITT-ahk shtait dee ZON-neh im ZEW-d'n.
At noon the sun stands in the south.

Dem Süden gegenüber ist der Norden.
Daim ZEW-d'n gay-ggen-EW-b'r ist dehr NOHR-d'n.
Opposite south is north.

Osten, Westen, Süden und Norden sind die vier Himmelsrichtungen.
OST'*n*, VEST'*n*, ZEW-*d'n* oont NOHR-*d'n zint dee feer* HIMM-'*ls-reekh-toon-g'n.*
East, West, South and North are the four directions.

Im Sommer geht die Sonne sehr früh auf und sehr spät unter.
Im ZOMM'*r gait dee* ZON-*neh zair frew aouf oont zair shpait* OON-*t'r.*
In summer the sun rises very early and sets very late.

Die Tage sind lang.
Dee TAH-*ggeh zint lahnk.*
The days are long.

Geht die Sonne im Winter früh auf?
Gait dee ZON-*neh im* VINT'*r frew aouf?*
Does the sun rise early in winter?

Nein, sie geht sehr spät auf und sehr früh unter,
Nine, zee gait zair shpait aouf oont zair frew OON-*t'r,*
No, it rises very late and sets very early,

die Tage sind kurz.
dee TAH-*ggeh zint koorts.*
the days are short.

Während des Tages arbeiten wir;
VAY-*r'nd dess* TAH-*g's* AHR-*bigh-t'n veer;*
We work during the day;

während der Nacht schlafen wir.
VAY-*r'nd dehr Nahkht* SHLAH-*f'n veer.*
we sleep at night.

Wir legen uns am Abend ins Bett,
Veer LAY-*g'n oons ahm* AH-*b'nt ins Bett,*
We go to bed in the evening,

wir gehen schlafen.
veer GAY-*h'n* SHLAH-*f'n.*
we go to sleep.

Wann legen Sie sich schlafen?
Vahn LAY-*g'n Zee zeekh* SHLAH-*f'n?*
When do you lie down to sleep?

Wann stehen Sie auf?
Vahn SHTAY-*h'n Zee aouf?*
When do you get up?

Am Morgen stehen wir auf,
Ahm MOHR-*g'n* SHTAY-*h'n veer aouf,*
In the morning we get up,

wir waschen und kämmen uns,
veer VAH-*sh'n oont* KAIM-*m'n oons,*
we wash and comb ourselves,

wir kleiden uns an
veer KLIGH-*d'n oons ahn*
we dress ourselves

und dann frühstücken wir.
oont dahn FREW-*shtew-k'n veer.*
and then we have breakfast.

Ich wasche und kämme mich.
Ikh VAH-*sheh oont* KAIM-*meh mikh.*
I wash and comb (my hair).

Wann kleiden Sie sich an?
Vahn KLIGH-*d'n Zee zeekh ahn?*
When do you dress yourself?

Wann kleide ich mich aus?
Vahn KLIGH-*deh ikh mikh aous?*
When do I undress myself?

NOTE to Student: "I dress myself" is *ich kleide mich an.* *Mich* is a reflexive pronoun corresponding to "myself". Other reflexive forms are: *uns* for "ourselves"—*sich* for "itself, himself, herself, themselves, yourself, yourselves."

THINKING IN GERMAN
(Answers on page 259)

1. Wie teilen wir die vierundzwanzig Stunden ein?
2. Wann ist es hell, und wann ist es dunkel?
3. Ist es am Abend hell?
4. Woher kommt das Tageslicht?
5. Scheint die Sonne während der Nacht?
6. Wann arbeiten wir?
7. Wann gehen wir ins Theater?
8. Wann geht der Mond auf?
9. Wann schalten wir das elektrische Licht ein?
10. Ist es im Kino hell oder dunkel?
11. Was sehen Sie während der Nacht am Himmel?
12. Geht die Sonne im Sommer früh auf?
13. In welcher Jahreszeit sind die Tage lang?
14. Warum sind die Tage im Winter kurz?
15. Sind die Nächte in den Wintermonaten länger als die Tage?
16. Womit zünden Sie die Zigarette an?
17. Wann geht ein Kind schlafen?
18. Schläft ein Kind lang?

19. Schlafen Sie am Sonntag länger als an Wochentagen?

20. Wie lange arbeitet man im Büro?

21. Arbeiten Sie gern?

22. Können Sie während des Tages schlafen?

23. Ist das Licht des Mondes so stark wie das der Sonne?

24. Kann man die Sterne zählen?

25. Wann sehen Sie den Mond?

26. Wo geht die Sonne auf und wo geht sie unter?

27. Wie heissen die vier Himmelsrichtungen?

28. Frühstücken Sie am Abend?

29. Ist es jetzt Abend oder Morgen?

30. Ist die Sonne am Strand heiss?

31. Nehmen Sie ein Sonnenbad?

32. Wann ziehen Sie sich an?

33. Kämmen Sie sich oft?

ÜBUNG NR. 25

Das Wetter
Dahs VETT'r
The weather

Der Himmel ist grau;
Dehr HIMM'*l ist graou;*
The sky is gray;

er ist mit Wolken bedeckt;
air ist mit VOHL-*k'n beh-*DEKKT;
it is covered with clouds;

es fängt an zu regnen.
ess fenkt ahn tsoo REHG-*n'n.*
it is starting to rain.

Dicke Tropfen fallen herab.
DICK-*eh* TROPP-*f'n* FAHL-*l'n hair-*AHP.
Thick drops are falling.

NOTICE THE SPLIT VERB! The verb *anfangen* means "to begin". However, this verb, like many others in German, comes apart at the seams in most of its uses, as above. For example, we say: *Es fängt an zu regnen*—"It is starting to rain" as well as *es hört auf zu regnen—(aufhören)*—"it stops raining". Remember: *die Sonne geht auf (aufgehen)*—"the sun is rising" or *die Sonne geht unter (untergehen)*—"the sun is setting". *Ich stehe auf (aufstehen)*—"I get up"; *wir schalten das Licht ein—(einschalten)*—"we switch on the light"; *wir schalten es aus (ausschalten)*—"we turn it off", etc. Such verbs are reassembled in the past tense as you will find out soon.

Machen Sie Ihren Regenschirm auf!
MAH-*kh'n Zee* EE-*r'n* RAY-*g'n-sheerm aouf!*
Open your umbrella!

Er schützt gegen den Regen.
Air shewtst GAY-*g'n dain* RAY-*g'n.*
It protects (you) from the rain.

Jetzt sind wir gegen den Regen geschützt,
Yetst zint veer GAY-*g'n dain* RAY-*g'n* ggeh-SHEWTST,
Now we are protected from the rain,

aber die Strasse ist nass.
AH-*b'r dee* SHTRAH-*sseh ist nahss.*
but the street is wet.

Ist das Wetter gut?
Ist dahs VETT'*r goot?*
Is the weather good?

Nein, wir haben schlechtes Wetter.
Nine, veer HAB-*b'n* SHLEKH-*tess* VETT'*r.*
No, we have bad weather.

Es ist zu schlechtes Wetter, um auszugehen.
Ess ist tsoo SHLEKH-*tess* VETT'*r, oom* AOUS-*tsoo-gay-h'n.*
The weather is too bad to go out.

Es ist zu nass, um spazierenzugehen.
*Ess ist tsoo nahss, oom shpah-*TSEE-*r'n-tsoo-gay-h'n.*
It is too wet to go for a stroll.

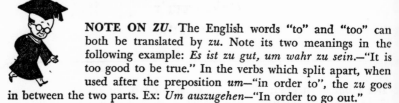

NOTE ON ZU. The English words "to" and "too" can both be translated by *zu*. Note its two meanings in the following example: *Es ist zu gut, um wahr zu sein.*—"It is too good to be true." In the verbs which split apart, when used after the preposition *um*—"in order to", the *zu* goes in between the two parts. Ex: *Um auszugehen*—"In order to go out."

Wir wollen in das Haus zurückgehen,
Veer VOLL'*n in dahs House tsoo-*REWK-*gay-h'n,*
We want to go back into the house,

im Zimmer ist es angenehm warm.
im TSIMM'*r ist ess* AHN-*ggeh-naim vahrm.*
it is agreeably warm in the room.

Unsere Kleider sind nass.
OON-*z'reh* KLIGH-*d'r zint nahss.*
Our clothes are wet.

Wir ziehen die nassen Kleider aus
Veer TSEE-*h'n dee* NAHSS'*n* KLIGH-*d'r aous*
We take off the wet clothes

und ziehen trockene Kleider an.
oont TSEE-*h'n* TROKK-'*neh* KLIGH-*d'r ahn.*
and put on dry clothes.

Wir ziehen uns um.
Veer TSEE-*h'n oons oom.*
We change clothes.

Ziehen Sie sich um, wenn Ihre Kleider nass sind?
TSEE-*h'n Zee zeekh oom, venn* EE-*reh* KLIGH-*d'r nahss zint?*
Do you change clothes when they are wet?

Wechseln Sie die Schuhe?
VEKK-*s'ln Zee dee* SHOO-*heh?*
Do you change your shoes?

Sehen Sie aus dem Fenster!
ZAY-*h'n Zee aous daim* FEN-*st'r!*
Look out of the window!

Es ist nicht mehr Winter,
Ess ist nikht mair VINT'*r,*
It is no longer winter,

aber wir haben Wetter wie im Dezember.
AH-*b'r veer* HAH-*b'n* VETT'*r vee im Deh-*TSEHM-*b'r.*
but we have weather as in December.

Es ist jetzt sehr kalt.
Ess ist yetst zair kahlt.
It is very cold now.

Setzen Sie sich an die Heizung und wärmen Sie sich!
ZET-*s'n Zee zikh ahn dee* HIGH-*tsoonk oont* VAIR-*m'n Zee zikh!*
Sit down close to the radiator and warm up!

Ich gehe zum Kamin, dort brennt ein Feuer.
Ikh GAY-*heh tsoom Kah-*MEEN*, dohrt brent ine* FOY-*ehr.*
I go to the fireplace; a fire is burning there.

Das Feuer ist sehr schwach.
Dahs FOY-*ehr ist zair shvahkh.*
The fire is very weak.

Das Mädchen kann Hoiz und Kohle nachlegen!
Dahs MAIT-*kh'n kahn Hohlts oont* KOH-*leh* NAHKH-*lay-g 1!*
The maid can throw on wood and coal!

Ist Ihnen jetzt warm genug?
Ist EE-*n'n yetst vahrm ggeh-*NOOK?*
Are you warm enough now?

Halten Sie Ihre Füsse an den Kamin!
HAHLT'*n Zee* EE-*reh* FEW-*sseh ahn dain Kah-*MEEN!*
Hold your feet close to the fireplace!

Frieren Sie noch?   **Nein, ich danke Ihnen, ich friere nicht mehr.**
FREE-*r'n Zee nohkh?*   *Nine, ikh* DAHN-*keh* EE-*n'n, ikh* FREE-*reh nikht mair.*
Are you still freezing?   No, I thank you, I am not freezing any more.

Ziehen Sie Ihre Schuhe aus, sie sind ganz nass!
TSEE-*h'n Zee* EE-*reh* SHOO-*heh aous, zee zint gahnts nahss!*
Take off your shoes, they are all wet!

Was für hässliches Wetter!
Vahss fewr HESS-*lee-khes* VETT'*r!*
What ugly weather!

Jetzt fängt es noch an zu schneien!
Yetst fenkt ess nohkh ahn tsoo SHNIGH'*n!*
Now it is even beginning to snow!

Es ist nicht gut, kalte Füsse zu haben.
Ess ist nikht goot, KAHL-*teh* FEW-*sseh tsoo* HAH-*b'n.*
It is not good to have cold feet.

Im Winter tragen wir dicke Kleider, im Sommer dünne.
Im VINT'*r* TRAH-*g'n veer* DICK-*eh* KLIGH-*d'r, im* ZOMM'*r* DEW-*neh.*
In winter we wear thick clothes, in summer thin ones.

Dicke Kleider sind schwer,
DICK-*eh* KLIGH-*d'r zint shvair,*
Thick clothes are heavy,

dünne Kleider sind leicht.
DEW-*neh* KLIGH-*d'r zint lighkht.*
thin clothes are light.

Im Sommer machen wir Türen und Fenster auf, es ist warm.
Im ZOMM'*r* MAH-*kh'n veer Tew-r'n oont* FEN-*st'r aouf, ess ist vahrm.*
In summer we open door and windows, it is warm.

Im Winter schliessen wir Türen und Fenster
Im VINT'*r* SHLEESS'*n veer* TEW-*r'n oont* FEN-*st'r*
In winter we close doors and windows

und setzen uns an den Kamin oder an die Heizung.
oont ZETS'*n oons ahn dain Kah-*MEEN OH-*d'r ahn dee* HIGH-*tsoonk.*
and sit near the fireplace or the radiator.

Im Sommer ist es warm.
Im ZOMM'*r ist ess vahrm.*
In summer it is warm.

Wie ist es im Winter?
Vee ist ess im VINT'*r?*
How is it in winter?

Tragen Sie im Winter einen Mantel?
TRAH-*g'n Zee im* VINT'*r* EYE-*n'n* MAHN-*t'l?*
Do you wear an overcoat in winter?

Warum tragen Sie im Sommer dünne Kleider?
VAH-*room* TRAH-*g'n Zee im* ZOMM'*r* DEW-*neh* KLIGH-*d'r?*
Why do you wear thin clothes in summer?

Ist es in Afrika heiss?
Ist ess in AH-*free-kah highss?*
Is it warm in Africa?

Ist es am Nordpol kalt?
Ist ess ahm NOHRT-*pohl kahlt?*
Is it cold at the North Pole?

Ist es am Südpol wärmer als am Nordpol?
Ist ess ahm ZEWD-*pohl* VAIR-*m'r ahls ahm* NOHRT-*pohl?*
Is it warmer at the South Pole than at the North Pole?

Wann tragen Sie Überschuhe?
Vahn TRAH-*g'n Zee* EW-*b'r-shoo-heh?*
When do you wear rubbers?

Wenn ich dicke Kleider trage, so ist mir warm.
Venn ikh DICK-*eh* KLIGH-*d'r* TRAH-*ggeh, zoh ist meer vahrm.*
When I wear thick clothes, I am warm.

Wenn ich im Winter dünne Kleider trage, friere ich, mir ist kalt.
Venn ikh im VINT'r DEW-*neh* KLIGH-*d'r* TRAH-*ggeh,* FREE-*reh ikh, meer ist kahlt.*
When I wear thin clothes in winter, I freeze: I am cold.

Wenn mir warm ist, setze ich mich an das offene Fenster.
Venn meer vahrm ist, ZET-*tseh ikh mikh ahn dahs* OFF-'*neh* FEN-*st'r*
When I am warm, I sit by the open window.

Wenn mir kalt ist, schliesse ich Türen und Fenster.
Venn meer kahlt ist, SHLEE-*sseh ikh* TEW-*r'n oont* FEN-*st'r.*
When I am cold, I close doors and windows.

REMEMBER: In German, you are never cold, hot or warm. It is cold, hot or warm *to you.* Ex: *Es ist mir kalt* or *mir ist kalt*—"I am cold." *Es ist ihm warm* or *ihm ist warm*—"He is warm." *Es ist uns heiss* or *uns ist heiss*—"We are hot." The pronoun forms in such a construction are: "to me"— *mir;* "to us"—*uns;* "to you" sing—*Dir;* "to you"—*Ihnen;* "to him" (it)—*ihm;* "to them"—*ihnen;* "to her"—*ihr.* Pay attention to the capital letters in *Ihnen*—"to you".

Wir sehen aus dem Fenster.
Veer ZAY-*h'n aous daim* FEN-*st'r.*
We look out of the window.

Sehen Sie den Mann, der über die Strasse geht?
ZAY-*h'n Zee dain Mahn, dehr* EW-*b'r dee* SHTRAH-*sseh gait?*
Do you see the man who is crossing the street?

Er muss seinen Hut mit der Hand festhalten.
Air mooss ZIGH-*n'n Hoot mit dehr Hahnt* FESST-*hahl-t'n.*
He must hold his hat with (his) hand.

Es geht ein starker Wind.
Ess gait ine SHTAHR-*k'r Vint.*
A strong wind is blowing.

Es ist sehr windig.
Ess ist zair VIN-*dikh.*
It is very windy.

Dieser Wind macht das Wetter noch unangenehmer.
DEEZ'r *Vint mahkht dahs* VETT'r *nohkh* OON-*ahn-ggeh-nay-m'r.*
This wind makes the weather still more disagreeable.

Der Wind vertreibt aber auch die Wolken;
*Dehr Vint fair-*TRIGHPT AH-*b'r aoukh dee* VOHL-*k'n;*
However, the wind is also chasing the clouds away;

es regnet jetzt weniger stark.
ess RAIG-*net yetst* VAY-*nee-g'r shtark.*
now it is raining less violently.

Trinken Sie heissen oder kalten Kaffee?
TRIN-*k'n Zee* HIGH-*ss'n* OH-*d'r* KAHL-*t'n Kah*-FEH?
Do you drink hot or cold coffee?

Ich trinke ihn heiss.
Ikh TRIN-*keh een highss.*
I drink it hot.

Wenn der Topf sehr warm ist, können Sie ihn nicht berühren,
Venn dehr Toppf zair vahrm ist, KUH-*n'n Zee een nikht beh*-REW-*r'n,*
When the pot is very warm, you cannot touch it,

        er ist heiss.
        air ist highss.
        it is hot.

Im Sommer ist es heiss (warm),
Im ZOMM-*'r ist ess highss (vahrm),*
In summer it is hot (warm),

im Frühling ist es kühl,
im FREW-*link ist ess kewl,*
in spring it is cool,

im Winter kalt.
im VINT-*'r kahlt.*
in winter it is cold.

Ist es in New York im Sommer heiss?
Ist ess in New York im ZOMM-*'r highss?*
Is it hot in New York in summer?

Ja, gewöhnlich ist es dort heiss.
Yah, ggeh-VUHN-*likh ist ess dohrt highss.*
Yes, usually it is hot there.

Ist es im Winter in Hamburg kalt?
Ist ess im VINT-*'r in* HAHM-*boork kahlt?*
Is it cold in winter in Hamburg?

Gewiss ist es dort kalt.
Ggeh-VISS *ist ess dohrt kahlt.*
It certainly is cold there.

Am Nordpol ist es immer kalt, Winter und Sommer.
Ahm NOHRT-*pohl ist ess* IMM-*'r kahlt,* VINT-*'r oont* ZOMM-*'r.*
At the North Pole it is always cold, winter and summer.

Es ist dort nie warm.
Ess ist dohrt nee vahrm.
It is never warm there.

Im Winter schneit es oft, im Sommer nie.
Im VINT-*'r shnight ess offt, im* ZOMM-*'r nee.*
In wintertime it snows often, in summer never.

Im April schneit es manchmal.
Im Ah-PREEL *shnight ess* MAHNKH-*mahl.*
It snows sometimes in April.

Schneit es oft in den Alpen?
Shnight ess offt in dain AHL-*p'n?*
Does it often snow in the Alps?

Sprechen Sie manchmal deutsch?
SHPREH-*kh'n Zee* MAHNKH-*mahl doitsh?*
Do you sometimes speak German?

Sprechen Sie russisch?
SHPREH-*kh'n Zee* ROOS-*sish?*
Do you speak Russian?

    Ich spreche manchmal deutsch, aber nie russisch.
    Ikh SHPREH-*kheh* MAHNKH-*mahl doitsh,* AH-*b'r nee* ROOS-*sish.*
    I sometimes speak German, but never Russian.

    Gehen Sie oft in die Oper?
    GAY-*h'n Zee offt in dee* OH-*p'r?*
    Do you go to the opera often?

    Nein, ich gehe sehr selten in die Oper.
    Nine, ikh GAY-*heh zair* ZELL-*t'n in dee* OH-*p'r.*
    No, I very seldom go to the opera.

THINKING IN GERMAN

(Answers on page 259)

1. Ist Ihnen warm, soll ich das Fenster aufmachen?

2. Frieren Sie, wenn Sie im Winter ohne Mantel ausgehen?

3. Wie ist der Himmel bei schlechtem Wetter?

4. Regnet es, wenn der Himmel mit Wolken bedeckt ist?

5. Regnet es, wenn es friert?

6. Was fällt im Winter vom Himmel?

7. Was haben Sie in der Hand, um sich gegen Regen zu schützen?

8. Wogegen schützt Sie der Mantel?

9. Haben Sie einen Regenmantel?

10. Wie ist das Wetter heute?

11. Ist es hier zu warm?

12. Schneit es zuweilen im Hochsommer?

13. Ist es warm im Spätherbst?

14. Ist Ihnen im Frühling manchmal kalt?

15. Wieviel Grad haben wir heute?

16. Wann heizt man die Zimmer?

17. Woher kommt die Wärme?

18. Scheint die Sonne im Dezember so warm wie im Juli?

19. Wann gehen Sie baden?

20. In welcher Jahreszeit ziehen Sie dicke Kleider an?

21. Ist es im März sehr windig?

22. Was tun Sie, wenn Ihre Kleider und Schuhe sehr nass sind?

23. Ziehen sich die Damen oft um?

24. Ist es in Cuba gewöhnlich heiss?

25. Wohin setzen Sie sich, wenn Ihnen kalt ist?

26. Geben die Sterne Wärme?

27. Gehen Sie bei schlechtem Wetter manchmal aus?

28. Gehen Sie bei Regenwetter ohne Schirm aus?

29. Was ziehen Sie im Winter an?

30. Was ist besser: Warm und nass oder kalt und trocken?

ÜBUNG NR. 26

Hast Du das Neueste gehört?
Hahst Doo dahs NOY-*ess-teh ggeh*-HUHRT?
Have you heard the latest?

ATTENTION: In German you address members of your family and good friends, as well as children, with the familiar *Du*—"you" in the singular, *Ihr* in the plural. *Du* corresponds to the Quaker "thou", which is still used in prayers. The verb changes accordingly—the ending of the singular takes *st* and the plural *t*. Ex: *Du gehst—Ihr geht*—"you go". Don't forget the capital letter in both cases. The cases are: *Du, Dir, Dich—Ihr, Euch, Euch.*

ER: **Guten Morgen, mein Liebling! Wie hast Du geschlafen?**
AIR: GOOT'*n* MOHR-*g'n, mine* LEEB-*link! Vee hahst Doo ggeh*-SHLAH-*f'n?*
HE: Good morning, my darling! How did you sleep?

SIE: **Danke, es geht. Die Katzen haben mich zweimal geweckt.**
ZEE: DAHN-*keh, ess gait. Dee* KAH-*ts'n* HAH-*b'n mikh* TSVIGH-*mahl ggeh*-VEKKT.
SHE: Thanks, so-so. The cats woke me up twice.

147

ER: **Hat der Briefträger die Post schon gebracht?**
AIR: *Haht dehr* BREEF-*treh-g'r dee Posst shohn ggeh-*BRAHKHT?
HE: Has the mailman brought the mail already?

SIE: **Ich habe noch nicht nachgesehen,**
ZEE: *Ikh* HAH-*beh nohhk nikht* NAHKH-*ggeh-zay-h'n,*
SHE: I have not looked for it yet,

ich habe das Frühstück gemacht.
ikh HAH-*beh dahs* FREW-*shtewk ggeh-*MAHKHT.
I have been making the breakfast.

ER: **Das ist lieb von Dir. Ich bin hungrig.**
AIR: *Dahs ist leep fonn Deer. Ikh bin* HOON-*grikh.*
HE: That is nice of you. I am hungry.

 IMPORTANT NOTE: The past tense is formed in German with the auxiliary verbs *haben* and *sein* together with the past participle. In this chapter we find the verbs using the auxiliary verb *haben*. Just try to remember all the verbs but keep in your mind, that *all* reflexive verbs take exclusively the auxiliary *haben*. *Ich setze mich—ich habe mich gesetzt—* "I sit down", "I sat down".

SIE: **Da ist die Zeitung, ich habe sie Dir geholt.**
ZEE: *Dah ist dee* TSIGH-*toonk, ikh* HAH-*beh zee Deer ggeh-*HOHLT.
SHE: Here is the paper, I have fetched it for you.

ER: **Danke. Ich habe inzwischen eine Tasse Kaffee getrunken,**
AIR: DAHN-*keh. Ikh* HAH-*beh in-*TSVEE-*sh'n* EYE-*neh* TAH-*sseh Kah-*FEH *ggeh-*TROON-*k'n,*
HE: Thanks. I have drunk a cup of coffee in the meanwhile,

aber ich habe noch nicht genug gehabt.
AH-*b'r ikh* HAH-*beh nohhk nikht ggeh-*NOOK *ggeh-*HAHPT.
but I have not yet had enough.

Kann ich noch eine Tasse haben?
Kahn ikh nohhk EYE-*neh* TAH-*sseh* HAH-*b'n?*
Can I have another cup?

SIE: **Hier. Heute hast Du, Gott sei Dank, drei Brötchen gegessen.**
ZEE: *Here.* HOY-*teh hahst Doo, Goht zigh Dahnk, drigh* BRUHT-*kh'n ggeh-*GGESS'*n.*
SHE: Here. Today thank goodness you have eaten three rolls.

ER: **Du hast sie wohl gezählt?**
AIR: *Doo hahst zee vohl ggeh-*TSAILT?
HE: You really counted them?

SIE: **Nein, aber ich habe fünf Brötchen auf den Teller**
ZEE: *Nine, AH-b'r ikh HAH-beh fewnf BRUHT-kh'n aouf dain TELL'r*
SHE: No, but I put 5 rolls on the dish

gelegt und es sind nur noch zwei da.
ggeh-LAIGT oont ess zint noor nohkh tsvigh dah.
and there are only two left.

ER: **(liest die Zeitung) Hast Du schon sowas gehört?**
AIR: *(leest dee TSIGH-toonk) Hahst Doo shohn ZOH-vahss ggeh-HUHRT?*
HE: (reading the paper) Have you ever heard of such a thing?

In Sizilien hat es geschneit.
In See-TSEEL-yen haht ess ggeh-SHNIGHT.
It has snowed in Sicily.

SIE: **Mama hat das schon aus Rom geschrieben.**
ZEE: *Mah-MAH haht dahs shohn aous Rome ggeh-SHREE-b'n.*
SHE: Mama has already written about it from Rome.

Hast Du den Brief nicht gelesen?
Hahst Doo dain Breef nikht ggeh-LAY z'n?
Haven't you read the letter?

ER: **Was, meine Mutter hat geschrieben?**
AIR: *Vahss, MIGH-neh MOOTT'r haht ggeh-SHREE-b'n?*
HE: What, has my mother written?

SIE: **Ja, Deine Mutter.**
ZEE: *Yah, DIGH-neh MOOTT'r.*
SHE: Yes, your mother.

ER: **So? Was hat sie berichtet?**
AIR: *Zoh? Vahss haht zee beh-REEKH-t't?*
HE: Oh? What did she report?

SIE: **Sie hat heute den Zug genommen, um hierher zu fahren.**
ZEE: *Zee haht HOY-teh dain Tsook ggeh-NOMM'n, oom here-HAIR tsoo FAH-r'n.*
SHE: She took the train today to come here.

ER: **Das ist aber schön!**
AIR: *Dahs ist AH-b'r shuhn!*
HE: That is nice!

Sie hat uns fast zwei Jahre lang nicht besucht.
Zee haht oons fahst tsvigh YAH-reh lahnk nikht beh-ZOOKHT.
She has not visited us for almost two years.

SIE: **Hast Du mir bei Tietz die neuen Strümpfe gekauft?**
ZEE: *Hahst Doo meer by Teets dee* NOY'*n* SHTREWM-*pfeh ggeh-*KAOUFT?
SHE: Have you bought me the new stockings at Tietz?

ER: **Grosser Gott, das habe ich ganz vergessen.**
AIR: GROH-*ss'r Goht, dahs* HAH-*beh ikh gahnts fair-*GGESS'*n.*
HE: Good Lord, that I completely forgot.

Ich habe gestern zu viel zu tun gehabt, ich habe es nicht tun können.
Ikh HAH-*beh* GGEST-'*rn tsoo feel tsoo toon ggeh-*HAHPT, *ikh hah-beh ess nikht toon* KUH-*n'n.*
I had too much to do yesterday, I have not been able to do it.

NOTE: The auxiliary verbs *können*—"can"; *müssen*—"must"; *sollen*—"should"; *dürfen*—"to be permitted to"; and the verbs *lassen*—"let"; *brauchen*—"need"; *heissen*—"to order"; *helfen*—"help"; *hören*—"hear"; *sehen*—"see" and *wollen*—"to wish" or "to want" all form their past with *haben.* They use the infinitive form in place of the past participle, along with the infinitive form of another verb.
If the verbs *können,* etc., are used independently (not as auxiliary verbs), they form the past tense normally.

SIE: **Du hast wieder zu viel gearbeitet. Du Armer!**
ZEE: *Doo hahst* VEE-*d'r tsoo feel ggeh-*AHR-*bigh-tet. Doo* AHR-*m'r!*
SHE: You have again worked too much. You poor dear!

ER: **Ich habe in der Zeitung gelesen, dass bei Tietz**
AIR: *Ikh* HAH-*beh in dehr* TSIGH-*toonk ggeh-*LAY-*z'n, dahss by Teets*
HE: I have read in the paper, that there is a

Ausverkauf ist. Zieh' Dich schnell an,
AOUS-*fair-kaouf ist. Tseeh deekh shnell ahn,*
sale at Tietz. Dress quickly,

wir gehen zu Tietz und kaufen, was Du brauchst.
veer GAY-*h'n tsoo Teets oont* KAOU-*f'n, vahss Doo braoukhst.*
we are going to Tietz's store and buy whatever you need.

SIE: **Da hast Du eine gute Idee gehabt.**
ZEE: *Dah hahst Doo* EYE-*neh* GOO-*teh Ee-*DAY *ggeh-*HAHPT.
SHE: There you have had a good idea.

THINKING IN GERMAN

(Answers on page 260)

1. Wie haben die Beiden geschlafen?
2. Wer bringt die Post?
3. Haben Sie heute Ihre Zeitung zum Kaffee gelesen?
4. Wann haben Sie das letzte Mal gegessen?
5. Wenn acht Brötchen auf dem Teller waren, bevor Sie zwei gegessen haben, wieviele Brötchen bleiben übrig?
6. Haben Sie schon einmal einen deutschen Brief geschrieben?
7. Haben Sie schon Sizilien besucht?
8. Wie lange haben Sie sich in Europa aufgehalten?
9. Haben Sie auch auf dem Lande gelebt?
10. Haben Sie immer gehalten, was Sie versprochen haben?
11. Haben Sie alles behalten, was Sie gelernt haben?
12. Haben Sie vergessen, wie Sie heissen?
13. Haben Sie alles verstanden, was Sie gelesen haben?
14. Wer hat Amerika entdeckt?
15. Wo haben Sie deutsch gelernt?

ÜBUNG NR. 27

Salzburger Festspiele
ZAHLTS-*boor-g'r* FESST-*shpee-leh*
The Salzburg Festival

NOTE: Here is the past tense with *sein*. The verbs used in this chapter form their past tense with *sein*—"to be". This tense, like the past with *haben*—"to have", is used when the action has been completed in the past. Practically all verbs of motion form the past with *sein*. Ex: *Ich bin gegangen*—"I have gone"; *ich bin gelaufen*—"I have run"; *ich bin gekommen*—"I have come", etc.

In addition, the verb "to be"—*sein*, forms the past with itself as an auxiliary. Ex: *Ich bin gewesen*—"I have been."

HERR ROTH: **Fräulein Franzen persönlich, welche**
HERR ROHT: FROY-*line* FRAHN-*ts'n* per-ZUHN-*likh,* VEL-*kheh*
MR. ROTH: Miss Franzen in person, what a

152

Überraschung! Sie sind lange nicht hier gewesen.
*Ew-b'r-*RAH-*shoonk! Zee zint* LAHN-*ggeh nikht here ggeh-*VAY-*z'n.*
surprise! You have not been here for a long time.

FRÄULEIN FRANZEN: **Ich bin doch im April nach Salzburg gefahren.**
FROY-*line* FRAHN-*ts'n: Ikh bin dohkh im Ah-*PREEL *nahkh* ZAHLTS-*boork
ggeh-*FAH-*r'n.*

MISS FRANZEN: I went to Salzburg in April, you know.

HERR ROTH: **Also sind Sie doch endlich in Österreich gewesen.**
AHL-*zoh zint Zee dohkh* END-*likh in* UH-*st'r-righkh ggeh-*VAY-*z'n.*
So you finally have been in Austria.

Wie ist es gewesen? Hat es sich gelohnt?
*Vee ist ess ggeh-*VAY-*z'n? Haht ess zikh ggeh-*LOHNT?
How was it? Was it worthwhile?

FRÄULEIN FRANZEN: **Es ist mir dieses Mal gelungen,**
Ess ist meer DEEZ'*s Mahl ggeh-*LOONG'*n,*
I succeeded this time

für wenig Geld einen herrlichen Sommer zu verbringen.
fewr VAY-*nikh Ggelt* EYE-*n'n* HERR-*likh'n* ZOMM'*r tsoo fair-*BRING'*n.*
in spending a magnificent summer for little money.

HERR ROTH: **Wie teuer ist Sie das zu stehen gekommen?**
Vee TOY-'*r ist Zee dahs tsoo* SHTAY-*h'n ggeh-*KOMM'*n?*
How expensive was it for you?

FRÄULEIN FRANZEN: **Ich bin sehr billig weggekommen. Freunde sind mit**
Ikh been zair BILL-*ik vek-*ggeh-*komm'n.* FROIN-*deh zint mit*
I got off very inexpensively. Friends went

dem Wagen gefahren und haben mich mitgenommen.
daim VAH-*g'n ggeh-*FAH-*r'n oont* HAH-*b'n mikh* MIT-*ggeh-nomm'n.*
by car and took me with them.

Meine Tante in Salzburg hat mich schon
MIGH-*neh* TAHN-*teh in* ZAHLTS-*boork haht mikh shohn*
My aunt in Salzburg has invited me

so oft eingeladen und so bin ich bei ihr als Gast geblieben.
zoh offt INE-*ggeh-lah-d'n oont zoh bin ikh by eer ahls Gahst ggeh-*
BLEE-*b'n.*
so often, so I stayed as her guest.

HERR ROTH: **Sind die Festspiele wirklich so schön gewesen**
Zint dee FESST-*shpee-leh* VEERK-*likh zoh shuhn ggeh-*VAY-*z'n*
Was the festival really as beautiful

wie in der Zeitung gestanden ist?
vee in dair TSIGH-*toonk ggeh-*SHTAHN-*d'n ist?*
as described in the paper?

FRÄULEIN FRANZEN: **Das glaube ich! Die besten Sänger aus**
Dahs GLAOU-*beh ikh! Dee* BEST*'n* ZENG*'r aous*
I believe that! (Indeed it was!) The best singers in

der ganzen Welt sind dort aufgetreten.
dehr GAHN-*ts'n Vellt zint dohrt* AOUF-*ggeh-treh-t'n.*
the whole world appeared there.

NOTE ON IDIOMS: *Das glaube ich!* literally translated means "I believe that!" We use this expression, if we want to stress the verity or correctness of a statement, as we use in English: "But definitely!"—"Indeed it was!"

HERR ROTH: **Haben Sie auch "Rosenkavalier" gesehen?**
HAH-*b'n Zee aoukh* "ROH-*z'n-kah-vah-leer*" *ggeh-*ZAY-*h'n?*
Did you also see "Rosenkavalier"?

FRÄULEIN FRANZEN: **Das ist der Höhepunkt der Festpiele gewesen.**
Dahs ist dehr HUH-*heh-poonkt dehr* FESST-*shpee-leh ggeh-*VAY-*z'n.*
That was the highlight of the festival.

Richard Strauss ist persönlich gekommen
REE-*khahrt Shtraouss ist pair-*ZUHN-*likh ggeh-*KOMM*'n*
Richard Strauss came personally

un zu dirigieren.—Und wie ist es Ihnen gegangen?
*oom tsoo dee-ree-*GGEAR*'n.—Oont vee ist ess* EE-*n'n ggeh-*GAHNG*'n?*
to conduct.—And how have you been?

HERR ROTH: **Mein Sommer ist wie immer vergangen.**
Mine ZOMM*'r ist vee* IMM*'r fair-*GAHNG*'n.*
My summer went off as always.

Ich bin nach Rügen gefahren und ich bin jeden Tag
Ikh bin nahkh REW-*g'n ggeh-*FAHR*'n oont bin* YAY-*d'n Tahk*
I travelled to Rügen and went swimming

baden gegangen, wie es sich gehört.
BAH-*d'n ggeh-*GAHNG*'n, vee ess sikh ggeh-*HUHRT.
every day, as is customary.

EXPRESSIONS TO REMEMBER: *Es lohnt sich—*"it is worthwhile", "it pays"; *es kommt mich teuer zu stehen—* "it is becoming very expensive to me"; *billig wegkommen* —"to get off inexpensively"; *wie es sich gehört—*"as it should be" or "as is customary"; *es gehört sich—*"it is proper".

FRÄULEIN FRANZEN: **Ist nichts Aufregendes vorgefallen?**
Ist nikhts AOUF-*reh-g'n-d's* FOHR-*ggeh-fahll'n?*
Did nothing exciting happen?

Ist niemand gestorben oder fortgezogen?
Ist NEE-*mahnt ggeh-*SHTOHR-*b'n* OH-*d'r* FOHRT-*ggeh-tsoh-g'n?*
Did nobody die or move away?

Ich weiss gar nichts!
Ikh vice gahr nikhts!
I know absolutely nothing!

HERR ROTH: **Die alte Frau Weghuber ist im Juli gestorben**
Dee AHL-*teh Fraou* VAIK-*hoo-b'r ist im* YOO-*lee ggeh-*SHTOHR-*b'n*
Old Mrs. Weghuber died in July

und das Fräulein Zimbler ist von Berlin weggezogen.
oont dahs FROY-*line* TSIM-*bl'r ist fonn Behr-*LEEN VEK-*ggeh-tsoh-g'n.*
and Miss Zimbler moved away from Berlin.

Sonst ist nichts passiert.
*Zonnst ist nikhts pahs-*SEERT.
Nothing else happened.

Wann sind Sie angekommen?
Vahn zint Zee AHN-*ggeh-komm'n?*
When did you arrive?

FRÄULEIN FRANZEN: **Gestern bin ich zurückgeflogen. Ich habe einen**
GGEST-*'rn bin ikh tsoo-*REWK-*ggeh-floh-g'n.* Ikh HAH-*beh* EYE-*n'n*
I flew back yesterday. I spent

herrlichen Sommer verbracht und ich bin sehr glücklich gewesen.
HERR-*lee-kh'n* ZOMM-*'r fair-*BRAHKHT *oont ikh bin zair* GLEWK-*likh ggeh-*
VAY-*z'n.*
a glorious summer and I was very happy.

HERR ROTH: **Und dennoch ist das Sprichwort richtig:**
Oont DEN-*nohkh ist dahs* SHPREEKH-*vohrt* REEKH-*tik:*
The old saying is still true, however:

Überall gut, zuhause am besten.
EW-*b'r-ahl goot, tsoo-*HAOU-*zeh ahm* BEST-*'n.*
Everywhere is good, but home is best.

THINKING IN GERMAN

(Answers on page 260)

1. Wo ist Fräulein Franzen im Sommer gewesen?
2. Ist es ihr gelungen, mit wenig Geld einen schönen Sommer zu verbringen?
3. Wer hat das Fräulein eingeladen?
4. Ist sie lange bei der Tante geblieben?
5. Hat sich die Reise gelohnt?
6. Ist ein berühmter Dirigent nach Salzburg gekommen?
7. Ist Herr Roth viel baden gegangen?
8. Sind Sie schon einmal nach Europa gefahren?
9. Was ist im Jahre 1492 passiert?
10. Wann ist Georg Washington gestorben?
11. Wann ist die Mayflower in Amerika angekommen?
12. Sind Sie schon einmal über den Ozean geflogen?
13. Sind die Sterne gestern abend am Himmel gestanden?
14. Ist der Dreizehnte im vorigen Monat auf einen Freitag gefallen?
15. Wann sind Sie geboren?

ÜBUNG NR. 28

Was wird morgen geschehen?
Vahss veert MOHR-*g'n ggeh*-SHAY-*h'n?*
What will happen tomorrow?

HERR KRAUSE: **Sind Sie heute sehr beschäftigt, Herr Doktor?**
Herr KRAOU-*zeh:* *Zint Zee* HOY-*teh zair beh*-SHEFF-*tikt, Herr* DOCK-*tohr?*
MR. KRAUSE: Are you very busy today, Doctor?

DR. PETERS: **Heute nicht so sehr; aber morgen werde ich**
DOCK-*tohr* PEH-*tehrs:* HOY-*teh nikht zoh zair;* AH-*b'r* MOHR-*g'n* VAIR-*deh ikh*
DR. PETERS: Not so much today; but tomorrow I shall be

den ganzen Tag zu tun haben.
dehn GAHN-*ts'n Tahk tsoo toon* HAH-*b'n.*
busy all day long.

HERR KRAUSE: **Was werden Sie denn machen?**
Vahss VAIR-*d'n Zee denn* MAH-*kh'n?*
What will you then do?

 NOTE on Titles: In German you don't address a doctor as "Doctor So-and-So" but as "Mr. Doctor So-and-So". This does not apply exclusively to doctors of medicine. In Germany, you call all lawyers, professors, philosophers and other graduates who have the equivalent of a Ph.D., an LLB or any other advanced degree *Herr Doktor.*

DR. PETERS: **Das werde ich Ihnen gleich sagen, wenn Sie es hören wollen.**
Dahs VAIR-*deh ikh* EE-*n'n glighkh* ZAH-*g'n, venn Zee ess* HUH-*r'n*
VOLL'*n.*
I'll tell you that right now, if you care to hear it.

HERR KRAUSE: **Ich werde aufmerksam zuhören.**
Ikh VAIR-*deh* AOUF-*mairk-zahm* TSOO-*huh-r'n.*
I shall listen attentively.

DR. PETERS: **Ich werde morgen sehr früh aufstehen, sozusagen mit den
Hühnern.**
Ikh VAIR-*deh* MOHR-*g'n zair frew* AOUF-*shtay-h'n,* ZOH-*tsoo-zah-g'n mit
dehn* HEW-*n'rn.*
I shall get up very early, so to speak with the chickens.

 NOTE on the Future Tense: *Die Zukunft*—"the future"
tense is formed with the auxiliary verb *werden* and the
infinitive. *Ich werde essen*—"I shall eat"; *ich werde gehen*
—"I shall go". It is used exactly as is the English future
tense. Isn't it a relief to find something really easy? This
lesson is a breather for you.

HERR KRAUSE: **Und wann wird das sein?**
Oont vahn veert dahs zine?
And when will that be?

DR. PETERS: **Um sechs Uhr, wenn Sie sich gerade aufs andere Ohr legen
werden.**
*Oom zeks Oor, venn Zee zikh ggeh-*RAH-*deh aoufs* AHN-*d'reh Ohr*
LAY-*g'n* VAIR-*d'n.*
At six o'clock, just when you'll be lying on the other ear.

**Dann werde ich das Radio einstellen und meine Morgenübungen
machen.**
Dahn VAIR-*deh ikh dahs* RAHD-*yoh* INE-*shtell'n oont* MIGH-*neh* MOHR-*g'n-
ew-boong'n* MAH-*kh'n.*
Then I'll turn on the radio and do my morning exercises.

HERR KRAUSE: **Deswegen werden Sie so früh aus dem Bett steigen?**
DESS-*veh-g'n* VAIR-*d'n Zee zoh frew aous daim Bett* SHTIGH-*g'n?*
Just for that you'll climb out of bed that early?

DR. PETERS: **Jawohl, das tue ich jeden Morgen.**
*Yah-*VOHL, *dahs* TOO-*eh ikh* YEH-*d'n* MOHR-*g'n.*
Certainly, I do it every morning.

Ich werde dann frühstücken, meine Berlitz-Aufgabe durchnehmen
Ikh VAIR-*deh dahn* FREW-*shtewk'n,* MIGH-*neh* BEHR-*lits-aouf-gah-beh*
DOORKH-*neh-m'n*
I'll have breakfast, do my Berlitz exercise

und Tennis spielen gehen.
oont TEN-*niss* SHPEE-*l'n* GAY-*h'n.*
and then go to play tennis.

HERR KRAUSE: **Da werden Sie aber schnell müde werden!**
Dah VAIR-*d'n Zee* AH-*b'r shnell* MEW-*deh* VAIR-*d'n!*
You will get tired fast though!

Und was haben Sie dann vor?
Oont vahss HAH-*b'n Zee dahn fohr?*
And what are your plans then?

DR. PETERS: **Ich werde in mein Büro schauen, die Post lesen**
Ikh VAIR-*deh in mine Bew*-ROH SHAOU'*n, dee Posst* LAY-*z'n*
I'll have a look in my office, read the mail

und einige wichtige Telefongespräche erledigen.
oont EYE-*nee-ggeh* VIKH-*tee-ggeh Teh-leh*-FOHN-*ggeh-shpray-kheh air-*
LEH-*deeg'n.*
and make a few important telephone calls.

HERR KRAUSE: **Werden Sie zu Mittag heimgehen oder mit uns essen?**
VAIR-*d'n Zee tsoo* MIT-*tahk* HIME-*gay-h'n* OH-*d'r mit oons* ESS'*n?*
Will you go home at noon or will you eat with us?

DR. PETERS: **Um eins werde ich meine Kanzlei verlassen und gern mit**
Ihnen essen.
Oom eyenss VAIR-*deh ikh* MIGH-*neh kahn*-TSLIGH *fair*-LAHSS'*n oont gairn*
mit EE-*n'n* ESS'*n.*
At one o'clock I'll leave my office and shall gladly lunch with you.

Dann werde ich zum Kunstmaler Schiefer gehen.
Dahn VAIR-*deh ikh tsoom* KOONST-*mah-l'r* SHEE-*f'r* GAY-*h'n.*
Then I'll go to Schiefer the painter's.

Werden Sie mich begleiten?
VAIR-*d'n Zee mikh beh*-GLIGH-*t'n?*
Will you accompany me?

HERR KRAUSE: **Ich werde gern mit Ihnen gehen,**
Ikh VAIR-*deh gairn mit* EE-*n'n* GAY-*h'n,*
I'll gladly go with you,

wenn Sie mir verraten, was ich dort sehen werde.
venn Zee meer fair-RAH-*t'n, vahss ikh dohrt* ZAY-*h'n* VAIR-*deh.*
if you tell me what I'll see there.

DR. PETERS: **Schiefer wird mein Portrait anfangen und ich werde**
SHEE-*f'r veert mine Pohr*-TREH AHN-*fahng'n oont ikh* VAIR-*deh*
Schiefer is going to start my picture and I shall

ihm den ganzen Nachmittag für mein Bild sitzen müssen.
eem dehn GAHN-*ts'n* NAHKH-*mit-tahk fewr mine Bilt* ZEETS'*n* MEWSS'*n.*
have to sit for my painting all afternoon.

HERR KRAUSE: **Gut, das wird mir sicherlich gefallen.**
Goot, dahs veert meer ZEE-*kh'r-likh ggeh*-FAHLL'*n.*
Good, this certainly will be to my liking.

Abends werden wir dann zusammen ins Theater gehen.
AH-*b'nts* VAIR-*d'n veer dahn tsoo*-ZAHMM'*n ins Teh*-AH-*t'r* GAY-*h'n.*
Then in the evening we shall go to the theatre together.

Wir werden unsere Karten vorher nehmen.
Veer VAIR-*d'n* OON-*z'reh* KAHR-*t'n* FOHR-*hair* NAY-*m'n.*
We shall buy our tickets in advance.

Während des Zwischenaktes werden wir
VAY-*r'nt dess* TSWISH'*n-ahk-tess* VAIR-*d'n veer*
During the intermission we shall

das berühmte Theaterfoyer besichtigen.
dahs beh-REWM-*teh Teh*-AH-*t'r-foh-ah-yeh beh*-ZIKH-*teeg'n.*
examine the famous theatre foyer.

DR. PETERS: **Die Vorstellung wird zeitig aus sein.**
Dee FOHR-*shtell-oonk veert* TSIGH-*tikh aous zine.*
The performance will be over early.

Wir werden dann zu mir gehen und einen kleinen Imbiss nehmen.
Veer VAIR-*d'n dahn tsoo meer* GAY-*h'n oont* EYE-*n'n* KLIGH-*n'n* EEM-*biss*
NAY-*m'n.*
We shall go then to my place and have a little snack.

 EXPRESSIONS to Remember: *Zeitig* means "early". *Aus*
means "over" used with the verb *sein*. *Die Stunde ist aus*—
"the lesson is over." *Das Lied ist aus*—"the song has ended."

HERR KRAUSE: **Das wird mir leider nicht möglich sein.**
Dahs veert meer LIGH-*d'r nikht* MUHG-*likh zine.*
Unfortunately, that will not be possible for me.

Ich werde um elf Uhr im Restaurant Trocadero sein müssen,
Ikh VAIR-*deh oom elf Oor im Reh-staou-*RAHNT *Troh-kah-*DEH-*roh zine*
MEWSS'*n,*
I'll have to be at the Trocadero restaurant at 11 o'clock,

weil mich Herr Eckner dort erwarten wird.
*vile mikh Herr Eck-nehr dohrt air-*VAHR-*t'n veert.*
because Mr. Eckner will be waiting for me there.

DR. PETERS: **Wissen Sie, was wir da tun werden?**
VISS'*n Zee, vahss veer dah toon* VAIR-*d'n?*
Do you know what we'll do?

Sie werden Herrn Eckner, den ich kenne, telegraphieren,
Zee VAIR-*d'n Herrn* ECK-*nehr, dehn ikh* KEN-*neh, teh-leh-grah-*FEE-*r'n,*
You shall wire to Mr. Eckner whom I know,

er soll direkt in meine Wohnung kommen.
*air zohll dee-*RECKT *in* MIGH-*neh* VOH-*noonk* KOMM'*n.*
that he should come directly to my apartment.

HERR KRAUSE: **Er wird aber mit Frau und Tochter kommen!**
Air veert AH-*b'r mit Fraou oont* TOHKH-*t'r* KOMM'*n!*
But he is coming with his wife and daughter!

DR. PETERS: **Umso besser! Meine Frau und meine Tochter werden sich**
OOM-*zoh* BESS'*r!* MIGH-*neh Fraou oont* MIGH-*neh* TOHKH-*t'r* VAIR-*d'n zikh*
All the better! My wife and my daughter will be only

nur freuen, die Damen kennen zu lernen.
noor FROY'*n, dee* DAH-*m'n* KEN-*n'n tsoo* LAIR-*n'n.*
too glad to meet the ladies.

Bleiben die Eckners den ganzen Sommer in der Stadt?
BLIGH-*b'n dee* ECK-*n'rs dehn* GAHN-*ts'n* ZOMM'*r in dehr Shtaht?*
Are the Eckners going to remain in town all summer?

HERR KRAUSE: **Nein, sie werden vier Wochen auf dem Lande verbringen**
Nine, zee VAIR-*d'n feer* VOH-*kh'n aouf daim* LAHN-*deh fair-*BRING'*n*
No, they will spend four weeks in the country

und dann eine Reise nach Paris antreten.
oont dahn EYE-*neh* RIGH-*zeh nahkh Pah-*REES *AHN-treh-t'n.*
and then start out on a trip to Paris.

DR. PETERS: **Werden sich die Herrschaften auf französisch verständigen**
können?
VAIR-*d'n zikh dee* HERR-*shahf-t'n aouf frahn-*TSUH-*seesh fair-*SHTEN-*deeg'n*
KUHN-*n'n?*
Will these people be able to make themselves understood in French?

HERR KRAUSE: **Ich glaube das wird ihnen nicht schwer fallen,**
Ikh GLAOU-*beh dahs veert* EE-*n'n nikht shvehr* FAHLL'*n,*
I think that it will not be difficult for them,

denn sie haben bei Berlitz einen kompletten Kurs genommen.
denn zee HAH-*b'n by* BEHR-*lits* EYE-*n'n kohm-*PLETT'*n Koors ggeh-*
NOMM'*n.*
as they have taken a complete course at Berlitz.

DR. PETERS: **Da werden sie wirklich keine Schwierigkeiten**
Dah VAIR-*d'n zee* VEERK-*likh* KIGH-*neh* SHWEE-*reekh-kigh-t'n*
Then they really won't have any difficulty

mit der Sprache haben.
mit dehr SHPRAH-*kheh* HAH-*b'n.*
with the language.

HERR KRAUSE: **Es wird spät, ich werde jetzt gehen müssen.**
Ess veert shpait, ikh VAIR-*deh yetst* GAY-*h'n* MEWSS'*n.*
It is getting late, I shall have to go now.

Werde ich Sie heute noch sehen?
VAIR-*deh ikh Zee* HOY-*teh nohkh* ZAY-*h'n?*
Shall I see you again today?

DR. PETERS: **Ich fürchte, wir werden schon bis Morgen warten müssen.**
Ikh FEWRKH-*teh, veer* VAIR-*d'n shohn biss* MOHR-*g'n* VAHR-*t'n* MEWSS'*n.*
I am afraid we shall have to wait till tomorrow.

Auf Wiedersehen!
Aouf VEE-*d'r-zay-h'n!*
Till we meet again!

Werde ich einmal ein Filmstar in Hollywood sein?
Wen werde ich heiraten?

Was werde ich heute bei Frau Huber zu essen bekommen?

Wird der Professor heute abend pünktlich zum Essen kommen?

(LIESE) (PROFESSOR) (FRAU HUBER)

THINKING IN GERMAN
(Answers on page 261)

1. Woran denkt Liese?
2. Woran denkt Frau Huber?
3. Wohin wird der Professor heute Abend gehen?
4. Wozu ladet Herr Krause Herrn Dr. Peters ein?
5. Wird dieser die Einladung annehmen?
6. Wo werden die Herren am nächsten Tage speisen?
7. Wann wird Herr Dr. Peters aufstehen?
8. Wann werden sie die Theaterkarten nehmen?
9. Was werden sie im Zwischenakt tun?
10. Wem wird Herr Krause telegraphieren?
11. Werden die Eckners aufs Land gehen?
12. Wann wird die Theatervorstellung aus sein?
13. Werden Sie den Sommer in der Stadt verbringen?
14. Was wird Herr Dr. Peters in seinem Büro machen?
15. Wann wird er seine Kanzlei verlassen?
16. Warum werden die Eckners in Frankreich französisch sprechen können?

ÜBUNG NR. 29

Die Tiere
Dee TEE-*reh*
The animals

Menschen und Tiere bewegen sich, sie leben.
MEN-*sh'n oont* TEE-*reh beh*-VEH-*g'n zikh, zee* LEH-*b'n.*
Men and animals move: they live.

Um zu leben, müssen sie atmen, essen und trinken;
Oom tsoo LEH-*b'n* MEWSS'*n zee* AHT-*m'n,* ESS'*n oont* TRIN-*k'n;*
To live, they must breathe, eat and drink;

ohne Luft und ohne Speise und Trank können sie nicht leben, sie sterben.
OH-*neh Looft oont* OH-*neh* SHPIGH-*zeh oont Trahnk* KUH-*n'n zee nikht*
    LEH-*b'n, zee* SHTAIR-*b'n.*
without air and without food and drink they cannot live: they die.

Der Mensch und die meisten Tiere haben fünf Sinne.
Dehr Mensh oont dee MIGH-*st'n* TEE-*reh* HAH-*b'n fewnf* ZIN-*neh.*
Man and most animals have five senses.

Die fünf Sinne sind: Das Gesicht, das Gehör, der Geruch,
Dee fewnf ZIN-*neh zint: Dahs Ggeh-*ZIKHT*, dahs Ggeh-*HUHR*, dehr Ggeh-*
ROOKH,
The five senses are: sight, hearing, smell,

der Geschmack und das Gefühl.
*dehr Ggeh-*SHMAHK *oont dahs Ggeh-*FEWL.
taste and touch.

Die Organe des Gesichts sind die Augen;
*Dee Ohr-*GAH-*neh dess Ggeh-*ZIKHTS *zint dee* AOU-*g'n;*
The organs of sight are the eyes;

die des Gehörs sind die Ohren.
*dee dess Ggeh-*HUHRS *zint dee* OH-*r'n.*
those of hearing are the ears.

Die Nase ist das Geruchsorgan, der Geschmack liegt in der Zunge
Dee NAH-*zeh ist dahs Ggeh-*ROOKHS-*ohr-gahn, dehr Ggeh-*SHMAHK *leegt in
dehr* TSOON-*ggeh*
The nose is the organ of smell, the sense of taste lies in the tongue

und das Gefühl ist über den ganzen Körper verbreitet.
*oont dahs Ggeh-*FEWL *ist* EW-*b'r dehn* GAHN-*ts'n* KUHR-*p'r fehr-*BRIGH-*tet.*
and the sense of touch is spread over the entire body.

Mit dem Gesicht nehmen wir die Farbe, die Form,
*Mit dahm Ggeh-*ZIKHT NAY-*m'n veer dee* FAHR-*beh, dee Form,*
Through sight we perceive color, form,

die Dimension, Ort und Lage der Gegenstände wahr.
*dee Dee-mehn-see-*OHN*, Ohrt oont* LAH-*ggeh dehr* GGEH-*g'n-shtenn-deh vahr.*
dimension, place and position of objects.

Durch das Gehör vernehmen wir Laute und Geräusche,
*Doorkh dahs Ggeh-*HUHR *fehr-*NAY-*m'n veer* LAOU-*teh oont Ggeh-*ROY-*sheh,*
Through hearing we perceive sounds and noises,

durch das Gefühl empfinden wir die Kälte des Eises
*doorkh dahs Ggeh-*FEWL *ehm-*PFEEN-*d'n veer dee* KELL-*teh dess* IGH-*zehs*
through touch we feel the cold of ice

und die Wärme der Heizung, wir fühlen Schmerz,
oont dee VAIR-*meh dehr* HIGH-*tsoonk, veer* FEW-*l'n Shmairts,*
and the heat of the radiator; we feel pain

wenn wir uns verbrennen.
*venn veer oons fair-*BRENN-*n'n.*
when we burn ourselves.

Wir fühlen auch, ob ein Gegenstand hart oder weich ist.
Veer FEW-*l'n aoukh, op ine* GGEH-*g'n-shtahnt hahrt* OH-*d'r vighkh ist.*
We feel also if an object is hard or soft.

> **Wir teilen die Tiere in Vierfüssler, Vögel,**
> *Veer* TIGH-*l'n dee* TEE-*reh in* FEER-*fewss-lehr,* FUH-*g'l,*
> We divide the animals into quadrupeds, birds,

> **Fische, Reptilien und Insekten ein.**
> FISH-*eh, Rehp*-TEEL-*yen oont In*-SEK-*t'n ine.*
> fish, reptiles and insects.

> **Die Vierfüssler leben auf dem Festland;**
> *Dee* FEER-*fewss-lehr leh-b'n aouf daim* FEHST-*lahnt;*
> Quadrupeds live on the ground;

sie haben vier Füsse zum Gehen, Laufen und Springen;
zee HAH-*b'n feer* FEW-*sseh tsoom* GAY-*h'n,* LAOU-*f'n oont* SHPRING-*n;*
they have four legs to walk, to run and to jump;

> **ihr Körper ist mit Haaren bedeckt.**
> *eer* KUHR-*p'r ist mit* HAH-*r'n beh*-DEKT.
> their bodies are covered with hair.

Vierfüssler sind: Das Pferd, der Ochs, die Kuh, der Esel,
FEER-*fewss-lehr zint: Dahs Pfehrt, dehr Ox, dee Koo, dehr* EH-*z'l,*
Some quadrupeds are: The horse, the ox, the cow, the donkey,

der Hund, die Katze; das sind Haustiere.
dehr Hoont, dee KAHT-*seh; dahs zint* HAOUS-*tee-reh.*
the dog, the cat; these are domestic animals.

Der Löwe, der Tiger, der Bär, der Wolf und
Dehr LUH-*veh, dehr* TEE-*g'r, der Behr, dehr Vohlf oont*
The lion, the tiger, the bear, the wolf and

der Fuchs sind wilde Tiere oder Raubtiere.
dehr Fooks zint VEEL-*deh* TEE-*reh* OH-*d'r* RAOUP-*tee-reh.*
the fox are wild animals, or beasts of prey.

Die Gemse ist eine Bergziege, die in den Alpen lebt.
Dee GGEM-*zeh ist* EYE-*neh* BAIRK-*tsee-ggeh, dee in dehn* AHL-*p'n lehpt.*
The chamois is a mountain goat which lives in the Alps.

Die Vögel leben auf dem Lande und in der Luft,
Dee FUH-*g'l leh-b'n aouf daim* LAHN-*deh oont in dehr Looft,*
The birds live on the ground and in the air,

sie haben zwei Füsse und zwei Flügel, mit denen sie fliegen.
zee HAH-*b'n tsvigh* FEW-*sseh oont tsvigh* FLEW-*g'l, mit* DEH-*n'n zee* FLEE-*g'n.*
they have two legs, and two wings with which they fly.

Sie haben einen Schnabel, mit dem sie essen.
Zee HAH-*b'n* EYE-*n'n* SHNAH-*b'l mit daim zee* ESS'*n.*
They have a beak with which they eat.

Ihr Körper ist mit Federn bedeckt.
Eer KUHR-*p'r ist mit* FAY-*d'rn beh-*DEKT.
Their body is covered with feathers.

Einige Vögel: Das Huhn, die Ente, der Pfau, die Gans,
EYE-*nee-ggeh* FUH-*g'l: Dahs Hoon, dee* EHN-*teh, dehr Pfaou, dee Gahns,*
Some birds: The hen, the duck, the peacock, the goose,

der Truthahn, der Adler, der Papagei, der Strauss, die Eule usw.
dehr TROOT-*hahn, dehr* AHD-*l'r, dehr Pap-pah-*GGIGH, *dehr Shtraouss, dee*
OY-*leh oont-zoh-*VIGH-*tehr.*
the turkey, the eagle, the parrot, the ostrich, the owl, etc.

Der Mensch und diese zwei Tierarten haben rotes, warmes Blut
Dehr Mensh oont DEE-*zeh tsvigh* TEER-*ahrt-t'n* HAH-*b'n* ROH-*tehs,* VAHR-*mehs*
     Bloot
Man and these two kinds of animals have red, warm blood

und ein Herz, durch welches das Blut kreist;
oont ine Hairts, doorkh VELL-*khehs dahs Bloot krighst;*
and a heart through which the blood circulates;

**sie haben eine Lunge zum Atmen und einen Magen zur Verdauung der
Nahrung.**
zee HAH-*b'n* EYE-*neh* LOON-*ggeh tsoom* AHT-*men oont* EYE-*n'n* MAH-*g'n tsoor*
     *Fair-*DAOU-*oonk dehr* NAH-*roonk.*
they have lungs for breathing and a stomach for the digestion of the food.

Wenn eines dieser Organe bei uns nicht normal funktioniert,
Venn EYE-*nes* DEEZ'*r Ohr-*GAH-*neh by oons nikht nohr-*MAHL
     *foonk-tsee-oh-*NEERT,
If one of these organs does not function normally for us,

          sind wir krank und gehen zum Doktor.
          zint veer krahnk oont GAY-*h'n tsoom* DOCK-*tohr.*
          we are sick and go to see a doctor.

Die Fische leben im Wasser. Sie haben weder Füsse noch Flügel,
Dee FISH-*eh* LEH-*b'n im* VAH-*ss'r. Zee* HAH-*b'n* VAY-*d'r* FEW-*sseh nohkh*
     FLEW-*g'l,*
Fish live in the water. They have neither legs nor wings;

sie sind mit Flossen versehen, mit deren Hilfe sie schwimmen.
zee zint mit FLOSS'*n fehr-*ZEH'*n, mit* DEH-*r'n* HIL-*feh zee* SHVIMM'*n.*
they are provided with fins, with whose aid they swim.

Der Haifisch ist der gefährlichste Raubfisch.
Dehr HIGH-*fish ist dehr ggeh-*FAIR-*likh-steh* RAOUP-*fish.*
The shark is the most dangerous fish of prey.

Wenn Sie beim Baden einen Haifisch erblicken, dann rufen Sie:
Venn Zee bighm BAH-*d'n* EYE-*n'n* HIGH-*fish air*-BLIKK'*n, dahn* ROO-*f'n Zee:*
If you sight a shark while bathing, then you call out:

"Vorsicht! Haifische!"
*"*FOHR-*sikht!* HIGH-*fish-eh!"*
"Look out! Sharks!"

USEFUL PHRASES: The following interjections and commands are commended to use, with the hope that you will not need some of them:

Zu Hilfe!—"Help!"   *Polizei!*—"Police!"
Achtung!—"Look out!"   *Hinaus!*—"Get out!"
Halt!—"Stop!"   *Vorsicht!*—"Caution!"

Die Schlange ist ein Reptil (Kriechtier);
Dee SHLAHN-*ggeh ist ine Repp*-TEEL (KREEKH-*teer);*
The serpent is a reptile;

sie hat keine Füsse, sie kriecht auf dem Bauche.
zee haht KIGH-*neh* FEW-*sseh, zee kreekht aouf daim* BAOU-*kheh.*
it has no legs, it crawls on its belly.

Das Krokodil lebt in den grossen Flüssen der Tropen.
*Dahs Kroh-koh-*DEEL *lehpt in dehn* GROHSS'*n* FLEWSS'*n dehr* TROH-*p'n.*
The crocodile lives in the large rivers of the tropics.

Der Frosch lebt im Wasser und auf dem Lande.
Dehr Frosh lehpt im VAH-*ss'r oont aouf daim* LAHN-*deh.*
The frog lives in the water and on the ground.

Die Biene erzeugt Honig und die Seidenraupe erzeugt Seide;
Dee BEE-*neh air*-TSOIKT HOH-*nikh oont dee* ZIGH-*d'n-raou-peh air*-TSOIKT
ZIGH-*deh;*
The bee produces honey and the silkworm produces silk;

diese Insekten sind nützlich.
DEE-*zeh In-*SEK-*t'n zint* NEWTS-*likh.*
these insects are useful.

Die Fliege und die Mücke sind jedoch schädliche Insekten.
Dee FLEE-*ggeh oont dee* MEWK-*keh zint yeh-*DOHKH SHAID-*lee-kheh In-*SEK-*t'n.*
The fly and the mosquito, however, are harmful insects.

THINKING IN GERMAN

(Answers on page 261)

1. Können die Pflanzen sich bewegen?
2. Was müssen die Tiere tun, um zu leben?
3. Können wir leben, ohne zu essen?
4. Muss der Löwe trinken?
5. Was brauchen wir zum Leben?
6. Wie heissen die 5 Sinne?
7. Wie heisst das Organ des Geruchs?
8. Wie teilen wir die Tiere ein?
9. Wie heissen die wichtigsten Haustiere?
10. Was ist der Unterschied zwischen den Vögeln und den Vierfüsslern?
11. Ist das Huhn nützlich?
12. Womit fliegen die Vögel?
13. Welches sind die Atmungsorgane?
14. Womit verdauen wir?
15. Sind Sie gesund?
16. Wann sind wir krank?
17. Fliegt die Schlange?
18. Wo lebt der Frosch?
19. Ist die Biene nützlich?
20. Ist der Haifisch gefährlich?

Der Mensch und seine Empfindungen
Dehr Mensh oont ZIGH-*neh Ehm*-PFEEN-*doong'n*
Man and his feelings

Ist der Mensch den Tieren überlegen?
Ist dehr Mensh dehn TEE-*r'n ew-b'r*-LAY-*g'n?*
Is man superior to the animals?

Manche Tiere haben besser entwickelte Sinne als der Mensch.
MAHN-*kheh* TEE-*reh* HAH-*b'n* BESS'*r aint*-VIKK'*l-teh* ZIN-*neh ahls dehr Mensh.*
Some animals have better developed senses than man.

So zum Beispiel hat der Adler schärfere Augen.
Zoh tsoom BIGH-*shpeel haht dehr* AHD-*lehr* SHAIR-*feh-reh aoug'n,*
Thus for instance the eagle has sharper eyes,

der Fisch schwimmt weitaus besser, das Pferd rennt viel schneller und
dehr Fish shvimmt VIGHT-*aous* BESS'*r, dahs Pfehrt rent feel* SHNELL'*r oont*
the fish swims far better, the horse runs much faster and

der Elefant ist viel stärker als mehrere Menschen zusammengenommen.
*dehr Eh-leh-*FAHNT *ist feel* SHTAIR-*k'r ahls* MAY-*reh-reh* MEN-*sh'n tsoo-*
ZAHMM'*n-ggeh-nomm'n.*
the elephant is much stronger than several men together.

Dennoch ist der Mensch den meisten Tieren durch seinen Verstand
DEHN-*nohkh ist dehr Mensh dehn* MIGH-*st'n* TEE-*r'n doorkh* ZIGH-*n'n Fair-*
SHTAHNT
Nevertheless man is superior to most animals through his

überlegen. Man sagt, dass der Löwe der König der Tiere ist.
*ew-b'r-*LAY-*g'n. Mahn zahkt, dahss dehr* LUH-*veh dehr* KUH-*neekh dehr*
TEE-*reh ist.*
mind. They say that the lion is the king of the animals.

Der Mensch allerdings ist die Krone der Schöpfung
*Dehr Mensh ahl-l'r-*DEENKS *ist dee* KROH-*neh dehr* SHUHP-*foonk*
Man, however, is the crown of creation

wegen seines hochentwickelten Gehirns.
VAY-*g'n* ZIGH-*nes* HOHKH-*ent-vikk'l-t'n Ggeh-*HEERN'*s.*
because of his highly developed brain.

Wir denken mit dem Gehirn, das sich in unserem Kopf befindet.
Veer DEN-*k'n mit daim Ggeh-*HEERN, *dahs sikh in* OON-*z'r'm Koppf beh-*
FIN-*det.*
We think with the brain, which is located in our head.

Ohne zu denken, können wir nicht richtig sprechen.
OH-*neh tsoo* DEHN-*k'n,* KUH-*n'n veer nikht* RIKH-*tikh* SHPREH-*kh'n.*
Without thinking we cannot speak correctly.

In unserem Gehirn haben wir Gedanken und Ideen.
In OON-*z'r'm Ggeh-*HEERN HAH-*b'n veer Ggeh-*DAHN-*k'n oont Ee-*DAY'*n.*
In our brain we have thoughts and ideas.

Wir teilen unsere Gedanken und Ideen anderen Personen durch die
Sprache mit.
Veer TIGH-*l'n* OON-*z'reh Ggeh-*DAHN-*k'n oont Ee-*DAY'*n* AHN-*d'r'n Pehr-zoh-n'n*
doorkh dee SHPRAH-*kheh mit.*
We communicate our thoughts and ideas to other persons through speech.

Wir können an Anwesende und Abwesende denken.
Veer KUH-*n'n ahn* AHN-*veh-zehn-deh oont* AHP-*veh-zehn-deh* DEN-*k'n.*
We are able to think of people present and absent.

Sie denken gerade an Ihre deutsche Aufgabe.
Zee DEN-*k'n ggeh-*RAH-*deh ahn* EE-*reh* DOIT-*sheh* AOUF-*gah-beh.*
You are now thinking of your German lesson.

Wenn Sie an etwas anderes denken, können Sie mich nicht gut verstehen.
Venn Zee ahn ETT-*vahss* AHN-*d'res* DEN-*k'n,* KUH-*n'n Zee mikh nikht goot fair-*SHTAY-*h'n.*
If you are thinking of something else, you cannot understand me well.

Woran denken Sie, wenn Sie einen gedeckten Tisch sehen?
*Voh-*RAHN DEHN-*k'n Zee, venn Zee* EYE-*n'n ggeh-*DEKK-*t'n Tish* ZAY-*h'n?*
Of what do you think when you see a table set?

Wenn jemand gut, schnell und viel denkt,
Venn YEH-*mahnt goot, shnell oont feel denkt,*
If someone thinks well, fast and much,

dann nennen wir ihn intelligent oder klug.
dahn NEN-*n'n veer een in-tehl-lee-*GGEHNT OH-*d'r klook.*
then we call him intelligent or clever.

Kluge Menschen lernen leicht.
KLOO-*ggeh* MEN-*sh'n* LAIR-*n'n lighkht.*
Clever people learn easily.

Ist der Esel gescheit?	**Nein, der Esel ist dumm.**
Ist dehr EH-*z'l ggeh-*SHIGHT?	*Nine, dehr* EH-*z'l ist doomm.*
Is the donkey clever?	No, the donkey is stupid.

Was wir gelernt haben, wissen wir. Was wir wissen, verstehen wir.
*Vahss veer ggeh-*LAIRNT HAH-*b'n,* VISS'*n veer. Vahss veer* VISS'*n, fair-*SHTAY-*h'n veer.*
What we have learned, we know. What we know, we understand.

Was ich gesehen oder gehört habe, das kenne ich.
*Vahss ikh ggeh-*ZAY-*h'n* OH-*d'r ggeh-*HUHRT HAH-*beh, dahs* KEN-*neh ikh.*
What I have seen or heard, I know.

Ich kenne Ihren Namen; kennen Sie meinen Namen?
Ikh KEN-*neh* EE-*r'n* NAH-*m'n;* KEN-*n'n Zee* MIGH-*n'n* NAH-*m'n?*
I know your name; do you know my name?

Sie wissen, was ich in meiner Hand habe, weil Sie es sehen.
Zee VISS'*n, vahss ikh in* MIGH-*n'r Hahnt* HAH-*beh, vile Zee ess* ZAY-*h'n.*
You know what I have in my hand, because you see it.

Sie wissen nicht, was ich in der Tasche habe.
Zee VISS'*n nikht, vahss ikh in dehr* TAH-*sheh* HAH-*beh.*
You don't know what I have in the pocket.

Wir behalten nicht alles, was wir lernen.
*Veer beh-*HAHL-*t'n nikht* AHL-*less, vahss veer* LAIR-*n'n.*
We do not retain all we learn.

Was wir nicht behalten können, das vergessen wir.
*Vahss veer nikht beh-*HAHL-*t'n* KUH-*n'n, dahs fair-*GGESS*'n veer.*
What we cannot retain, we forget.

Haben Sie alles behalten, was sie hier gelesen haben?
HAH-*b'n Zee* AHL-*less beh-*HAHL-*t'n, vahss Zee here ggeh-*LAY-*z'n* HAH-*b'n?*
Have you retained all you have read here?

> **Vergessen Sie leicht Namen und Zahlen?**
> *Fair-*GGESS*'n Zee lighkht* NAH-*m'n oont* TSAH-*l'n?*
> Do you forget names and numbers easily?

NOTE the difference! *Ich kann deutsch* means "I know how to speak German." *Ich kann schwimmen* means "I know how to swim." Otherwise *ich kann* means "I am able to" or "I can". *Ich kenne* means "I know". *Ich kenne Namen, Zahlen, Städte, Menschen.*—"I know names, numbers, cities, people," when I have seen or heard of them. Yet *ich weiss, was ich sage*—"I know what I am saying" or *Ich weiss, was ich gelernt habe*—"I know what I have learned."

Die Gefühle und Empfindungen sind bei den Menschen
*Dee Ggeh-*FEW-*leh oont Ehm-*PFIN-*doong'n zint by dehn* MEN-*sh'n*
The feelings and sensations in man are

stärker als bei den Tieren.
SHTAIR-*k'r ahls by dehn* TEE-*r'n.*
stronger than in animals.

Die Tiere haben ihre Jungen gern, doch die Liebe
Dee TEE-*reh* HAH-*b'n* EE-*reh* YOON-*g'n ggehrn, dohkh dee* LEE-*beh*
Animals like their young, yet the love

der Mutter zu ihren Kindern ist viel stärker.
dehr MOOTT*'r tsoo* EE-*r'n* KIN-*d'rn ist feel* SHTAIR-*k'r.*
of a mother for her children is much stronger.

Wir lieben unsere Familie, unsere Heimat.
Veer LEE-*b'n* OON-*z'reh Fah-*MEEL-*yeh,* OON-*z'reh* HIGH-*maht.*
We love our family, our homeland.

Wenn wir etwas Angenehmes erleben, freuen wir uns.
Venn veer ETT-*vahss* AHN-*ggeh-neh-mess air-*LEH-*b'n,* FROY-*'n veer oons.*
If something pleasant happens to us, we are glad.

Wenn uns was Unangenehmes zustösst, sind wir traurig.
Venn oons vahss OON-*ahn-ggeh-neh-mess* TSOO-*shtuhsst, zint veer* TRAOU-*rikh.*
If something unpleasant happens to us, we are sad.

Wenn man sagt, dass Sie gut sprechen, sind Sie froh.
Venn mahn zahkt, dahss Zee goot SHPREH-*kh'n, zint Zee froh.*
If they say that you speak well, you are glad.

> **Wenn Sie hören, dass Ihr Freund krank ist,**
> *Venn Zee* HUH-*r'n, dahss Eer Froint krahnk ist,*
> If you hear that your friend is sick,
>
> **dann sind Sie traurig, Sie bedauern ihn.**
> *dahn zint Zee* TRAOU-*rikh, Zee beh-*DAOU-*ehrn een.*
> then you are sad, you feel sorry for him.

Sie sagen: "Es tut mir leid. Ich hoffe, Sie sind morgen wieder gesund".
Zee ZAH-*g'n: "Ess toot meer light. Ikh* HOFF-*eh, Zee zint* MOHR-*g'n* VEE-*d'r* ggeh-*ZOONT".*
You say: "I am sorry. I hope you will be well again tomorrow."

 USEFUL PHRASES: *Es tut mir leid*—"I am sorry." *Leider* means "unfortunately". *Ich bedauere sehr*—"I regret very much." *Sehr gern*—"gladly." *Mit Vergnügen!*—"With pleasure!"

Ein anderes Gefühl ist die Furcht.
Ine AHN-*deh-ress Ggeh-*FEWL *ist dee Foorkht.*
Another sensation is fear.

Die kleinen und schwachen Tiere fürchten die grösseren und stärkeren.
Dee KLIGH-*n'n oont* SHVAH-*kh'n* TEE-*reh* FEWRKH-*t'n dee* GRUHS-*seh-r'n oont* SHTAIR-*keh-r'n.*
The small and weak animals are afraid of the larger and stronger ones.

Kinder haben Furcht vor der Dunkelheit.
KIN-*d'r* HAH-*b'n Foorkht fohr dehr* DOON-*k'l-hight.*
Children are afraid of the dark.

Viele Mädchen fürchten sich vor Spinnen, Mäusen und Schlangen.
FEE-*leh* MAID-*kh'n* FEWRKH-*t'n zikh fohr* SHPIN-*n'n,* MOY-*z'n oont* SHLAHNG-*'n.*
Many girls are afraid of spiders, mice and snakes.

Wenn jemand sich vor nichts fürchtet, ist er mutig.
Venn YEH-*mahnt zikh fohr nikhts* FEWRKH-*teht, ist air* MOO-*tikh.*
If somebody is not afraid of anything, he is brave.

War Wilhelm Tell mutig?
Vahr VEEL-*hehlm Tell* MOO-*tikh?*
Was William Tell brave?

Haben Sie Angst vor Mäusen?
HAH-*b'n Zee Ahnkst fohr* MOY-*z'n?*
Are you afraid of mice?

Angenehme Dinge gefallen uns, unangenehme missfallen uns.
AHN-*ggeh-neh-meh* DIN-*ggeh ggeh-*FAHL-*l'n oons,* OON-*ahn-ggeh-neh-meh miss-*FAHL-*l'n oons.*
We like pleasant things; we dislike unpleasant ones.

Schönes Wetter gefällt mir.
SHUH-*ness* VETT'*r ggeh*-FELLT *meer.*
I like nice weather.

Den Strassenlärm habe ich nicht gern.
Dehn SHTRAH-*ss'n-lairm* HAH-*beh ikh nikht ggehrn.*
I do not like the noise from the street.

Wenn etwas uns sehr missfällt, ärgern wir uns.
Venn ETT-*vahss oons zehr miss*-FELLT, AIR-*g'rn veer oons.*
If we dislike something very much, we are annoyed.

> **Wir sind ärgerlich.**
> *Veer zint* AIR-*g'r-likh.*
> We are angry.

Wenn wir sehr ärgerlich sind, sind wir zornig.
Venn veer zehr AIR-*g'r-likh zint, zint veer* TSOHR-*neekh.*
When we are very angry, we are furious.

Komische Dinge, Menschen oder Ereignisse machen uns lachen.
KOH-*mee-sheh* DING'*eh,* MEN-*sh'n* OH-*d'r Air*-IGHG-*niss-eh* MAH-*kh'n oons*
   LAH-*kh'n.*
Funny things, people or occurrences make us laugh.

Lachen Sie über Charlie Chaplin?
LAH-*kh'n Zee* EW-*b'r* TCHAHR-*lie* TCHAH-*plin?*
Do you laugh at Charlie Chaplin?

Das Gegenteil von Lachen ist Weinen.
Dahs GAY-*g'n-tighl fonn* LAH-*kh'n ist* VIGH-*n'n.*
The opposite of laughing is crying.

Kleine Kinder weinen oft.
KLIGH-*neh* KIN-*d'r* VIGH-*n'n offt.*
Little children cry often.

Manchmal weinen wir vor Lachen.
MAHNKH-*mahl* VIGH-*n'n veer fohr* LAH-*kh'n.*
Sometimes we cry from laughing.

Wenn wir sehr traurig sind, weinen wir bittere Tränen.
Venn veer zehr TRAOU-*reekh zint,* VIGH-*n'n veer* BITT'*reh* TRAY-*n'n.*
If we are very sad we cry bitter tears.

Was ist angenehmer, ein Kind, das weint
Vahss ist AHN-*ggeh-neh-m'r, ine Kint dahs vighnt*
What is more pleasant, a child who cries

> **oder ein Kind, das lacht?**
> OH-*d'r ine Kint, dahs lahkht?*
> or a child who laughs?

THINKING IN GERMAN

(Answers on page 262)

1. Ist der Professor traurig?   2. Worüber freut er sich?

3. Warum weint Liese?   4. Lacht Frau Huber?

5. Warum ist sie traurig?   6. Ist der Mensch den Tieren überlegen?

7. Denken Sie an Ihre deutsche Übung, wenn Sie nicht zuhause sind?

8. Kann man sprechen ohne zu denken?   9. Was weiss man?

10. Was kann man?   11. Kennen Sie Deutschland?

12. Kann Liese deutsch?   13. Können Sie lesen?

14. Wissen Sie, wieviele Zähne ich habe?   15. Vergessen Sie schnell?

16. Können wir die Sterne zählen?   17. Liebt man seine Mutter?

18. Haben Sie deutsche Musik gern?

19. Weinen Sie, wenn Sie sich freuen?

20. Haben Sie Furcht vor Katzen? 21. Liebt die Katze den Hund?

22. Gefällt Ihnen der Winter?   23. Sind Sie ärgerlich, wenn es regnet?

24. Haben die Tiere Verstand?

Wenn man reist
Venn mahn righst
When we travel

Deutschland ist ein Land.
DOITSH-*lahnt ist ine Lahnt.*
Germany is a country.

Frankreich ist ein Land.
FRAHNK-*righkh ist ine Lahnt.*
France is a country.

Einige Länder Europas sind:
EYE-*nee-ggeh* LEN-*d'r Oy*-ROH-*pahs zint:*
A few countries in Europe are:

England	**die Schweiz**	**Spanien**
ENNG-*lahnt*	*dee Shvights*	SHPAHN-*yenn*
England	Switzerland	Spain
Italien	**Russland**	**Österreich**
*Ee-*TAHL-*yenn*	ROOSS-*lahnt*	UH-*st'r-righkh*
Italy	Russia	Austria

Die Vereinigten Staaten und Kanada liegen in Nordamerika,
Dee Fer-ine-ik-t'n shtah-t'n oont kah-nah-dah lee-g'n in nort-ah-meh-ree-kah,
The United States and Canada are in North America,

> **China und Japan sind in Asien.**
> *khee-nah oont yah-pahn zint in ahz-yenn.*
> China and Japan are in Asia.

> **Argentinien ist in Südamerika.**
> *Ahr-ggen-teen-yenn ist in sewt-ah-meh-ree-kah.*
> Argentina is in South America.

> **Die grössten Städte der Welt sind:**
> *Dee gruhss-t'n shtet-teh dehr Vellt zint:*
> The biggest cities in the world are:

New York	London	Paris	Moskau	Berlin
New York	*lohn-dohn*	*Pah-rees*	*mohs-kaou*	*Behr-leen*
New York	London	Paris	Moscow	Berlin
Kalkutta	**Chicago**	**Tokio**	**Rom**	**Wien.**
Kahl-koo-tah	*Tshee-kah-goh*	*toh-kee-oh*	*Rohm*	*Veen.*
Calcutta	Chicago	Tokio	Rome	Vienna.

Wenn wir uns von einem Land in ein anderes
Venn veer oons fonn eye-n'm Lahnt in ine ahn-d'ress
If we go from one country to another

oder von einer Stadt in eine andere begeben,   **reisen wir.**
oh-d'r fonn eye-n'r Shtaht in eye-neh ahn-d'reh beh-ggeh-b'n,   *rye-z'n veer.*
or from one city to another,   we travel.

Wir können mit der Eisenbahn, mit dem Schiff, dem Autobus,
Veer kuh-n'n mit dehr eye-z'n-bahn, mit daim Shiff, daim aou-toh-booss,
We can travel by railroad, by ship, by bus,

> **mit dem Auto oder im Flugzeug reisen.**
> *mit daim aou-toh oh-d'r im flook-tsoik righ-z'n.*
> by automobile or by plane.

> **Für weite Reisen und um Zeit zu gewinnen,**
> *Fewr vigh-teh righ-z'n oont oom Tsight tsoo ggeh-vinn'n,*
> For long trips and in order to gain time,

> **nehmen wir das Flugzeug.**
> *nay-m'n veer dahs flook-tsoik.*
> we take the plane.

Wenn wir nicht weit zu fahren haben, nehmen wir die Bahn oder den Wagen.
Venn veer nikht vite tsoo FAH-*r'n* HAH-*b'n,* NAY-*m'n veer dee Bahn* OH-*d'r dain* VAH-*g'n.*
If we have not far to go, we take the railroad or the car.

Einige Autobusse fahren ziemlich schnell.
EYE-*nee-ggeh* AOU-*toh-booss-eh* FAH-*r'n* TSEEM-*likh shnell.*
Some busses go quite fast.

Bevor wir abreisen, müssen wir unsere Koffer packen.
*Beh-*FOHR *veer* AHP-*righ-z'n,* MEWSS'*n veer* OON-*z'reh* KOFF'*r* PAHK-*k'n.*
Before we leave, we must pack our suitcases.

Wir legen alles, was wir auf der Reise brauchen, in unsere Koffer.
Veer LAY-*g'n* AHL-*less, vahss veer aouf dehr* RIGH-*zeh* BRAOU-*kh'n, in* OON-*z'reh* KOFF'*r.*
We put every thing we need during our journey in our suitcases.

Wir müssen Kleider und Wäsche mitnehmen,
Veer MEWSS'*n* KLIGH-*d'r oont* VEH-*sheh* MIT-*nay-m'n,*
We must take along clothing and linen;

wir brauchen Schuhe und viele andere Dinge.
veer BRAOU-*kh'n* SHOO-*heh oont* FEE-*leh* AHN-*d'reh* DING-*eh.*
we need shoes and many other things.

Nehmen Sie eine Schuhbürste mit?
NAY-*m'n Zee* EYE-*neh* SHOO-*bewr-steh mit?*
Do you take a shoe brush along?

Haben Sie einen Kamm oder eine Haarbürste?
HAH-*b'n Zee* EYE-*n'n Kahm* OH-*d'r* EYE-*neh* HAHR-*bewr-steh?*
Have you a comb or a hairbrush?

Wir packen unsere Koffer und lassen sie hinuntertragen.
Veer PAHK-*k'n* OON-*z'reh* KOFF'*r oont* LAHSS'*n zee hin-*OON-*t'r-trah-g'n.*
We pack our suitcases and have them carried down.

> **Wir lassen ein Taxi rufen.**
> *Veer* LAHSS'*n ine* TAHK-*see* ROOF'*n.*
> We have a taxi called.

> **Wir sagen dem Chauffeur:**
> *Veer* ZAH-*g'n daim Shoh-*FUHR:
> We tell the driver:

> **Fahren Sie zum Nordbahnhof!**
> FAHR'*n Zee tsoom* NOHRT-*bahn-hohf!*
> Drive to the North Station.

Schnell, bitte, ich habe Eile!
Shnell, BIT-teh, ikh HAH-beh EYE-leh!
Quickly, please, I am in a hurry!

EXPRESSION TO REMEMBER: *Ich habe Eile—*"I am in a hurry" or *ich bin in Eile—ich habe es eilig.*

Auf dem Bahnhof müssen wir zuerst eine Fahrkarte lösen.
Aouf daim BAHN-hohf MEWSS'n veer tsoo-AIRST EYE-neh FAHR-kahr-teh LUH-z'n.
At the station we must first buy a ticket.

Wir gehen zum Schalter und sagen zum Beamten:
Veer GAY-h'n tsoom SHAHL-t'r oont ZAH-g'n tsoom Beh-AHM-t'n:
We go to the window and tell the clerk:

Bitte, geben Sie mir eine erste nach München!
BIT-teh, GAY-b'n Zee meer EYE-neh AIR-steh nahkh MEWN-kh'n!
Please, give me one first (class) to Munich.

Der Kassier fragt: Einfach oder Rückfahrkarte?
Dehr Kahs-SEER frahkt: INE-fahkh OH-d'r REWK-fahr-kahr-teh?
The clerk asks: One way or round-trip?

Nehmen Sie eine Rückfahrkarte, wenn Sie bald zurückfahren, sie ist billiger.
NAY-m'n Zee EYE-neh REWK-fahr-kahr-teh, venn Zee bahlt tsoo-REWK-fah-r'n, zee ist BILL-ig'r.
Take a round-trip ticket, if you are returning soon, it is cheaper.

Sie fragen:	**Was kostet die Karte?**	**Sie bezahlen.**
Zee FRAH-g'n:	*Vahss KOHS-t't dee KAHR-teh?*	*Zee beh-TSAH-l'n.*
You ask:	How much is the ticket?	You pay.

Der Zug hält am Bahnsteig.	**Er hat mehrere Wagen.**
Dehr Tsook hellt ahm BAHN-shtike.	*Air haht MEH-reh-reh VAH-g'n.*
The train is standing at the platform.	It has several cars.

Sie steigen ein.	**Sie sehen mehrere Abteile.**
Zee SHTIGH-g'n ine.	*Zee ZAY-h'n MEH-reh-reh AHP-tigh-leh.*
You get aboard.	You see several compartments.

Sie fragen in dem ersten Abteil:	**Ist hier ein Platz frei, bitte?**
Zee FRAH-g'n in daim AIR-st'n AHP-tile:	*Ist here ine Plahts fry, BIT-teh?*
You ask in the first compartment:	Is there a vacant seat here, please?

Wenn ein Platz nicht besetzt ist, dann belegen Sie ihn.
*Venn ine Plahts nikht beh-*ZETST *ist, dahn beh-*LAY-*g'n Zee een.*
If a seat is not occupied, you put (something) on it.

Manchmal müssen Sie den Zug wechseln, das nennt man:
MAHNKH-*mahl* MEWSS*'n Zee dain Tsook* VEK-*s'ln, dahs nennt mahn:*
Sometimes you must change trains; this is called:

> **Umsteigen.**
> OOM-*shtigh-g'n.*
> to transfer.

> **Der Zug hält in einer Station.**
> *Dehr Tsook hellt in* EYE-*n'r Shtahts-*YOHN.
> The train stops at a station.

Sie fragen den Schaffner:	**Wie lange hält der Zug hier?**
Zee FRAH-*g'n dain* SHAHFF-*n'r:*	*Vee* LAHN-*ggeh hellt dehr Tsook here?*
You ask the conductor:	How long does the train stop here?

> **Der Schaffner antwortet:**
> *Dehr* SHAHFF-*n'r* AHNT-*vohr-t't:*
> The conductor answers:

Nur zwei Minuten Aufenthalt, bitte nicht auszusteigen!
*Noor tsvigh Mee-*NOO-*t'n* AOUF-*'nt-hahlt,* BIT-*teh nikht* AOUS-*tsoo-shtigh-g'n!*
Only two minutes stop, please do not get off!

REMEMBER: *einsteigen*—"to go aboard", *aussteigen*—"to get off" and *umsteigen*—"to transfer or change trains", *sich anziehen*—"to dress", *sich ausziehen*—"to undress", *sich umziehen*—"to change clothes".

Wenn Sie am Bestimmungsort ankommen, nehmen Sie ein Taxi.
*Venn Zee ahm Beh-*SHTIMM-*oonks-ohrt* AHN-*komm'n,* NAY-*m'n Zee ine* TAHK-*see.*
When you arrive at your destination, you take a taxi.

> **Sie fahren zu einem Hotel.**
> *Zee* FAH-*r'n tsoo* EYE-*n'm Hoh-*TELL.
> You drive to a hotel.

> **Sie sagen zu dem Hotelbeamten:**
> *Zee* ZAH-*g'n tsoo daim Hoh-*TELL-*beh-ahm-t'n:*
> You ask the hotel clerk:

> **Haben Sie ein Zimmer mit Bad?**
> HAH-*b'n Zee ine* TSIMM*'r mit Baht?*
> Have you a room with bath?

Ich werde eine Woche bleiben.
Ikh VAIR-*deh* EYE-*neh* VOH-*kheh* BLIGH-*b'n.*
I shall stay a week.

Sie fragen nach dem Preis des Zimmers.
Zee FRAH-*g'n nahkh daim Price dess* TSIMM'*rs.*
You ask about the price of the room.

Sie gehen auf Ihr Zimmer.
Zee GAY-*h'n aouf Eer* TSIMM'*r.*
You go to your room.

Wenn Sie sich in einer fremden Stadt verirren,
Venn Zee zikh in EYE-*n'r* FREM-*d'n Shtaht fair-*EAR-*r'n,*
If you get lost in a strange city,

müssen Sie einen Polizisten fragen:
MEWSS'*n Zee* EYE-*n'n Poh-lee-*TSIST'*n* FRAH-*g'n:*
you must ask a policeman:

Verzeihung, können Sie mir sagen, wie ich am
*Fair-*TSIGH-*hoonk,* KUH-*n'n Zee meer* ZAH-*g'n, vee ikh ahm*
Excuse me, can you tell me the

kürzesten zum Hotel Imperial komme?
KEWR-*tseh-st'n tsoom Hoh-*TELL *Im-pair-*YAHL KOMM-*meh?*
shortest (way) to the Hotel Imperial?

NOTE on the Cities' Finest: *der Polizist* is the policeman. You can call him *Wachtmeister* also. In Vienna they are addressed as *Herr Wachmann* and in Germany *Herr Schutzmann. Die Polizei* is "the police" but it is singular, and not plural as in English.

Wenn Sie den Polizisten nicht verstehen, sagen Sie:
*Venn Zee dain Poh-lee-*TSIST'*n nikht fair-*SHTAIH'*n,* ZAH-*g'n Zee:*
If you do not understand the policeman, you say:

Bitte, sprechen Sie langsamer, ich verstehe nicht gut deutsch.
BIT-*teh,* SHPREH-*kh'n Zee* LAHNK-*zah-m'r, ikh fair-*SHTAY-*heh nikht good doitsh.*
Please speak more slowly, I do not understand German well.

In einer grossen Stadt gibt es viele Geschäfte.
In EYE-*n'r* GROHSS'*n Shtaht ggipt ess* FEE-*leh Ggeh-*SHEFF-*teh.*
In a big city there are many stores.

Sie bekommen Bücher in der Buchhandlung.
*Zee beh-*KOMM'*n* BEW-*kh'r in dehr* BOOKH-*hahnd-loonk.*
You get books at the book store.

Der Grünzeughändler verkauft Gemüse und Obst.
Dehr GREWN-*tsoik-hend-l'r* *fair*-KAOUFT *Ggeh*-MEW-*zeh oont Ohpst.*
The greengrocer sells vegetables and fruits.

Fleisch gibt es beim Fleischer (Metzger).
Flighsh ggipt ess bighm FLIGH-*sh'r* (METS-*g'r*).
There is meat at the butcher's.

Im Gemischtwarengeschäft bekommen Sie: Mehl, Zucker, Kaffee, Gewürze.
Im Ggeh-MISHT-*vahr'n-ggeh-shefft beh*-KOMM'*n Zee: Mail,* TSOOK'*r, Kah*-FEH, *Ggeh*-VEWR-*tseh.*
At the grocer's, you get flour, sugar, coffee, spices.

Gute Wurstwaren und Schinken sowie Schweizer Käse
GOO-*teh* VOORST-*vahr'n oont* SHINK'*n zoh-vee* SHVIGH-*ts'r* KAY-*zeh*
You can find good sausages and ham as well as Swiss cheese

finden Sie im Delikatessengeschäft.
FINN-*d'n Zee im Deh-lee-kah-*TESS'*n-ggeh-shefft.*
in the delicatessen.

Medikamente sind in der Apotheke zu haben.
*May-dee-kah-*MEN-*teh zint in dehr Ah-poh-*TAY-*keh tsoo* HAH-*b'n.*
Medicines are to be had in the pharmacy.

In den grossen Kaufhäusern (Warenhäusern) finden Sie alles.
In dain GROHSS'*n* KAOUF-*hoy-z'rn* (VAHR'*n-hoy-z'rn*) FINN-*d'n Zee* AHL-*less.*
In the big department stores you find everything.

Im Warenhaus fragen Sie nach der Abteilung, die Sie suchen.
Im VAHR'*n-haous* FRAH-*g'n Zee nahkh dehr* AHP-*tigh-loonk, dee Zee* ZOO-*kh'n.*
In the department store you ask for the department you are looking for.

Wenn Sie einen Hut brauchen, lassen Sie sich die Hutabteilung zeigen.
Venn Zee EYE-*n'n Hoot* BRAOU-*kh'n,* LAHSS'*n Zee zikh dee* HOOT-*ahp-tigh-loonk* TSIGH-*g'n.*
If you need a hat you are shown the hat department.

Der Verkäufer fragt Sie: **"Womit kann ich dienen?"**
*Dehr Fair-*KOY-*f'r frahgt Zee:*   *"Voh-*MIT *kahn ikh* DEE-*n'n?"*
The salesman asks you: "How may I serve you?"

Sie müssen ihm Ihre Kopfweite sagen.
Zee MEWSS'*n eem* EE-*reh* KOPPF-*vigh-teh* ZAH-*g'n.*
You must tell him your head-size.

Sie probieren den Hut an.
*Zee proh-*BEE-*r'n dain Hoot ahn.*
You try the hat on.

Wenn er Ihnen passt und gefällt, kaufen Sie ihn.
Venn air EE-*n'n pahsst oont ggeh-*FELLT, KAOU-*f'n Zee een.*
If it fits and you like it, you buy it.

Wenn der Preis zu hoch ist, fragen Sie:
Venn dehr Price tsoo hohkh ist, FRAH-*g'n Zee:*
If the price is too high, you ask:

Haben Sie nichts Billigeres?
HAH-*b'n Zee nikhts* BILL-*ee-ggeh-ress?*
Have you nothing cheaper?

Sie lassen die Ware einpacken.
Zee LAHSS'*n dee* VAH-*reh* INE-*pahk-k'n.*
You have the merchandise wrapped up.

Sie verlassen das Geschäft und gehen in Ihr Hotel zurück.
*Zee fair-*LAHSS'*n dahs Ggeh-*SHEFFT *oont* GAY-*h'n in Eer Hoh-*TELL *tsoo-*
REWK.
You leave the store and go back to your hotel.

THINKING IN GERMAN

(Answers on page 262)

1. Wie heissen die grössten Städte Europas?
2. Welches ist die grösste Stadt in den Vereinigten Staaten?
3. Wo liegt Montreal?
4. Ist Berlin weit von London?
5. Wie reisen Sie am liebsten?
6. Wo kaufen Sie die Fahrkarte?
7. Was fragen Sie, wenn Sie ein Abteil betreten?
8. Was nehmen Sie auf die Reise mit?
9. Packen Sie allein Ihre Koffer?
10. Wie fahren Sie zur Bahn?
11. Reist man im Flugzeug bequemer?
12. Reisen die Engländer viel?
13. Wo wohnen Sie in einer fremden Stadt?
14. Verstehen Sie gut deutsch?
15. Was sehen Sie in einer grossen Stadt?
16. Wo kaufen Sie Fleisch?
17. Welches sind die grössten Kaufhäuser in New York?
18. Was tun Sie, wenn Sie sich in einer fremden Stadt verirren?
19. Was verlangen Sie im Hotel?
20. Wenn Sie einen Hut brauchen, was sagen Sie zum Verkäufer?
21. Wonach fragt er?
22. Was sagen Sie, wenn der Preis zu hoch ist?
23. Passt Ihnen jeder Hut?

ÜBUNG NR. 32

Die Einladung
Dee INE-*lah-doonk*
The invitation

RITTER: **Guten Tag, alter Freund! Wie geht es Ihnen?**
RITT'r: GOO-*t'n Tahk,* AHL-*t'r Froint! Vee gait ess* EE-*n'n?*
RITTER: Hello, old friend! How are you?

Es freut mich unendlich, Sie wiederzusehen!
*Ess froit mikh oon-*END-*likh, Zee* VEE-*d'r-tsoo-zay-h'n!*
I am pleased no end to see you again!

NOTE on Greetings: When you meet a friend you may say: *Es freut mich, Sie zu sehen! (wiederzusehen)*—"Pleased to see you." When you meet someone for the first time: *Sehr erfreut, Sie kennen zu lernen.*—"Very pleased to make your acquaintance", and when you leave a new acquaint-ance *Sehr erfreut, Ihre Bekanntschaft gemacht zu haben (Sie ken-nengelernt zu haben)*—"Very pleased to have met you." Many people just say: *Sehr erfreut!* or *Sehr angenehm!*—corresponding roughly to our "charmed".

SCHMITT: **Ganz meinerseits, Herr Ritter. Ich habe Sie lange**
SHMITT: *Gahnts MIGH-n'r-zights, Herr RITT'r. Ikh HAH-beh Zee LAHN-ggeh*
SCHMITT: The pleasure is all mine, Mr. Ritter. I have not seen you for

nicht gesehen. Wie geht es Ihnen?
nikht ggeh-ZAY-h'n. Vee gait ess EE-n'n?
a long time. How are you?

RITTER: **Danke, ich kann nicht klagen. Seit wann sind Sie in Frankfurt?**
DAHN-keh, ikh kahn nikht KLAH-g'n. Zight vahn zint Zee in FRAHNK-foort?
Thanks, I cannot complain. How long have you been in Frankfurt?

SCHMITT: **Ich bin vor einer Woche hier angekommen.**
Ikh bin fohr EYE-n'r VOH-kheh here AHN-ggeh-komm'n.
I arrived here a week ago.

Ich habe hier geschäftlich zu tun. Was machen Sie hier?
Ikh HAH-beh here ggeh-SHEFFT-likh tsoo toon. Vahss MAH-kh'n Zee here?
I have some business to do here. What are you doing here?

Sie wohnen doch in Wien, wenn ich mich nicht irre?
Zee VOH-n'n dohkh in Veen, venn ikh mikh nikht EAR-reh?
You live in Vienna, if I am not mistaken?

RITTER: **Jawohl, ich bin zu Besuch hier.**
Yah-VOHL, ikh bin tsoo Beh-ZOOKH here.
Yes, I am here on a visit.

Ich muss sehr bald wieder nach Wien zurückfahren.
Ikh mooss zair bahlt VEE-d'r nahkh Veen tsoo-REWK-fah-r'n.
I must go back to Vienna very soon.

Halten Sie sich länger hier auf?
HAHL-t'n Zee zikh LENG'r here aouf?
Will you be staying here longer?

SCHMITT: **Keineswegs. Ich bin soeben im Begriff,**
KIGH-ness-vaiks. Ikh bin zoh-AY-b'n im Beh-GRIFF,
Not at all. I am just about

mir eine Fahrkarte nach Wien zu lösen.
meer EYE-neh FAHR-kahr-teh nahkh Veen tsoo LUH-z'n.
to get myself a ticket to Vienna.

RITTER: **Das ist ja grossartig! Können wir nicht die Reise**
Dahs ist yah GROHSS-ahr-tikh! KUH-n'n veer nikht dee RYE-zeh
This is indeed splendid! Can't we make the trip

gemeinsam machen? Was halten Sie davon?
ggeh-MINE-zahm MAH-kh'n? Vahss HAHL-t'n Zee dah-FONN?
together? What do you think of that?

SCHMITT: **Das ist eine gute Idee! Ich war noch nie in der**
Dahs ist EYE-neh GOO-teh Ee-DAY! Ikh vahr nohkh nee in dehr
That is a good idea! I have never been in the

österreichischen Haupstadt. Wenn ich mit Ihnen
UH-st'r-righ-khish'n HAOUPT-shtaht. Venn ikh mit EE-n'n
Austrian capital. If I

fahre, habe ich gleich einen Fremdenführer an der Hand.
FAH-reh, HAH-beh ikh glighkh EYE-n'n FREM-d'n-few-r'r ahn dehr Hahnt.
go with you, I'll have a guide right at hand.

RITTER: **Sie waren noch nie in Wien?**
Zee VAH-r'n nohkh nee in Veen?
You have never been in Vienna?

Ist Ihre Mutter denn nicht Wienerin?
Ist EE-reh MOOTT'r denn nikht VEE-neh-rin?
Isn't your mother Viennese?

SCHMITT: **Das stimmt schon. Ich bin aber noch nie dazugekommen,**
Dahs shtimmt shohn. Ikh bin AH-b'r nohkh nee dah-TSOO-ggeh-komm'n,
That is correct. Yet I have never got around

die Heimat meiner Mutter zu besuchen. Doch jetzt will ich die
dee HIGH-maht MIGH-n'r MOOTT'r tsoo beh-ZOO-kh'n. Dohkh yetst vill ikh dee
to visit my mother's homeland. But now I shall avail myself

Gelegenheit benutzen, um meine Verwandten in Wien
Ggeh-LAY-g'n-hite beh-NOOT-z'n, oom MIGH-neh Fair-VAHN-t'n in Veen
of the opportunity to get acquainted with my relatives in Vienna.

kennenzulernen. Ich habe meine Cousinen noch nie gesehen.
KENN'n-tsoo-lair-n'n. Ikh HAH-beh MIGH-neh Koo-ZEE-n'n nohkh nee ggeh-ZAY-h'n.
I have never seen my cousins.

 NOTE: *Der Cousin*—"cousin" is the male cousin while the feminine is called *die Cousine.* True German words for these relatives exist, like *Vetter* and *Base,* yet the French words are far more commonly used by the Germans themselves.

RITTER: **Dann ist es allerdings höchste Zeit, das nachzuholen.**
Dahn ist ess ahll'r-DINKS HUHK-steh Tsight, dahs NAHKH-tsoo-hoh-l'n.
Then it is high time to make up for that.

Gleichzeitig können Sie mich besuchen, ich möchte
GLIGHKH-tsigh-tikh KUH-n'n Zee mikh beh-ZOO-kh'n, ikh MUHKH-teh
At the same time you can visit me, I would like

Sie meiner Frau vorstellen.
Zee MIGH-*n'r Fraou* FOHR-*shtell'n.*
to present you to my wife.

SCHMITT: Da sage ich nicht nein. Ich nehme Ihre liebenswürdige
Dah ZAH-*ggeh ikh nikht nine. Ikh* NAY-*meh* EE-*reh* LEE-*b'ns-vewr-dee-ggeh*
I cannot refuse that. I accept your kind

Einladung mit Dank an. Gehen wir gleich hier in das
INE-*lah-doonk mit Dahnk ahn.* GAY-*h'n veer glighkk here in dahs*
invitation with thanks. Let us go into this travel

Reisebüro, um unsere Karten zu bestellen.
RYE-*zeh-bew-roh, oom* OON-*z'reh* KAHR-*t'n tsoo beh-*SHTELL*'n.*
office here at once to order our tickets.

RITTER: Gut, ich liebe auch schnelle Entschlüsse.
Goot, ikh LEE-*beh aoukh* SHNELL-*eh Ent-*SHLEW-*sseh.*
Good, I like quick decisions too.

Sie kennen doch sicher das Sprichwort:
Zee KENN'n *dohkh* ZEE-*kh'r dahs* SHPRIKH-*vohrt:*
You certainly know the proverb:

"Was Du heute kannst besorgen,
"Vahss Doo HOY-*teh kahnst beh-*ZOHR-*g'n,*
"What you can take care of today,

das verschiebe nicht auf morgen!"
*dahs fair-*SHEE-*beh nikht aouf* MOHR-*g'n!"*
don't put off until tomorrow!"

SCHMITT: Ich kenne auch ein anderes Sprichwort,
Ikh KENN-*eh aoukh ine* AHN-*d'ress* SHPRIKH-*vohrt,*
I know another proverb too,

das ähnlich klingt. Es lautet:
dahss AIN-*likh klinkt. Ess* LAOU-*t't:*
that sounds similar. It goes:

"Morgen, morgen, nur nicht heute, sagen alle faulen Leute."
*"*MOHR-*g'n,* MOHR-*g'n, noor nikht* HOY-*teh,* ZAH-*g'n* AHL-*leh* FAOU-*l'n* LOY-*teh."*
"Tomorrow, tomorrow, only not today, all the lazy people say."

RITTER: Da wir jedoch nicht faul sind,
*Dah veer yeh-*DOHKH *nikht faoul zint,*
However, as we are not lazy.

besorgen wir unsere Fahrscheine unverzüglich.
*beh-*ZOHR-*g'n veer* OON-*z'reh* FAHR-*shigh-neh* OON-*fair-tsewg-likh.*
we shall get our tickets without delay.

Wie wollen Sie nach Wien fahren?
Vee VOLL'*n Zee nahkh Veen* FAH-*r'n?*
How do you want to travel to Vienna?

SCHMITT: **Ich möchte natürlich fliegen, das geht am schnellsten**
Ikh MUHKH-*teh nah-*TEWR-*likh* FLEE-*g'n, dahs gait ahm* SHNELL-*st'n*
Naturally I want to fly, that is the fastest

und ist auch am angenehmsten.
oont ist aoukh ahm AHN-*ggeh-naim-st'n.*
and also the most comfortable way.

RITTER: **Da sieht man den fortschrittlichen Amerikaner!**
Dah zeet mahn dain FOHRT-*shritt-lee-kh'n Ah-meh-ree-*KAH-*n'r!*
There you see the progressive American!

Ich bin noch ein wenig altmodisch und fahre am
Ikh bin nohkh ine VAY-*nikh* AHLT-*moh-dish oont* FAH-*reh ahm*
I am still a little old-fashioned and like best to travel

liebsten mit der guten, alten Eisenbahn!
LEEP-*st'n mit dehr* GOO-*t'n* AHL-*t'n* EYE-*z'n-bahn!*
on the good old railroad!

SCHMITT: **Ich habe nichts gegen die Eisenbahn oder gegen**
Ikh HAH-*beh nikhts* GAY-*g'n dee* EYE-*z'n-bahn* OH-*d'r* GAY-*g'n*
I have nothing against the railroad or against

Schiffe, wenn ich Zeit und Musse habe.
SHIFF-*eh, venn ikh Tsight oont* MOOSS-*eh* HAH-*beh.*
ships, if I have time and leisure.

Sonst nehme ich ausnahmslos das Flugzeug.
Zohnst NAY-*meh ikh* AOUS-*nahms-lohs dahs* FLOOK-*tsoik.*
Otherwise I invariably take the plane.

Ich hoffe, Sie haben doch keine Angst, zu fliegen?
Ikh HOFF-*eh, Zee* HAH-*b'n dohkh* KIGH-*neh Ahnkst, tsoo* FLEE-*g'n?*
You are not afraid to fly, I hope?

RITTER: **Eigentlich nicht. Aber um aufrichtig zu sein,**
EYE-*g'nt-likh nikht.* AH-*b'r oom* AOUF-*rikh-tikh tsoo zine,*
As a matter of fact, no. But to be candid,

muss ich gestehen, dass meine Frau energisch dagegen ist.
*mooss ikh ggeh-*SHTAY-*h'n, dahss* MIGH-*neh Fraou en-*NERR-*ggish dah-*
GGEH-*g'n ist.*
I must admit, that my wife is energetically against it.

Sie verfolgt die Flugzeugabstürze in den
*Zee fair-*FOHLKT *dee* FLOOK-*tsoik-ahp-shtewr-tseh in dain*
She follows the plane crashes in the

Zeitungen sehr genau und will nicht, dass ich mein
TSIGH-*toon-g'n zair ggeh-*NAOU *oont vill nikht, dahss ikh mine*
papers very closely and does not want me to

Leben leichtsinnig aufs Spiel setze, wie sie es hinstellt.
LAY-*b'n* LIGHKHT-*zinn-ikh aoufs Shpeel* ZET-*tseh, vee zee ess* HIN-*shtellt.*
risk my life foolishly, as she puts it.

SCHMITT: Glauben Sie nicht, dass das ein wenig übertrieben ist?
GLAOU-*b'n Zee nikht, dahss dahs ine* VAY-*nikh ew-b'r-*TREE-*b'n ist?*
Don't you think that that is a little exaggerated?

Ich möchte Ihnen gerne eine Frage stellen:
Ikh MUHKH-*teh* EE-*n'n* GAIR-*neh* EYE-*neh* FRAH-*ggeh* SHTELL'*n:*
I should like to put a question to you:

Wo sterben die meisten Leute?
Voh SHTAIR-*b'n dee* MIGH-*st'n* LOY-*teh?*
where do most people die?

IDIOMS TO REMEMBER: *an der Hand haben*—"to have handy", *dazukommen*—"to get around to it", *unverzüglich*—"without delay", *aufs Spiel setzen*—"to put at stake" or "to risk".

RITTER: Im Bett natürlich.
*Im Bett nah-*TEWR-*likh.*
In bed, of course.

SCHMITT: Sie haben aber keine Furcht, jeden Abend ins Bett zu steigen.
Zee HAH-*b'n* AH-*b'r* KIGH-*neh Foorkht,* YAY-*d'n* AH-*b'nt ince Bett tsoo*
SHTIGH-*g'n.*
And yet you are not afraid to climb into your bed every night.

RITTER: Das ist ein gutes Beispiel, das werde ich meiner Frau erzählen.
Dahss ist ine GOO-*tess* BIGH-*shpeel, dahss* VAIR-*deh ikh* MIGH-*n'r Fraou*
*air-*TSAY-*l'n.*
That is a good example, I'll tell it to my wife.

SCHMITT: Also, wie ist es, fliegen wir?
AHL-*zoh, vee ist ess,* FLEE-*g'n veer?*
Now, how about it, do we fly?

RITTER: **Abgemacht, wir fliegen!**
AHP-*ggeh-mahkht, veer* FLEE-*g'n!*
Right, we fly!

(Im Reisebüro.)
(*Im* RYE-*zeh-bew-roh.*)
(In the travel office.)

DER SCHALTERBEAMTE: **Guten Tag, meine Herren.**
Dehr SHAHL-*t'r-beh-ahm-teh:* GOO-*t'n Tahk,* MIGH-*neh* HERR'*n.*
THE CLERK: Good day, gentlemen.

Womit kann ich Ihnen dienen?
*Voh-*MIT *kahn ikh* EE-*n'n* DEE-*n'n?*
What can I do for you?

RITTER: **Wir möchten gerne zwei Flugplätze nach Wien haben.**
Veer MUHKH-*t'n* GAIR-*neh tsvigh* FLOOK-*plett-tseh nakh Veen* HAH-*b'n.*
We would like to have two plane tickets to Vienna.

SCHALTERBEAMTER: **Gern. Für welchen Tag, bitte?**
SHAHL-*t'r-beh-ahm-t'r: Gairn. Fewr* VEL-*kh'n Tahk,* BIT-*teh?*
CLERK: Gladly. For which day, please?

SCHMITT: **Der kommende Montag passt uns!**
Dehr KOMM'*n-deh* MOHN-*tahk pahsst oons!*
Next Monday suits us!

SCHALTERBEAMTER: **Gewiss, meine Herren! Montag haben wir**
*Ggeh-*VISS, MIGH-*neh* HERR'*n!* MOHN-*tahk* HAH-*b'n veer*
Certainly, gentlemen! Monday we have

zwei Flüge, einen um 9 Uhr und
tsvigh FLEW-*ggeh,* EYE-*n'n oom noine Oor oont*
two flights, one at 9 o'clock and

einen andern um 11 Uhr Vormittag.
EYE-*n'n* AHN-*d'rn oom elf Oor* FOHR-*mit-tahk.*
another one at 11 o'clock A.M.

Das erste Flugzeug geht direkt nach Wien,
Dahs AIR-*steh* FLOOK-*tsoik gait dee-*REKT *nach Veen,*
The first plane goes directly to Vienna,

das zweite macht Zwischenlandungen in
dahs TSVIGH-*teh mahkht* TSVISH'*n-lahn-doong'n in*
the second stops in

Stuttgart und München.
SHTOOTT-*gahrt oont* MEWN-*kh'n.*
Stuttgart and Munich.

RITTER: **Ich glaube, wir nehmen lieber das erste Flugzeug.**
Ikh GLAOU-*beh, veer* NAY-*m'n* LEE-*b'r dahs* AIR-*steh* FLOOK-*tsoik.*
I think we would rather take the first plane.

Beim Landen wird mir immer schlecht und so
Bighm LAHN-*d'n veert meer* IMM'*r shlekht oont zoh*
Upon landing, I always get sick and so

möchte ich die beiden Zwischenlandungen vermeiden.
MUHKH-*teh ikh dee* BIGH-*d'n* TSVISH'*n-lahn-doon-g'n faire-*MIGH-*d'n.*
I'd like to avoid the two stops.

SCHMITT: **Was kostet die Reise?**
Vahss KOHSS-*t't dee* RYE-*zeh?*
What does the trip cost?

BEAMTER: **Ein Flug kostet 200 Mark,**
Ine Flook KOHSS-*t't* TSVIGH-*hoon-d'rt Mark,*
One way costs 200 marks,

ein Rückfahrschein kostet 350 Mark.
ine REWK-*fahr-shine* KOHSS-*t't* DRIGH-*hoon-d'rt-fewnf-tsikh Mark.*
a round-trip ticket costs 350 marks.

RITTER: **Ich nehme nur die einfache Karte,**
Ikh NAY-*meh noor dee* INE-*fah-kheh* KAHR-*teh,*
I shall take only the one-way ticket,

ich bin in Wien zuhause und weiss nicht,
*ikh bin in Veen tsoo-*HAOU-*zeh oont vice nikht,*
I am at home in Vienna and I do not know

wann ich wieder nach Frankfurt reisen werde.
vahn ikh VEE-*d'r nahkh* FRAHNK-*foort* RYE-*z'n* VAIR-*deh.*
when I shall be going to Frankfurt again.

SCHMITT: **Ich nehme hin und zurück.**
Ikh NAY-*meh hin oont tsoo-*REWK.
I'll take the round trip.

BEAMTER: **Wo wohnen die Herren?**
Voh VOH-*n'n dee* HERR'*n?*
Where are the gentlemen staying?

SCHMITT: **Ich wohne im Hotel Excelsior am Bahnhofsplatz.**
Ikh VOH-*neh im Hoh-*TELL *Ex-*TSELL-*zee-ohr ahm* BAHN-*hohfs-plahts,*
I am staying at the Hotel Excelsior at the Station Square.

RITTER: **Und ich bin im Monopol abgestiegen.**
*Oont ikh bin im Moh-noh-*POHL AHPP-*ggeh-shtee-g'n.*
And I am staying at the Monopol.

BEAMTER: **Danke bestens. Unser Autobus wird Sie also**
DAHN-*keh* BESS-*t'ns.* OON-*z'r* AOU-*toh-booss veert Zee* AHL-*zoh*
Thanks very much. Our bus will then pick you up

am Montag um sechs Uhr früh abholen.
ahm MOHN-*tahk oom zeks Oor frew* AHPP-*hoh-l'n.*
on Monday at 6 in the morning.

SCHMITT: **Um sechs Uhr? Das ist ja mitten in der Nacht!**
Oom zeks Oor? Dahs ist yah MITT'*n in dehr Nahkht!*
At 6 o'clock? That's really in the middle of the night!

Warum, wenn das Flugzeug erst um 9 Uhr abgeht?
*Vah-*ROOM*, venn dahs* FLOOK-*tsoik airst oom noin Oor* AHPP-*gait?*
Why, if the plane leaves only at 9 o'clock?

BEAMTER: **Der Autobus braucht eine Stunde zum Flugplatz**
Dehr AOU-*toh-booss braoukht* EYE-*neh* SHTOON-*deh tsoom* FLOOK-*plahts*
The bus takes one hour to the Rhine-Main

Rhein-Main. Ausserdem muss man Ihr Gepäck noch wiegen.
Rine-Mine. AOU-*ss'r-daim mooss mahn Eer Gay-*PECK *nohkh* VEE-*g'n.*
airport. Besides they must also weigh your luggage.

RITTER: **Auch scheint die Fluggesellschaft nicht zu wünschen,**
Aoukh shighnt dee FLOOK-*ggeh-zell-shahft nikht tsoo* VEWN-*sh'n,*
Then too the Airline Company does not seem to want

dass ihre Passagiere zu spät kommen.
dahss EE-*reh Pah-ssah-*ZHEE-*reh tsoo shpait* KOMM'*n.*
their passengers to come too late.

Deshalb raubt man uns unseren süssen Morgenschlummer!
DESS-*hahlp raoupt mahn oons* OON-*z'ren* SEWSS'*n* MOHR-*g'n-shloom'r!*
Therefore, they rob us of our sweet morning slumber!

IDIOMS: *Ich bin zu Besuch hier*—"I am here on a visit",
Ich habe keine Lust—"I do not feel like",—*es ist nichts los
hier*—"It is dull around here, there is nothing much going
on here." (This is amusing, as the literal meaning is—"there
is nothing loose here.")

THINKING IN GERMAN
(Answers on page 263)

1. Wo befinden sich Herr Ritter und Herr Schmitt?

2. Woher kommt Herr Ritter?

3. Seit wann ist Herr Schmitt in Frankfurt und was macht er da?

4. Ist Herr Ritter Deutscher?

5. Woher stammt Herr Schmitt mütterlicherseits?

6. Wohin will sich Herr Schmitt von Frankfurt begeben?

7. Wird sich Herr Schmitt länger in Frankfurt aufhalten?

8. Ist er schon einmal in Wien gewesen?

9. Wozu ladet ihn Herr Ritter ein?

10. Nimmt er Herrn Ritters Einladung an?

11. Wird Herr Ritter ihm als Führer dienen können?

12. Brauchen Sie einen Führer in New York?

13. Wohin begeben sich die beiden Herren, nachdem sie ihre Flugscheine gekauft haben?

14. Ist es leicht, eine Flugkarte für denselben Tag zu erhalten?

15. Was sagen Sie zum Schalterbeamten im Reisebüro?

16. Wie verlange ich eine Eisenbahnfahrkarte?

17. Wann fliegt das erste Flugzeug nach Wien ab?

18. Warum wählen sie das 9 Uhr Flugzeug?

19. Wo macht der andere Aeroplan eine Zwischenlandung?

20. Ist es angenehmer zu fliegen oder im Expresszug zu fahren?

21. Warum nimmt Herr Ritter keine Rückfahrkarte?

22. Wozu verlangt der Schalterbeamte die Adressen der Fluggäste?

23. Wohnen Sie in einer Grossstadt?

24. Wie ist Ihre Adresse?

25. Wann kommt der Autobus die Herren abholen?

26. Schlafen Sie gern lang am Morgen?

27. Warum ist es notwendig, dass die Reisenden zeitig aufstehen?

28. Wenn Sie zeitig aufstehen, sind Sie tagsüber sehr verschlafen?

ÜBUNG NR. 33

Der Abflug
Dehr AHPP-*flook*
The Take-off

(Der Fernsprecher klingelt)
(*Dehr* FAIRN-*shpreh-kh'r* KLING'*lt*)
(The telephone rings)

SCHMITT: **Hallo, wer dort? (Wer spricht?)**
*Hah-*LOH, *vair dohrt? (Vair shprikht?)*
Hello, who is there? (Who is speaking?)

TELEFONISTIN: **Guten Morgen! Es ist sechs Uhr vorbei, Herr Schmitt.**
*Tay-lay-foh-*NISS-*tin:* GOO-*t'n* MOHR-*g'n! Ess ist zeks Oor fohr-*BIGH, *Herr Shmitt.*
OPERATOR: Good morning! It is past six o'clock, Mr. Schmitt.

Ich habe bereits einmal vorher angerufen,
Ikh HAH-*beh beh-*RITES INE-*mahl* FOHR-*hair* AHN-*ggeh-roof'n,*
I have already called you once before.

ohne Antwort zu bekommen!
OH-*neh* AHNT-*vohrt tsoo beh-*KOMM'*n!*
without getting an answer!

SCHMITT: **Donnerwetter! Ich habe nicht wiel Zeiti**
DONN'*r-vett'r!* Ikh HAH-*beh nikht feel Tsight!*
Ye gods! I haven't much time!

Ich bin gleich unten, lassen Sie meine Rechnung vorbereiten!
Ikh bin glighkh OON-*t'n,* LAHSS'*n Zee* MIGH-*neh* REKH-*noonk* FOHR-*beh-rite'n.*
I'll be down at once, have my bill prepared.

IDIOMS: *Donnerwetter*—"Thunderstorm" is an exclamation which you may use to express your surprise—either agreeable or disagreeable. Translate it any way you like, from "Oops!" to "Nuts!"

TELEFONISTIN: **Sehr wohl. Ich werde sofort den Hausdiener**
Zair vohl. Ikh VAIR-*deh zoh-*FOHRT *dain* HAOUS-*dee-n'r*
Very well. I shall send the porter

um Ihr Gepäck schicken.
*oom Eer Ggeh-*PECK SHICK'*n.*
for your luggage at once.

(Im Hotelbüro)
*(Im Hoh-*TELL-*bew-roh)*
(At the hotel desk)

DER KASSIER: **Hier ist Ihre Rechnung, mein Herr, 80 Mark 25.**
*Dehr Kahs-*SEER: *Here ist* EE-*reh* REKH-*noonk, mine Herr,* AHKH-*tsikh Mark*
FEWNF-*oont-tsvahn-tsikh.*
THE CASHIER: Here is your bill, sir, 80 Marks 25.

SCHMITT: **Ist alles eingerechnet?**
Ist AHL-*less* INE-*ggeh-rekh-net?*
Is everything included?

KASSIER: **Jawohl, mein Herr. Ihre Speisen-Rechnung ist drin**
*Yah-*VOHL, *mine Herr.* EE-*reh* SHPIGH-*z'n-rekh-noonk ist drin*
Yes, sir. Your restaurant account is included

und auch Ihre Telefongespräche.
oont aoukh EE-*reh Teh-leh-*PHONE-*ggeh-shpreh-kheh.*
and so are your telephone calls.

SCHMITT: **Hier ist das Geld. Den Schlüssel habe ich in der Tür stecken lassen.**
Here ist dahs Gellt. Dain SHLEW-*s'l* HAH-*beh ikh in dehr Tewr* SHTEKK'*n*
LAHSS'*n.*
Here is the money. I left the key sticking in the door.

EXPRESSIONS TO REMEMBER: *Der Schlüssel steckt in der Tür.—"The key is (sticking) in the door." Ich lasse den Schlüssel stecken.—"I leave the key sticking (in the lock)."*

KASSIER: **Danke bestens! Angenehme Reise! Hausdiener!**
DAHN-*keh* BEST'*ns!* AHN-*ggeh-nay-meh* RYE-*zeh!* HAOUS-*dee-n'r!*
Thank you very much! A pleasant trip! Boy!

Bringen Sie Herrn Schmitt's Gepäck zum Wagen!
BRING'*n Zee Herrn Shmitts Ggeh-*PECK *tsoom* VAH-*g'n!*
Take Mr. Schmitt's luggage to the car!

SCHMITT: **Ich danke Ihnen! (zum Hausdiener)**
Ikh DAHN-*keh* EE-*n'n! (tsoom* HAOUS-*dee-n'r)*
Thank you! (To the porter)

Lassen Sie die kleine Tasche, die nehme ich selbst!
LAHSS'*n Zee dee* KLIGH-*neh* TAH-*sheh, dee* NAY-*meh ikh zellpst!*
Leave the small bag, I'll take it myself!

Sie enthält alle meine Papiere, die will ich nicht verlieren!
*Zee ent-*HELLT AHL-*leh* MIGH-*neh Pah-*PEE-*reh, dee vill ikh nikht fair-*
LEE-*r'n!*
It contains all my papers, I don't want to lose them!

(Im Auto)
(Im AOU-*toh)*
(In the car)

RITTER: **Was ist los, Freund Schmitt? Warum kommen Sie so spät?**
*Vahss ist lohs, Froint Shmitt? Vah-*ROOM KOMM'*n Zee zoh shpait?*
What is the matter, friend Schmitt? Why are you so late?

SCHMITT: **Ich habe verschlafen. In New York stehen wir nicht**
Ikh HAH-*beh fair-*SHLAH-*f'n. In New York* SHTAY-*h'n veer nikht*
I overslept. In New York we do not

so zeitig auf. Ich habe wie ein Murmeltier geschlafen.
zoh TSIGH-*tikh aouf. Ikh* HAH-*beh vee ine* MOOR-*m'l-teer ggeh-*SHLAH-*f'n.*
get up so early. I slept like a marmot.

IDIOMS:
Was ist los?—"What is the matter?", "What has happened?"
Ich bin spät daran—"I am late."
Verschlafen—"to oversleep".

(Am Flugplatz.)
(*Ahm* FLOOK-*plahts.*)
(At the air port.)

RITTER: **Unsere Namen sind Schmitt und Ritter.**
OON-*z'reh* NAH-*m'n zint Shmitt oont* RITT'*r.*
Our names are Schmitt and Ritter.

Wir wollen das 9 Uhr Flugzeug nach Wien nehmen.
Veer VOLL'*n dahs noin Oor* FLOOK-*tsoik nahhk Veen* NAY-*m'n.*
We want to take the 9 o'clock plane for Vienna.

ANGESTELLTER: **Jawohl, meine Herren, Ihre Namen sind auf**
AHN-*ggeh-shtell-t'r:*   *Yah-*VOHL, MIGH-*neh* HERR'*n,* EE-*reh* NAH-*m'n zint aouf*
CLERK: Yes, gentlemen, your names are on the

dem Verzeichnis. Wieviel wiegen Sie?
*daim Fair-*TSIGHKH-*niss. Vee-*FEEL VEE-*g'n Zee?*
list. How much do you weigh?

RITTER: **75 Kilo.**
FEWNF-*oont-zeep-tsikh* KEE-*loh.*
75 kilos.

SCHMITT: **Ich glaube, ich auch.**
Ikh GLAOU-*beh, ikh aoukh.*
I think I do too.

ANGESTELLTER: **Sie scheinen mir etwas schwerer zu sein, mein Herr!**
Zee SHIGH-*n'n meer* ETT-*vahss* SHVAY-*r'r tsoo zine, mine Herr!*
You look a bit heavier to me, sir!

Sagen wir lieber 80 Kilo.
ZAH-*g'n veer* LEE-*b'r* AHKHT-*tsikh* KEE-*loh.*
Let's say rather 80 kilos.

Wollen Sie jetzt, bitte, zur Gepäckwage gehen!
VOLL'*n Zee yetst,* BIT-*teh, tsoor Ggeh-*PECK-*vah-ggeh* GAY-*h'n!*
Please go to the baggage scale now!

SCHMITT: **Wieviel Gepäck darf man mitnehmen, ohne Übergewicht zu bezahlen?**
Vee-FEEL Ggeh-PECK dahrf mahn MIT-nay-m'n, OH-neh EW-b'r-ggeh-vikht tsoo beh-TSAH-l'n?
How much luggage can one take along, without paying for excess weight?

ANGESTELLTER: **25 Kilo, mein Herr.**
FEWNF-oont-tsvahn-tsikh KEE-loh, mine Herr.
25 kilos, sir.

RITTER: **Gehen wir ins Restaurant, ich sterbe vor Hunger.**
GAY-h'n veer ince Reh-staou-RAHNT, ikh SHTAIR-beh fohr HOON-g'r
Let's go to the restaurant, I am dying of hunger.

Ich hatte keine Zeit zu frühstücken.
Ikh HAHT-teh KIGH-neh Tsight tsoo FREW-shtew-k'n.
I had no time for breakfast.

SCHMITT: **Einverstanden. Im ersten Stock gibt es ein Restaurant.**
INE-f'r-shtahn-d'n. Im AIR-st'n Shtohk ggipt ess ine Reh-staou-RAHNT.
Right. There is a restaurant on the second floor.

NOTE: In Europe, the ground floor is not the first floor, as in the U.S. They start counting with the floor above the ground level, so that "First floor" to a German is "Second floor" to us.

(AUSRUFER): **Fluggäste für Flug 505 nach Wien einsteigen!**
(AOUS-*roof'r*): *FLOOK-ggess-teh fewr Flook FEWNF-hoon-d'rt-fewnf nahkh Veen INE-shtigh-g'n!*
(Announcer): Passengers for flight 505 to Vienna, all aboard!

SCHMITT: **Wie unangenehm! Jetzt werde ich nichts mehr essen können.**
Vee OON-ahn-ggeh-naim! Yetst VAIR-deh ikh nikhts mair ESS'n KUH-n'n.
How unpleasant! Now I won't be able to eat at all.

RITTER: **Sorgen Sie sich nicht! Ich glaube, Sie bekommen**
ZOHR-g'n Zee zikh nikht! Ikh GLAOU-beh, Zee beh-KOMM'n
Don't worry. I think that you will get

im Flugzeug zu essen!
im FLOOK-tsoik tsoo ESS'n!
something to eat on the plane!

THINKING IN GERMAN

(Answers on page 264)

1. Schläft Herr Schmitt, wenn der Fernsprecher läutet?
2. Wer ruft ihn an?
3. Steht er gerne so zeitig auf?
4. Wer wird das Gepäck zum Auto bringen?
5. Was tut Herr Schmitt nach dem Telefongespräch?
6. Wo lässt er den Schlüssel?
7. Mit wem spricht Herr Ritter im Hotelbüro?
8. Warum lässt er den Pagen nicht die Handtasche nehmen?
9. Wieviel Gewicht dürfen die Passagiere unentgeltlich mitführen?
10. Hat er etwas zu sich genommen, bevor er zum Flughafen gefahren ist?
11. Warum können die Herren nicht am Flughafen essen?
12. Was sagt Herr Ritter, wenn er erfährt, dass keine Zeit mehr zum Essen ist?
13. Werden an Bord des Flugzeuges Mahlzeiten serviert?
14. Wird Essen im Flugzeug herumgereicht?
15. Sind Sie schon einmal geflogen?
16. Wieviel wiegen Sie?
17. In welchem Stock wohnen Sie?
18. Können die Herren direkt nach Wien fliegen?
19. Haben Sie schon einmal verschlafen?

Die Ankunft.
Dee AHN-*koonft*
The arrival

(Im Flugzeug.)
(*Im* FLOOK-*tsoik.*)
(In the plane.)

SCHMITT: **Werden wir bald ankommen? Wie lange dauert's noch?**
VAIR-*d'n veer bahlt* AHN-*komm'n? Vee* LAHN-*ggeh* DAOU'*rts nohkh?*
Will we arrive soon? How much longer will it be?

RITTER: **Nicht mehr lange. Man kann schon kleine**
Nikht mair LAHN-*ggeh. Mahn kahn shohn* KLIGH-*neh*
Not so long any more. We can already see small

Städtchen sehen. Wien liegt hinter diesen Hügeln.
SHTETT-*kh'n* ZAY-*h'n*. *Veen leegt* HINT'*r* DEEZ'*n* HEW-*g'ln*.
towns. Vienna lies behind these hills.

SCHMITT: Ist das da unten die Donau?
Ist dahs dah OON-*t'n dee* DOH-*naou?*
Is that the Danube down there?

RITTER: Gewiss! Sie heisst zwar die blaue Donau,
*Gay-*VISS*! Zee highsst tsvahr dee* BLAOU-*eh* DOH-*naou,*
Certainly! Although it is called the Blue Danube,

sie ist aber schmutzig-grün und gar nicht blau.
zee ist AH-*b'r* SHMOOT-*sikh-grewn oont gahr nikht blaou.*
it is a dirty green, and not blue at all.

SCHMITT: Kann man den Kahlenberg sehen?
Kahn mahn dain KAH-*l'n-bairk* ZAY-*h'n?*
Can one see the Kahlenberg?

RITTER: Nein, den sehen Sie auf der Fahrt vom Flugplatz in die Stadt.
Nine, dain ZAY-*h'n Zee aouf dehr Fahrt fom* FLOOK-*plahts in dee Shtaht.*
No, you see it on your trip from the airport into the city.

SCHMITT: Das Flugzeug macht eine Wendung.
Dahs FLOOK-*tsoik mahkht* EYE-*neh* VENN-*doonk.*
The plane is making a turn.

RITTER: Ich glaube, wir landen.
Ikh GLAOU-*beh, veer* LAHN-*d'n.*
I think we are landing.

SCHMITT: Ist das die Hauptstadt?
Ist dahs dee HAOUPT-*shtaht?*
Is this the capital?

RITTER: Nein, das ist der Flughafen.
Nine, dahs ist dehr FLOOK-*hah-f'n.*
No, this is the airport.

Wir haben noch eine Stunde in die Stadt.
Veer HAH-*b'n nohkh* EYE-*neh* SHTOON-*deh in dee Shtaht.*
We have still one hour's drive to the city.

DER BEAMTE DER PASSKONTROLLE: Passrevision! Bitte,
*Dehr Beh-*AHM-*teh dehr* PAHSS-*kohn-trohl-leh:* PAHSS-*reh-vee-zee-ohn!* BIT-*teh,*
The immigration officer: Passport inspection! Please,

weisen Sie Ihre Pässe oder andere Reisepapiere vor!
VIGH-*z'n Zee* EE-*reh* PESS-*eh* OH-*d'r* AHN-*d'reh* RIGH-*zeh-pah-pee-reh fohr!*
show your passports or other travel-papers!

RITTER: **Ich bin Österreicher, hier sind meine Papiere.**
Ikh bin UH-*st'r-righ-kh'r, here zint* MIGH-*neh Pah-*PEE-*reh.*
I am Austrian, here are my papers.

PASSKONTROLLOR: **Danke! Gehen Sie jetzt zur Zollrevision hinüber!**
PAHSS-*kohn-trohl-lohr:* DAHN-*keh!* GAY-*h'n Zee yetst tsoor* TSOHLL-*reh-vee-
zee-ohn hin-*EW-*b'r!*
Passport inspector: Thanks! Now go over to the customs inspection.

SCHMITT: **Ich bin Amerikaner. Hier sind meine Papiere.**
*Ikh bin Ah-meh-ree-*KAH-*n'r. Here zint* MIGH-*neh Pah-*PEE-*reh.*
I am an American. Here are my papers.

BEAMTER: **Wie lange gedenken Sie in Österreich zu bleiben?**
*Beh-*AHM-*t'r: Vee* LAHN-*ggeh ggeh-*DEN-*k'n Zee in* UH-*st'r-righkh tsoo*
BLIGH-*b'n?*
Officer: How long do you intend to stay in Austria?

EXPRESSIONS TO REMEMBER:

Ich gedenke zu bleiben—"I intend to stay."
Ich gedenke ins Theater zu gehen—"I intend to go to the
theatre."

SCHMITT: **Höchstens zwei Wochen.**
HUHK-*st'ns tsvigh* VOKH-*'n.*
A maximum of two weeks.

BEAMTER: **Danke schön. Sie können durch die Sperre gehen.**
DAHN-*keh shuhn. Zee* KUH-*n'n doorkh dee* SHPERR-*eh* GAY-*h'n.*
Thanks. You may go through the gate.

(er stempelt den Pass)
(*air* SHTEM-*p'lt dain Pahss*)
(he stamps the passport)

SCHMITT: **Verzeihung, wo kann ich meine Reiseschecks einwechseln?**
*Fair-*TSIGH-*hoonk, voh kahn ikh* MIGH-*neh* RIGH-*zeh-sheks* INE-*vek-s'ln?*
Pardon me, where can I change my traveller's checks?

BEAMTER: **In der Halle ist eine Wechselstube der Nationalbank.**
In dehr HAHL-*leh ist* EYE-*neh* VEK-*s'l-shtoo-beh dehr Nah-tsee-oh-*NAHL-
bahnk.
In the lobby there is an exchange booth of the National Bank.

Der Beamte wird Ihnen den genauen Kurs angeben.
*Dehr Beh-*AHM-*teh veert* EE-*n'n dain ggeh-*NAOU-*n Koors* AHN-*ggeh-b'n.*
The teller will tell you the exact rate.

SCHMITT: **Danke bestens. Jetzt will ich nach meinem Gepäck sehen.**
DAHN-*keh* BEST'*ns. Yetst vill ikh nahkh* MIGH-*n'm Ggeh*-PECK ZAY-*h'n.*
Thanks very much. Now I shall look for my luggage.

(Draussen)
(DRAOUSS'*n*)
(Outside)

DER GEPÄCKTRÄGER: **Ihren Gepäckschein, bitte!**
Dehr Ggeh-PECK-*tray-g'r:*   EE-*r'n Ggeh*-PECK-*shine,* BIT-*teh!*
The Porter: Your baggage check, please!

SCHMITT: **Einen Moment, bitte! Ich muss ihn erst heraussuchen!**
EYE-*n'n Moh*-MENT, BIT-*teh! Ikh mooss een airst hair*-AOUS-*zookh'n!*
One moment, please! I must dig it out first!

Das scheint er zu sein! Die zwei braunen Koffer gehören mir!
Dahs shighnt air tsoo zine! Dee tsvigh BRAOU-*n'n* KOFF'*r ggeh*-HUH-*r'n
meer!*
This seems to be it! The two brown trunks belong to me!

GEPÄCKTRÄGER: **Einen Augenblick müssen Sie sich noch gedulden.**
EYE-*n'n* AOU-*g'n-blick* MEWSS'*n Zee zikh nohkh ggeh*-DOOL-*d'n.*
You must be patient for a moment.

Der Zollinspektor wird Sie gleich abfertigen.
Dehr TSOHLL-*in-shpeck-tohr veert Zee glighkh* AHPP-*fair-tee-g'n.*
The customs inspector will soon be through with you.

SCHMITT: **Was, schon wieder? Seit ich von New York weg bin,**
Vahss, shohn VEE-*d'r? Zite ikh fonn New York veck bin,*
What, again? Since I have been away from New York

muss ich nichts wie Koffer auf- und zumachen! Wie langweilig!
mooss ikh nikhts vee KOFF'*r* AOUF- *oont* TSOO-*mah-kh'n! Vee* LAHNK-
vigh-likh!
I've had to do nothing but open and close trunks. How boring!

(Zolluntersuchung.)
(TSOHLL-*oon-t'r-zoo-khoonk.*)
(Customs inspection.)

ZOLLINSPEKTOR: **Öffnen Sie diesen Koffer, bitte!**
TSOHLL-*in-shpeck-tohr:*   UHFF-*n'n Zee* DEEZ'*n* KOFF'*r,* BIT-*teh!*
Customs inspector: Open this trunk, please.

SCHMITT: **Das kann ich nicht tun!**
Dahs kahn ikh nikht toon!
I cannot do that!

ZOLLBEAMTER: **Warum nicht?**
*Vah-*ROOM *nikht?*
Why not?

SCHMITT: **Weil das nicht mein Koffer ist.**
Vile dahs nikht mine KOFF*'r ist.*
Because it is not my trunk.

Dieser da ist meiner, den mache ich Ihnen gern auf!
DEEZ*'r dah ist* MIGH*-n'r, dain* MAH*-kheh ikh* EE*-n'n gairn aouf!*
This one here is mine, I shall gladly open it for you!

ZOLLBEAMTER: **Oh, Verzeihung! Haben Sie Zigaretten, Alkohol oder Parfüm?**
*Oh, Fair-*TSIGH*-hoonk!* HAH*-b'n Zee Tsee-gah-*RETT*'n,* AHL*-koh-hohl* OH*-d'r Pahr-*FUHM*?*
Oh, pardon me! Have you cigarettes, alcohol or perfume?

SCHMITT: **Nur diese Zigarren hier und diese halbe**
Noor DEE*-zeh Tsee-*GAHRR*'n here oont* DEE*-zeh* HAHL*-beh*
Only these cigars here and this half

Flasche Weinbrand. Mir war im Flugzeug nicht gut.
FLAH*-sheh* VINE*-brahnt. Meer vahr im* FLOOK*-tsoik nikht goot.*
bottle of brandy. I did not feel well on the plane.

ZOLLBEAMTER: **Das ist in Ordnung. 50 Zigarren können Sie**
Dahs ist in OHRD*-noonk.* FEWNF*-tsikh Tsee-*GAHRR*'n* KUH*-n'n Zee*
That's all right. You can bring in 50 cigars

zollfrei einführen! Irgendwelche Geschenke?
TSOHLL*-frigh* INE*-few-r'n!* EER*-g'nt-vel-kheh Ggeh-*SHENK*-eh?*
duty free! Any gifts?

SCHMITT: **Ja, ein paar Kleinigkeiten, die ich meinen**
Yah, ine pahr KLIGH*-nikh-kight'n, dee ikh* MIGH*-n'n*
Yes, some small things I brought

Verwandten aus New York mitbringe.
*Fair-*VAHNT*'n aous New York* MIT*-bring-eh.*
along from New York for my relatives.

RITTER: **Da sind Sie ja, Herr Schmitt! Entschuldigen**
*Dah zint Zee yah, Herr Shmitt! Ent-*SHOOL*-dig'n*
Oh, there you are, Mr. Schmitt! Excuse

Sie meine Abwesenheit! Ich musste meine Frau anrufen.
Zee MIGH*-neh* AHPP*-vay-z'n-hight! Ikh* MOOSS*-teh* MIGH*-neh Frou* AHN*-roof'n.*
my absence! I had to call up my wife.

SCHMITT: **Das verstehe ich sehr gut. Sicher fahren Sie direkt nach Hause.**
Dahs fair-SHTAY-heh ikh zair goot. ZEE-*kh'r* FAH-*r'n Zee dee-*RECKT
nahkh HAOU-*zeh.*
I can understand that quite well. You are going home right away,
of course.

RITTER: **Ganz richtig. Und wo werden Sie absteigen?**
Gahnts RIKH-*tikh. Oont voh* VAIR-*d'n Zee* AHPP-*shtigh-g'n?*
Quite right. And where will you be staying?

Wohnen Sie bei Ihren Verwandten?
VOH-*n'n Zee by* EE-*r'n Fair-*VAHN-*t'n?*
Will you stay with your relatives?

SCHMITT: **Nein, das möchte ich nicht. Können Sie mir**
Nine, dahs MUHKH-*teh ikh nikht.* KUH-*n'n Zee meer*
No, I prefer not. Can you

ein gutes Hotel empfehlen?
ine GOO-*tess Hoh-*TELL *ehmp-*FAY-*l'n?*
recommend a good hotel?

RITTER: **Gewiss kann ich das. Ich rate Ihnen, im Hotel**
*Ggeh-*VISS *kahn ikh dahs. Ikh* RAH-*teh* EE-*n'n, im Hoh-*TELL
Certainly I can do that. I advise you to stop

"Brauner Hirsch" abzusteigen. Es liegt zentral,
*"*BRAOU-*n'r Heehrsh"* AHPP-*tsoo-shtigh-g'n. Ess leegt tsen-*TRAHL,
at the "Brauner Hirsch". It is centrally located,

hat allen Komfort der Neuzeit und hat fast nur amerikanische Gäste.
haht AHLL'*n Kom-*FOHR *dehr* NOY-*tsight oont haht fahst noor
ah-meh-ree-*KAH-*nee-sheh GGEST-*eh.*
has all modern conveniences and has almost exclusively American
guests.

SCHMITT: **Ich möchte aber lieber in einem typisch**
Ikh MUHKH-*teh* AH-*b'r* LEE-*b'r in* EYE-*n'm* TEW-*pish*
I would prefer to stay in a typical

österreichischen Hotel wohnen. Ich bin nicht nach Europa
UH-*st'r-righ-khish'n Hoh-*TELL *voh-*n'n. Ikh bin nikht nahkh* OY-ROH-
pah
Austrian hotel. I did not come to Europe

gekommen, um nur meine Landsleute zu treffen.
*ggeh-*KOMM'*n, oom noor* MIGH-*neh* LAHNTS-*loy-teh tsoo* TREFF'*n.*
to associate exclusively with my compatriots.

RITTER: **Dann sind Sie am besten im Hotel "Österreichischer Hof"**
Dahn zint Zee ahm BEST'*n im Hoh-*TELL *"*UH-*st'r-righ-khish'r Hohf"*
Then you would be best off at the "Austrian Court"

untergebracht. **Die Küche dort ist erstklassig.**
OON-*t'r-ggeh-brahkht. Dee* KEW-*kheh dohrt ist* AIRST-*klah-ssikh.*
hotel. The cuisine there is first class.

SCHMITT: **Ausgezeichnet! Ich fahre also zum**
AOUS-*ggeh-tsighkh-net! Ikh* FAH-*reh* AHL-*zoh tsoom*
Excellent! So I'm off to the

"Österreichischen Hof". Wann sehen wir einander?
"UH-*st'r-righ-khish'n Hohf". Vahn* ZAY-*h'n veer ine-*AHN-*d'r?*
"Austrian Court". When shall we see each other?

NOTE to Student: *Einander means* "each other." *Wir gehen miteinander*—"we go with each other", *sie sprechen durcheinander*—"they speak through each other" or "they speak at the same time." *Öl und Wasser können nicht zueinander kommen*—"Oil and water cannot come to each other" or "Oil and water cannot mix."

RITTER: **Geben Sie mir nur Zeit, nach Hause zu fahren**
GAY-*b'n Zee meer noor Tsight, nahkh* HAOU-*zeh tsoo* FAH-*r'n*
Just give me time to go home

und ein wenig nach dem Rechten zu sehen!
oont ine VAY-*nikh nahkh daim* REKH-*t'n tsoo* ZAY-*h'n!*
and look after things a bit.

Ich beabsichtige, Sie kurz nach Mittag in Ihrem
*Ikh beh-*AHP-*zikh-tee-ggeh, Zee koorts nahkh Mit-tahk in Ee-r'm*
I plan to pick you up at your

Hotel abzuholen, um Ihnen Wien zu zeigen.
HOH-*tell* AHP-*tsoo-hoh-l'n, oom* EE-*n'n Veen tsoo-*TSIGH-*g'n.*
hotel shortly past noon, to show you Vienna.

SCHMITT: **Abgemacht. Hier ist mein Taxi. Auf Wiedersehen, Herr Ritter!**
AHPP-*ggeh-mahkht. Here ist mine* TAHK-*see. Aouf* VEE-*d'r-zay-h'n, Herr*
RITT-*'r!*
Very well. Here is my taxi. Till we meet again, Mr. Ritter.

(Zum Chauffeur) Zum "Österreichischen Hof".
*(Tsoom Shoh-*FUHR) *Tsoom* "UH-*st'r-righ-khish'n Hohf".*
(To the driver) To the "Austrian Court".

(Im Hotel.)
*(Im Hoh-*TELL.)
(At the hotel.)

SCHMITT: **Guten Morgen.**
GOO-*t'n* MOHR-*g'n.*
Good morning.

DER ANGESTELLTE: **Meine Verehrung! Was wünscht der Herr?**
MIGH-*neh* Fair-AIR-*oonk! Vahss vewnsht dehr Herr?*
My respects! What does the gentleman wish?

NOTE: In Vienna, you will regularly be addressed by tradespeople and clerks with the introductory remark: *Meine Verehrung!* meaning literally "my veneration" or "homage". This is a throwback to the days of nobility, and the Viennese like to make anyone feel noble. It's very pleas-ant, but you will still pay for what you get, of course.

SCHMITT: **Ich möchte ein Vorderzimmer, womöglich mit Bad.**
Ikh MUHKH-*teh ine* FORHR-*d'r-tsimm'r, voh-*MUH*-glikh mit Baht.*
I'd like to have a front room, if possible with bath.

ANGESTELLTER: **Für wie lange ungefähr?**
Fewr vee LAHN-*ggeh* OON-*ggeh-fair?*
For approximately how long?

SCHMITT: **Ich werde höchstwahrscheinlich vierzehn Tage bleiben.**
Ikh VAIR-*deh huhkst-vahr-*SHINE*-likh* FEER-*tsain* TAH-*ggeh* BLIGH-*b'n.*
I shall most probably stay for two weeks.

ANGESTELLTER: **Ich weiss noch nicht, ob ich ein Zimmer nach vorn habe.**
Ikh vice nohkh nikht, ohp ikh ine TSIMM'*r nahkh fohrn* HAH-*beh.*
I do not know yet, whether I have a front room.

Aber eben ist im ersten Stock ein Doppelzimmer mit Bad
AH-*b'r* AY-*b'n ist im* AIR-*st'n Shtock ine* DOPP'*l-tsimm'r mit Baht*
But just now a double room with bath on the

freigeworden. Das ist Nr. 34 A.
FRIGH-*ggeh-vohr-d'n. Dahs ist* NOOM'*r* FEER-*oont-drigh-ssikh Ah.*
first floor has been vacated. This is Nr. 34 A.

SCHMITT: **Einen Augenblick, bitte! Wie teuer ist das Zimmer?**
EYE-*n'n* AOU-*g'n-block, *BIT-*teh! Vee* TOY'*r ist dahs* TSIMM'*r?*
One moment please! How expensive is this room?

ANGESTELLTER: **75 Schilling pro Tag.**
FEWNF-*oont-zeep-tsikh* SHILL-*ink proh Tahk.*
75 shillings a day.

SCHMITT: **Das lässt sich machen. Lassen Sie mein Gepäck aus dem Taxi holen**
Dahs lesst zikh MAH-*kh'n.* LAHSS'*n Zee mine Ggeh-*PECK *aous daim* TAHK-*see* HOH-*l'n*
That's reasonable. Have my luggage fetched from the taxi

und sofort auf mein Zimmer bringen! Ich möchte mich ein
oont zoh-FOHRT *aouf mine* TSIMM'*r* BRING'*n! Ikh* MUHKH-*teh mikh ine*
and brought up to my room immediately. I would like to freshen up a

bisschen herrichten und umziehen.
BISS-*kh'n* HAIR-*reekh-t'n oont* OOM-*tsee-h'n.*
bit and change clothes.

IDIOM: *Das lässt sich machen* means "that can be done"
in the same sense of our "all right". *Lassen Sie das Gepäck
holen.*—"Have the luggage brought in." *Sich herrichten*
means "to freshen up" or "to wash and comb the hair",
or, for the ladies, "to make up."

(Der Hausdiener bringt das Gepäck.)
(Dehr HAOUS-*dee-n'r brinkt dahs* Ggeh-PECK.*)*
(The porter brings the luggage.)

SCHMITT: **Wo ist mein Schirm?**
Voh ist mine Sheerm?
Where is my umbrella?

HAUSDIENER: **Verzeihung, ich habe keinen im Wagen gesehen!**
*Fair-*TSIGH-*hoonk, ikh* HAH-*beh* KIGH-*n'n im* VAH-*g'n ggeh-*ZAY-*h'n!*
Pardon me, I did not see one in the car!

SCHMITT: **Das ist eine schöne Geschichte! Jetzt**
Dahs ist EYE-*neh* SHUH-*neh Ggeh-*SHIKH-*teh! Yetst*
This is a fine how-do-you-do! Now

habe ich den Schirm im Flugzeug vergessen!
HAH-*beh ikh dain Sheerm im* FLOOK-*tsoik fair-*GGESS'*n!*
I've forgotten my umbrella in the plane!

HOTELANGESTELLTER: **Ich werde sofort das Fundbüro der**
*Hoh-*TELL-*ahn-gay-shtell-t'r: Ikh* VAIR-*deh zoh-*FOHRT *dahs* FOONT-*bew-roh
dehr*

Clerk: I shall have the lost-and-found department

Flugzeuggesellschaft anrufen lassen. Sie können
FLOOK-*tsoik-ggeh-zell-shahft* AHN-*roo-f'n* LAHSS'*n. Zee* KUH-*n'n*
of the airline called at once. You may

sicher sein, dass Sie Ihren Schirm zurückbekommen.
ZIKH'*r zine, dahss Zee* EE-*r'n Sheerm tsoo-*REWK-*beh-komm'n.*
rest assured that you'll get your umbrella back.

SCHMITT: **Ich will es hoffen. Jetzt schaffen Sie die Sachen auf mein
Zimmer!**
Ikh vill ess HOFF'*n. Yetst* SHAHFF'*n Zee dee* ZAH-*kh'n aouf mine*
TSIMM'*r!*
I hope so. Now take my things up to my room.

ANGESTELLTER: **(läutet die Tischglocke) Im Augenblick, mein Herr!**
*(LOY-*t't dee TISH-*glohk-eh) Im* AOU-*g'n-block, mine Herr!*
(ringing the counter bell) In a flash, sir!

Sie können den Anmeldeschein auch oben
Zee KUH-*n'n dain* AHN-*mel-deh-shine aoukh* OH-*b'n*
You may fill out your registration blank upstairs

ausfüllen und später herunterschicken.
AOUS-*fewll'n oont* SHPAIT'*r hair*-OON-*t'r shick'n.*
and send it down later.

NOTE to Globe-Trotters: The "Anmeldeschein" is a form which all hotel guests must fill out for the police in practically every European country. Don't let it frighten you—it's routine.

SCHMITT: Noch eines, bitte. Wo ist der Speisesaal?
Nohkh EYE-*ness,* BIT-*teh. Voh ist dehr* SHPIGH-*zeh-zahl?*
One more thing, please. Where is the dining room?

Ich bin ausgehungert wie ein Wolf. Ich habe
Ikh bin AOUS-*ggeh-hoon-g'rt vee ine Vohlf. Ikh* HAH-*beh*
I am hungry as a wolf. I have not

seit sechs Uhr früh nichts mehr zu mir genommen.
zite zeks Oor frew nikhts mair tsoo meer ggeh-NOMM'*n.*
had anything since six o'clock this morning.

ANGESTELLTER: Gleich hier, am Ende der Hotelhalle, links!
Glighkh here, ahm EN-*deh dehr Hoh*-TELL-*hahl-leh, links!*
Right here, at the end of the hotel lobby, to the left.

Sie können aber auch Ihr Essen aufs Zimmer bekommen!
Zee KUH-*n'n AH-b'r aoukh Eer* ESS'*n aoufs* TSIMM'*r beh*-KOMM'*n!*
However, you can have your meal sent up to your room!

SCHMITT: Nein, ich werde es noch ein paar Minuten aushalten.
Nine, ikh VAIR-*deh ess nohkh ine pahr Mee*-NOO-*t'n* AOUS-*hahl-t'n.*
No, I shall bear with it for a few more minutes.

Danke sehr!
DAHN-*keh zair!*
Thanks!

IDIOMS TO REMEMBER:

Ich gedenke zu	— "I intend to";
nach etwas sehen	— "to look after something", "to attend to";
ich muss nichts wie	— "I do nothing else but";
nach dem Rechten sehen	— "look after things";
zu sich nehmen	— "to take something", "to eat."

THINKING IN GERMAN
(Answers on page 264)

1. Was sehen Sie von einem Flugzeug aus?
2. Kommt der Aeroplan direkt in Wien an?
3. Welcher Fluss ist gleich neben dem Flugplatz zu sehen?
4. Was für Papiere muss man bei der Passkontrolle vorzeigen?
5. Wonach fragt der Zollinspektor?
6. Sind die Beamten freundlich zu Herrn Schmitt?
7. Warum sind Sie höflich?
8. Sind Zollbeamte immer höflich?
9. Wie lange gedenkt Herr Schmitt in Österreich zu bleiben?
10. Wo kann man Devisen wechseln?
11. Wird Herr Schmitt bei seinen Wiener Verwandten wohnen?
12. Warum will er nicht in das Hotel "Brauner Hirsch" gehen?
13. Fährt Herr Ritter mit seinem Freund in die Stadt?

14. Haben die beiden Herren eine Verabredung?

15. Was für ein Zimmer möchte Herr Schmitt im Hotel haben?

16. Wo isst man im Hotel?

17. Wer bringt das Gepäck auf die Zimmer?

18. Warum geht Herr Schmitt zuerst auf sein Zimmer?

19. Was hat er verloren oder vergessen?

20. Haben Sie schon einmal Ihren Schirm irgendwo stehen lassen?

21. Was geben Sie dem Gepäckträger?

22. In welchem Stock ist Herrn Schmitts Doppelzimmer?

23. Wann erwartet er Herrn Ritter?

24. Warum nehmen Sie Reiseschecks und nicht Banknoten, wenn Sie reisen?

25. Sind Reiseschecks im internationalen Verkehr praktischer als Banknoten?

ÜBUNG NR. 35

Der Einkauf
Dehr INE-*kaouf*
Shopping

RITTER: **Da bin ich und nicht einmal zu spät!**
*Dah bin ikh oont nikht ine-*MAHL *tsoo shpait!*
Here I am and not a bit too late!

Haben Sie schon zu Mittag gegessen?
HAH-*b'n Zee shohn tsoo* MIT-*tahk ggeh-*GGESS*'n?*
Have you already had lunch?

SCHMITT: **Das will ich glauben! Ich bin zu hungrig gewesen,**
Dahs vill ikh GLAOU-*b'n! Ikh bin tsoo* HOON-*grikh ggeh-*VAY-*z'n,*
I should say so! I was too hungry

um länger zu warten.
oom LENG-*'r tsoo* VAHR-*t'n.*
to wait any longer.

215

RITTER: **Und wie hat Ihnen das Essen gemundet?**
Oont vee haht EE-*n'n dahs* ESS'*n ggeh-*MOON-*det?*
And how did the food taste to you?

SCHMITT: **Sie haben nicht zu viel versprochen. Es war herrlich.**
Zee HAH-*b'n nikht tsoo feel fair-*SHPROH-*kh'n. Ess vahr* HERR-*likh.*
You did not promise too much. It was magnificent.

Die Küche ist wirklich prima hier.
Dee KEW-*kheh ist* VEERK-*likh* PREE-*mah here.*
The cuisine is really first class here.

RITTER: **Haben Sie vielleicht Palatschinken gegessen?**
HAH-*b'n Zee feel-*LIGHKHT *Pah-laht-*SHINK'*n ggeh-*GGESS'*n?*
Did you by any chance eat "Palatschinken"?

 CULINARY NOTE: *Palatschinken* are a kind of thin and fine pancake with jelly or cheese. It is a Viennese specialty, and, if you go to Vienna, order it by all means!

SCHMITT: **Ja, zwei Portionen sogar. Und vorher habe ich**
*Yah, tsvigh Pohrts-*YOH-*n'n zoh-*GAHR. *Oont* FOHR-*hair* HAH-*beh ikh*
Yes, two helpings too. And before that I had

eine Spezialität des Hauses gehabt, Hirn mit Nieren.
EYE-*neh Shpeh-tsee-ah-lee-*TAIT *dess* HAOU-*zess ggeh-*HAHPT, *Heern mit*
NEE'*r'n.*
a specialty of the house: Brains with kidneys.

Ich bin ganz begeistert.
*Ikh bin gahnts beh-*GUY-*st'rt.*
I am thoroughly delighted.

RITTER: **Wollen wir jetzt gehen?**
VOLL'*n veer yetst* GAY-*h'n?*
Shall we go now?

SCHMITT: **Sicher. Wo wollen Sie mich hinführen?**
ZEE-*kh'r. Voh* VOLL'*n Zee mikh* HIN-*few-r'n?*
Certainly. Where do you want to take me?

RITTER: **Ich denke, wir gehen ins Stadtzentrum;**
Ikh DEN-*keh, veer* GAY-*h'n ince* SHTAHT-*tsain-troom;*
I think that we should go to the center of the town;

das ist ganz in der Nähe.
dahs ist gahnts in dehr NAY-*heh.*
it is very close by.

SCHMITT: **Vor allem muss ich mir einen Hut kaufen.**
Fohr AHL-*lem mooss ikh meer* EYE-*n'n Hoot* KAOU-*f'n.*
First of all I must buy myself a hat.

Meinen Schirm habe ich irgendwo verloren.
MIGH-*n'n Sheerm* HAH-*beh ikh* EER-*ggent-voh fair-*LOH-*r'n.*
I have lost my umbrella somewhere.

Ausserdem ist jemand im Flugzeug während der
AOUSS'*r-daim ist* YEH-*mahnt im* FLOOK-*tsoik* VAY-*r'nd dehr*
Besides somebody in the plane was sitting on my hat

ganzen Reise auf dem Hut gesessen.
GAHN-*ts'n* RIGH-*zeh aouf daim Hoot ggeh-*ZESS'*n.*
during the whole trip.

Er sieht aus wie ein Pfannkuchen.
Air zeet aous vee ine PFAHN-*koo-kh'n.*
It looks like a pancake.

RITTER: **Gut, brechen wir auf!**
Goot, BREKH'*n veer aouf!*
Good, let's get on our way.

SCHMITT: **(auf der Strasse) Wo kommen nur die vielen Menschen her?**
(aouf dehr SHTRAH-*sseh) Voh* KOMM'*n noor dee* FEE-*l'n* MEN-*sh'n hair?*
(in the street) Where do all these people come from?

Der Verkehr hier ist fast so stark wie in New York.
*Dehr Fair-*KAIR *here ist fahst zoh shtahrk vee in New York.*
The traffic here is almost as heavy as in New York.

RITTER: **Wir kommen nun zum Stephansplatz.**
Veer KOMM'*n noon tsoom* SHTEH-*fahns-plahts.*
We are now coming to St. Stephan's Square.

Das ist der Mittelpunkt Wiens. Da sind wir.
Dahs ist dehr MITT'*l-poonkt Veens. Dah zint veer.*
This is the center of Vienna. Here we are.

SCHMITT: **Das ist wohl die berühmte Stephanskirche,**
*Dahs ist vohl dee beh-*REWM-*teh* SHTEH-*fahns-keer-kheh,*
That must be the famous Stephan's church

von der meine Mutter so oft erzählt hat?
fonn dehr MIGH-*neh* MOOTT'*r zoh offt air-*TSAILT *haht?*
my mother spoke about so often?

Sie hat gesagt, dass man seit hunderten von Jahren
*Zee haht ggeh-*ZAHKT, *dahss mahn zite* HOON-*d'r-t'n fonn* YAH-*r'n*
She said that they have been making repairs on this church for

an dieser Kirche Ausbesserungen vornimmt.
ahn DEEZ'*r* KEER-*kheh* AOUS-*bess-'roon-g'n* FOHR-*nimmt.*
hundreds of years.

RITTER: Da hat Ihre Mutter ganz recht gehabt.
Dah haht EE-*reh* MOOTT'*r gahnts rekht ggeh-*HAHPT.
Your mother was quite right.

Sehen Sie das Gerüst am linken Turm?
ZAY-*h'n Zee dahs Ggeh-*REWST *ahm* LINK'*n Toorm?*
Do you see the scaffolding on the left tower?

Man baut wieder um!—Und nun kommen wir in die
Mahn baout VEED'*r oom!—Oont noon* KOMM'*n veer in dee*
They are rebuilding!—And now we are coming to

Kärntnerstrasse, die elegante
KAIRNT-*n'r-shtrah-sseh, dee ele-*GAHN-*teh*
Kärntner Street, the elegant

Geschäftsstrasse in der Inneren Stadt.
*Ggeh-*SHEFTS-*shtrah-sseh in dehr* INN-*ren Shtaht.*
business street in the inner city.

SCHMITT: Hier kann ich wohl meine Einkäufe besorgen?
Here kahn ikh vohl MIGH-*neh* INE-*koy-feh beh-*ZOHR-*g'n?*
Can I make my purchases here?

RITTER: Jawohl, hier ist das Hutgeschäft Habig.
*Yah-*VOHL, *here ist dahs* HOOT-*ggeh-shefft* HAH-*bikh.*
Yes, here is the Habig hat store.

Hier bekommen Sie das Modernste in Herrenhüten.
*Here beh-*KOMM'*n Zee dahs Moh-*DAIRN-*steh in* HERR'*n-hew-t'n.*
Here you can get the latest in gentlemen's hats.

Gehen wir hinein!
GAY-*h'n veer hin-*INE!
Let's go in!

VERKÄUFER: Was kann ich dienen?
*Fair-*KOY-*f'r: Vahss kahn ikh* DEE-*n'n?*
SALESMAN: What may I show you?

SCHMITT: Ich brauche einen Hut.
Ikh BRAOU-*kheh* EYE-*n'n Hoot.*
I need a hat.

VERKÄUFER: Ich kann Ihnen einen grauen Borsalino empfehlen.
Ikh kahn EE-*n'n* EYE-*n'n* GRAOU'*n Bohr-zah-*LEE-*noh emp-*FAY-*l'n.*
I can recommend you a gray Borsalino.

Er ist federleicht und besonders haltbar.
Air ist FAY-*d'r-lighkht oont beh-*ZONN-*d'rs* HAHLT-*bahr.*
It is featherweight and particularly durable.

RITTER: **Vielleicht legen Sie dem Herrn Verschiedenes vor.**
*Feel-*LIGHKHT LAY-*g'n Zee daim Herrn Fair-*SHEE-*deh-ness fohr.*
Perhaps you can show the gentleman several.

VERKÄUFER: **Aber gern! Welche Grösse?**
AH-*b'r gairn!* VEL-*kheh* GRUH-*sseh?*
Gladly! What size?

SCHMITT: **Ich weiss nicht recht, in New York habe ich 7½ gehabt.**
Ikh vice nikht rekht, in New York HAH-*beh ikh* ZEE-*b'n ine-*HAHLP
*ggeh-*HAHPT.
I am not sure, in New York I have had Nr. 7½.

Aber hier rechnen Sie ja anders!
AH-*b'r here* REKH-*n'n Zee yah* AHN-*d'rs!*
However here you measure it differently!

VERKÄUFER: **Wenn Sie gestatten, werde ich Ihren Kopf messen.**
*Venn Zee ggeh-*SHTAHT-*t'n vair-deh ikh* EE-*r'n Koppf* MESS'*n.*
If you will permit me, I'll take your head measure.

So—Sie haben Grösse 56.
Zoh—Zee HAH-*b'n* GRUH-*sseh* ZEKS-*oont-fewnf-tsikh.*
There—you are size 56.

Wie gefällt Ihnen diese Marke?
*Vee ggeh-*FELLT EE-*n'n* DEE-*zeh* MAHR-*keh?*
How do you like this brand?

SCHMITT: **Gut, aber wie ist die Qualität?**
Goot, AH-*b'r vee ist dee Kwah-lee-*TAIT?
Good, but how is the quality?

VERKÄUFER: **Allererste Qualität, dafür kann ich garantieren.**
*Ahll'r-*AIR-*steh Kwah-lee-*TAIT, *dah-*FEWR *kahn ikh gah-rahn-*TEE-*r'n.*
First class quality, I can guarantee that.

Und er kostet nur 150 Schilling.
Oont air KOSS-*tet noor Hoon-d'rt-*FEWNF-*tsikh* SHILL-*ink.*
Furthermore, it costs only 150 shillings.

 NOTE on the Superlative: The prefix *aller-* means something like our "super". *Der Allerbeste* is "the very best", *der Allererste* is "the very first", *der Allerliebste* is "the most beloved."

SCHMITT: **Was meinen Sie, Herr Ritter, wie steht mir der Hut?**
Vahss MIGH-n'n Zee, Herr RITT'r, vee shtait meer dehr Hoot?
What do you think, Mr. Ritter, how does the hat fit me?

NOTE on Fashions: *Der Hut steht mir*—"The hat suits me", *die Farbe steht Ihnen gut*—"this color suits you well".

RITTER: **Ausgezeichnet. Ich kann Ihnen nur dazu raten.**
AOUS-ggeh-TSIGHKH-net. Ikh kahn EE-n'n noor dah-TSOO RAH-t'n.
Excellent. I can only advise you to (take) it.

SCHMITT: **Also gut. Ich nehme ihn. Sie brauchen ihn nicht**
AHL-zoh goot. Ikh NAY-meh een. Zee BRAOU-kh'n een nikht
Good then. I'll take it. You don't need

einzupacken, ich behalte ihn gleich auf.
INE-tsoo-pah-k'n, ikh beh-HAHL-teh een glighkh aouf.
to wrap it, I shall put it on immediately.

Werfen Sie den alten Hut weg!
VAIR-f'n Zee dain AHL-t'n Hoot vek!
Throw the old hat away!

VERKÄUFER: **Danke sehr. Hier ist Ihr Wechselgeld.**
DAHN-keh zair. Here ist Eer VEK-s'l-ggelt.
Thanks very much. Here is your change.

Bitte beehren Sie uns bald wieder!
BIT-teh beh-AIR'n Zee oons bahlt VEE-d'r!
Please, honor us again soon!

(Auf der Strasse.)
(Aouf dehr SHTRAH-sseh.)
(In the street).

RITTER: **Wir nähern uns jetzt der Ringstrasse.**
Veer NAY-h'rn oons yetst dehr RINK-shtrah-sseh.
Now, we are approaching Ringstrasse.

Da rechts sehen Sie schon das Opernhaus.
Dah raikhts ZAY-h'n Zee shohn dahs OH-p'rn-haous.
Here on the right you can already see the Opera House.

SCHMITT: **Ja, von der Oper hat meine Mutter immer geschwärmt.**
Yah, fonn dehr OH-*p'r haht* MIGH-*neh* MOOTT'*r* IMM'*r ggeh*-SHVAIRMT.
Yes, my mother always raved about the opera.

Sir erzählte uns oft von den Zeiten, da sie hier Caruso,
*Zee air-*TSAIL-*teh oons offt fonn dain* TSIGH-*t'n, dah zee here Caruso,*
She often told us about the times when she heard Caruso,

Adelina Patti und andere Grössen zum ersten Male gehört hat.
*Ah-deh-*LEE-*nah* PAHT-*tee oont* AHN-*d'reh* GRUHSS'*n tsoom* AIR-*st'n* MAH-
*leh ggeh-*HUHRT *haht.*
Adelina Patti and other celebrities here for the first time.

> **NOTE:** *Eine Grösse,* literally "a greatness", means a star or a celebrity; it could apply to G. B. Shaw, Eisenhower, or Babe Ruth.

RITTER: **So, hier sind wir auf der Ringstrasse.**
Zoh, here zint veer aouf dehr RINK-*shtrah-sseh.*
Well, here we are now on the Ringstrasse.

Sie ist ein breiter Boulevard, der im Kreise
Zee ist ine BRIGH-*t'r Bool-*VAHR, *dehr im* KRIGH-*zeh*
It is a wide boulevard, which goes around

um die Innere Stadt führt. Jeder Teil hat seinen
oom dee INN-*'reh Shtaht fewrt.* YAY-*d'r Tile haht* ZIGH-*n'n*
the inner city in a circle. Each part has its

eigenen Namen. Rechts von hier ist der Opernring,
EYE-*ggeh-n'n* NAH-*m'n. Rekhts fonn here ist dehr* OH-*p'rn-rink,*
own name. To our right is the Opera Ring,

links der Kärntnerring.
links dehr KAIRNT-*n'r-rink.*
to our left the Kärntner Ring.

SCHMITT: **Hier müssen doch die bekannten internationalen**
Here MEWSS'*n dohkh dee beh-*KAHN-*t'n* IN-*ter-nahts-yoh-nah-l'n*
The well-known international hotels must be

Hotels liegen, das Grand Hotel, das Hotel Bristol,
*Hoh-*TELLS *lee-g'n, dahs Grahnt Hoh-*TELL, *dahs Hoh-*TELL *Bristol,*
located here, the Grand Hotel, the Hotel Bristol,

das Imperial und andere?
*dahs Im-pehr-*YAHL *oont* AHN-*d'reh?*
the Imperial and others?

RITTER: **Ganz richtig. Und hier, hinter der Oper, ist**
Gahnts RIKH-*tikh. Oont here,* HINT'r *dehr* OH-*p'r, ist*
That's right. And here, behind the opera, is

das weltberühmte Hotel Sacher mit der famosen Küche.
dahs VELT-*beh-rewm-teh* Hoh-TELL *Zah-kh'r mit dehr fah-*MOH-*z'n* KEW-
kheh.
the world famed Hotel Sacher with its famous cuisine.

Haben Sie noch nie von der Sachertorte gehört?
HAH-*b'n Zee nohkk nee fonn dehr* ZAH-*kh'r-tohr-teh ggeh-*HUHRT?
Haven't you ever heard of the "Sacher cake"?

SCHMITT: **Und ob! Wir haben in New York in der 72.**
Oont opp! Veer HAH-*b'n in New York in dehr* TSVIGH-*oont-zeep-tsik-st'n*
Most certainly! We have a pastry shop in New York on West

Strasse West eine Konditorei, wo man eine
SHTRAH-*sseh Vest* EYE-*neh Kohn-dee-toh-*RYE, *voh mahn* EYE-*neh*
72nd street, where one can get a

gute Sachertorte mit Sahne bekommt.
GOO-*teh* ZAH-*kh'r-tohr-teh mit* ZAH-*neh beh-*KOMMT.
good Sacher cake with whipped cream.

 IDIOM: The above expression *und ob* is what you might call high class slang. It has the sense of "And how!" or "You bet!", but is perfectly proper.

Ich möchte gerne Ansichtskarten kaufen.
Ikh MUHKH-*teh* GAIR-*neh* AHN-*zikhts-kahr-t'n* KAOU-*f'n.*
I'd like to buy some picture post-cards.

Kann ich die hier irgendwo finden?
Kahn ikh dee here EER-*ggent-voh* FINN-*d'n?*
Can I find them here somewhere?

RITTER: **Aber gewiss, hier in dem Zeitungskiosk am**
AH-*b'r ggeh-*VISS, *here in daim* TSIGH-*toonks-k'yosk ahm*
Of course, here at the newsstand at the

Strassenübergang hat man die schönsten Künstlerkarten.
SHTRAH-*ss'n-ew-b'r-gahnk haht mahn dee* SHUHN-*st'n* KEWN-*stl'r-kahr-t'n.*
street-crossing they have the most beautiful art cards.

RITTER: **Es ist schon fünf Uhr vorbei!**
*Ess ist shohn fewnf Oor fohr-*BIGH!
It is already past five!

SCHMITT: **Ich hätte nie gedacht, dass es schon so spät sei!**
Ikh HET-*teh nee ggeh-*DAHKHT, *dahss ess shohn zoh shpait zigh!*
I would never have thought that it were so late!

NOTE ON SUBJUNCTIVE: The subjunctive (Konjunk-
tiv) is used far more frequently in German than in English
to express uncertainty, possibility, desire, wish or purpose.
Ex: *So sei es!*—"So be it!"; *Es ist möglich, dass es morgen
regne.*—"It is possible that it rain tomorrow." Furthermore,
it must appear in indirect speech. Ex: *Er sagt, er habe kein Geld.*—"He
says he has no money."

The personal endings for all tenses of the subjunctive are: *-e, -est, -en*, as
follows:

Take the subjunctive of *haben*, for instance:

ich, (er,) (sie,) (es)	*habe*
Du	*habest*
wir, (sie,) (Sie)	*haben*

However, the subjunctive of *sein* is irregular:

ich, (er,) (sie,) (es)	*sei*
Du	*seist*
wir, (sie,) (Sie)	*seien*

There is also a *past* subjunctive. Ex: *Ich wünschte, er wäre dort.*—"I wished
he were there."

You can often recognize the past subjunctive by the *Umlaut* of the vowels
a, o, u.

Ex: Indicative: *ich, (er,) (sie,) (es) hatte, war, wurde, zog, schrieb, etc.*
    Subjunctive: *ich, (er,) (sie,) (es) hätte, wäre, würde, zöge, schriebe, etc.*

RITTER: **Wenn es Ihnen recht ist, nehmen wir jetzt ein**
Venn ess EE-*n'n rekht ist,* NAY-*m'n veer yetst ine*
If you agree, we can take a

Taxi und machen eine kleine Rundfahrt.
TAHK-*see oont* MAH-*kh'n* EYE-*neh* KLIGH-*neh* ROONT-*fahrt.*
taxi now and make a small tour.

Ich möchte Ihnen gerne die wichtigsten Gebäude zeigen.
Ikh MUHKH-*teh* EE-*n'n* GAIR-*neh dee* VEEKH-*tik-st'n Ggeh-*BOY-*deh*
TSIGH-*g'n.*
I would like to show you the most important buildings.

SCHMITT: **Aber gewiss, Herr Ritter! Ich habe nichts vor.**
AH-*b'r ggeh-*VISS, *Herr* RITT'*r! Ikh* HAH-*beh nikhts fohr.*
Certainly, Mr. Ritter! I have no plans.

Hier hält gerade ein Taxi. Das können wir gleich nehmen.
Here hellt ggeh-RAH-deh ine TAHK-see. Dahs KUH-n'n veer glighkh NAY-m'n.
Here is a taxi stopping now. We can take it right away.

EXPRESSION TO REMEMBER: *Ich habe etwas vor*—"I have something before me" that means "I have something on my mind to do" or "I intend to do something." *Ich habe heute abend nichts Besonderes vor.*—"I have no definite plans for tonight."

RITTER: **Chauffeur, sind Sie frei?**
Shoh-FUHR, zint Zee frigh?
Driver, are you free?

CHAUFFEUR: **Steigen Sie nur ein, meine Herren! Wo soll's denn hingehen?**
Shoh-FUHR: SHTIGH-g'n Zee noor ine, MIGH-neh HERR'n! Voh zolls denn HIN-gay-h'n?
DRIVER: Get right in, gentlemen! Where do you want to go?

RITTER: **Ich möchte meinem Gast die Sehenswürdigkeiten**
Ikh MUHKH-teh MIGH-n'm Gahst dee ZAY-h'ns-vewr-dikh-kigh-t'n
I would like to show my guest the sights

der Stadt zeigen. Kann man Sie pro Stunde mieten?
dehr Shtaht TSIGH-g'n. Kahn mahn Zee proh SHTOON-deh MEE-t'n?
of the town. Can one hire you by the hour?

CHAUFFEUR: **Natürlich kann man das! Sagen wir, fünfzig**
Nah-TEWR-likh kahn mahn dahs! ZAH-g'n veer, FEWNF-tsikh
Of course you can! Let's say fifty

Schilling die Stunde!
SHILL-ink dee SHTOON-deh!
shillings an hour!

RITTER: **Das ist viel zu hoch! Ich bin kein Fremder,**
Dahs ist feel tsoo hohkh! Ikh bin kine FREMM-d'r,
This is much too high! I am not a foreigner,

mich brauchen Sie nicht zu rupfen!
mikh BRAOU-kh'n Zee nikht tsoo ROOP-f'n!
you need not fleece me!

CAUTION! "Don't be fleeced!"—*Lassen Sie sich nicht rupfen!* The word *rupfen* literally means "to pluck" as a chicken, but is also used as "to fleece" or "to swindle."

CHAUFFEUR: **Wir werden schon keinen Richter brauchen!**
Veer VAIR-*d'n shohn* KIGH-*n'n* RIKH-*t'r* BRAOU-*kh'n!*
We won't need a judge!

Sagen wir also vierzig Schilling,
ZAH-*g'n veer* AHL-*zoh* FEER-*tsikh* SHILL-*ink,*
Let's say then 40 shillings,

das ist mein letztes Wort!
dahs ist mine LETS-*tess Vohrt!*
that's my last word!

RITTER: **Abgemacht! Fahren Sie also den Ring entlang, in der**
AHP-*ggeh-mahkht!* FAH-*r'n Zee* AHL-*zoh dain Rink ent-*LAHNK, *in dehr*
It's a deal! Drive along the Ring then, in the

Richtung zum Schottentor! Und nicht zu schnell, bitte!
RIKH-*toonk tsoom* SHOTT'*n-tohr! Oont nikht tsoo shnell,* BIT-*teh!*
direction of the Schottentor! And not too fast, please!

CHAUFFEUR: **Ich verstehe schon! Sie wollen sozusagen**
*Ikh fair-*SHTEH-*heh shohn! Zee* VOLL'*n* ZOH-*tsoo-zah-g'n*
I understand! You want to act

den Fremdenführer machen.
dain FREMM-*d'n-few-r'r* MAH-*kh'n.*
as the tourist-guide, so to speak.

THINKING IN GERMAN

(Answers on page 265)

1. Wo beginnen die Herren ihren Spaziergang?
2. Wie ist der Strassenverkehr in Wien?
3. Wie heisst der Platz im Zentrum der Stadt?
4. In welchem Hutgeschäft kauft Herr Schmitt ein?
5. Welche Marke empfiehlt der Verkäufer?
6. Welche Grösse hat der Käufer?
7. Gefällt Herrn Schmitt die Qualität der Ware?
8. Packt der Verkäufer den Hut für Herrn Schmitt ein?
9. Hat Herr Schmitt schon von der Wiener Oper gehört?
10. Wo befinden sich die grossen internationalen Hotels?
11. Was kauft Herr Schmitt noch ein?
12. Wohin begibt er sich dann?
13. An welchem Gebäuden kommt er vorbei?
14. Geht er am Abend in ein Theater?
15. Wo wird er den Abend verbringen?
16. Nimmt Herr Schmitt Herrn Ritters Einladung an?
17. Wann werden die Herren einander wiedersehen?
18. Ist die Ringstrasse eine gerade Strasse?
19. Welches Hotel ist wegen seiner Küche berühmt?
20. Welche Spezialität serviert man in diesem Hotel?
21. Kennen Sie die Sachertorte?
22. Bekommt man sie in New York?

ÜBUNG NR. 36

Hier rechts, meine Herrschaften .....
Here rekhts, MIGH-*neh* HERR-*shahf-ten* .....
On your right, ladies and gentlemen .....

RITTER: **Hier rechts haben wir noch einmal das Opernhaus.**
Here rekhts HAH-*b'n veer nohkh* INE-*mahl dahs* OH-*p'rn-haous.*
Here to the right we have the opera house again.

Jetzt kommen wir zu dem interessantesten Teil
Yetst KOMM'*n veer tsoo daim int'-reh-*SAHN-*test'n Tile*
Now we come to the most interesting part

unserer Fahrt. Hier rechts sehen Sie das Goethe-Denkmal,
OON-*z'r'r Fahrt. Here rekhts* ZAY-*h'n Zee dahs* GUH-*teh Denk-mahl,*
of our trip. To the right you can see the Goethe memorial,

auf der anderen Seite steht das Schiller-Monument.
aouf dehr AHN-*d'r'n* ZIGH-*teh shtait dahs* SHILL'*r-Moh-noo-ment.*
over there on the other side stands the Schiller monument.

Die beiden Dichterfürsten sind nur durch die Ringstrasse getrennt.
Dee BIGH-*d'n* DIKH-*t'r-fewr-st'n zint noor doorkh dee* RINK-*shtrah-sseh*
*gay-*TRENT.
The two princes of poetry are separated only by the Ringstrasse.

Auf der rechten Seite beginnt jetzt der Burggarten.
Aouf dehr REKH-*t'n* ZIGH-*teh beh*-GGINT *yetst dehr* BOORK-*gahr-t'n.*
To our right the Burggarten is beginning.

SCHMITT: **Können Sie mir sagen, wie diese beiden grossen Gebäude,**
KUH-*n'n Zee meer* ZAH-*g'n, vee* DEE-*zeh* BIGH-*d'n* GROHSS*'n Ggeh*-BOY-*deh*,
Can you tell me what these two big buildings

mit dem Denkmal dazwischen, heissen?
mit daim DENK-*mahl dah*-TSVISH*'n,* HIGH-*ss'n?*
with the monument between them are called?

RITTER: **Das sind die beiden Staats-Museen, zuerst das**
Dahs zint dee BIGH-*d'n* SHTAHTS-*moo-zay-ehn, tsoo*-AIRST *dahs*
These are the two National Museums, first the

kunsthistorische und dann das naturhistorische Museum.
KOONST-*hiss-toh-rish-eh oont dahn dahs nah*-TOOR-*hiss-toh-rish-eh Moo*-
ZAY-*oom.*
Museum of the History of Art and then the Natural History Museum.

Das Monument in der Mitte stellt die
Dahs Moh-noo-MENT *in dehr* MITT-*eh shtellt dee*
The monument in the middle represents the

Kaiserin Maria Theresia mit ihren Generälen und Ratgebern vor.
KIGH-*z'r-in Mah*-REE-*ah Teh*-RAY-*zee-ah mit* EE-*r'n Ggeh-nay*-RAY-*l'n oont*
RAHT-*ggeh-b'rn fohr.*
Empress Maria Theresa with her generals and counsellors.

 NOTE to Student: Pay particular attention to the new tense used throughout this chapter—the imperfect. It is known in German as *das Imperfekt* or *die Mitvergangenheit.* It corresponds to the English imperfect but can also convey the sense of "used to". Ex: *Ich studierte*—"I was studying" or "I used to study."

Some verbs, called "weak verbs," form the imperfect in the following manner, *Leben—ich, (er), (sie), (es) lebte, du lebtest, wir, (sie), (Sie) lebten.*

Other verbs, called "strong verbs," however form their imperfect differently as you can see in the examples blow:

PRESENT	IMPERFECT
Ich bin	Ich war
Ich komme	Ich kam
Ich sehe	Ich sah
Ich sitze	Ich sass
Ich stehe	Ich stand
Ich gebe	Ich gab

etc. etc.

SCHMITT: **Maria Theresia? Sie war doch die Mutter des**
*Mah-*REE*-ah Teh-*RAY*-zee-ah? Zee vahr dohkh dee* MOOTT*'r dess*
Maria Teresa? Was she not the mother of the

volkstümlichsten österreichischen Kaisers Josef,
FOLKS*-tewm-likh-st'n* UH*-st'r-righ-khish'n* KIGH*-z'rs* YOH*-zeff,*
most popular Austrian Emperor, Joseph,

über den so viele Geschichten erzählt werden.
EW*-b'r dain zoh* FEE*-leh Ggeh-*SHIKH*-t'n air-*TSAILT VAIR*-d'n.*
about whom so many stories are told?

Mutter sprach stundenlang von ihm.
MOOTT*'r shprahkh* SHTOON*-d'n-lahnk fonn eem.*
Mother talked for hours about him.

RITTER: **Erzählte Ihre Mutter auch die Geschichte vom**
*Air-*TSAIL*-teh* EE*-reh* MOOTT*'r aoukh dee Ggeh-*SHIKH*-teh fom*
Did your mother also tell the story of

Kaiser Josef und dem Bahnwärter?
KIGH*-z'r* YOH*-zeff oont dehm* BAHN*-vair-t'r?*
Emperor Joseph and the railroad watchman?

SCHMITT: **Ich glaube, ja.**
Ikh GLAOU*-beh, yah.*
I think she did.

RITTER: **Jetzt habe ich Sie hereingelegt,**
Yetst HAH*-beh ikh Zee hair-*INE*-ggeh-laigt,*
Now I have fooled you,

zu Kaiser Josefs Zeiten gab es noch keine Bahn
tsoo KIGH*-z'r* YOH*-seffs* TSIGH*-t'n gahp ess nohkh* KIGH*-neh Bahn*
for at the time of Emperor Joseph there was not yet a railroad

und daher auch keinen Bahnwärter!
*oont dah-*HAIR *aoukh* KIGH*-n'n* BAHN*-vair-t'r!*
and therefore no railroad watchman!

 NOTE to Practical Jokers: *Jemand hereinlegen*—"to fool somebody". If you set a trap for somebody and you catch him, *Sie legen ihn herein.*

SCHMITT: **Das muss ich mir merken.**
Dahs mooss ikh meer MAIR*-k'n.*
I must remember that one.

RITTER: **Das grosse Tor hier zu unserer Rechten, mit den vielen Säulen,**
Dahs GROH-*sseh Tohr here tsoo* ONN-*z'r'r* REKH-*t'n, mit dain* FEE-*l'n* ZOY-*l'n,*
The big gate to our right, with the many columns,

ist das Burgtor, der Eingang zur Hofburg.
ist dahs BOORK-*tohr, dehr* INE-*gahnk tsoor* HOHF-*boork.*
is the castle gate, the entrance to the Imperial Palace.

Die Habsburger wohnten und regierten darin mehrere Jahrhunderte lang.
Dee HAHPS-*boor-g'r* VOHN-*t'n oont ray-*GGEER-*t'n dah-*RIN MEH-*reh-reh Yahr-*HOON-*d'r-teh lahnk.*
The Hapsburgs lived and governed in it for several centuries.

SCHMITT: **Das Gebäude dort im Vordergrund muss das**
*Dahs Ggeh-*BOY-*deh dohrt im* FOR-*d'r-groont mooss dahs*
The building there in the foreground must be

österreichische Parlament sein. Wir haben zuhause ein Bild davon!
UH-*st'r-righ-khish-eh Pahr-lah-*MENT *zine. Veer* HAH-*b'n tsoo-*HAOU-*zeh ine Bilt dah-*FONN!
the Austrian parliament. We have a picture of it at home!

RITTER: **Stimmt. Und nun fahren wir links am Rathaus und**
Shtimt. Oont noon FAH-*r'n veer links ahm* RAHT-*haous oont*
That's right. And now we are driving past the City Hall on the left and

rechts am Burgtheater vorbei.
rekhts ahm BOORK-*teh-ah-t'r fohr-*BIGH.
the Burg Theatre on the right.

SCHMITT: **Jetzt kann es nicht mehr weit zur Universität sein.**
*Yetst kahn ess nikht mair vite tsoor Oo-nee-vair-zee-*TAIT *zine.*
Now we cannot be very far from the University.

RITTER: **Hier sind wir schon!**
Here zint veer shohn!
Here we are already!

Und da sind wir beim Schottentor!
Oont dah zint veer bime SHOTT'*n-tohr!*
And here we are at the Schottentor!

SCHMITT: **Ja, das kenne ich, da bin ich vorbeigekommen,**
Yah, dahs KEN-*neh ikh, dah bin ikh fohr-*BIGH-*ggeh-komm'n,*
Yes, I know it, I passed by there,

als ich von der Endstation der Fluggesellschaft kam.
ahls ikh fonn dehr ENT-*stah-tsee-ohn dehr* FLOOK-*ggeh-zell-shahft kahm.*
when I came from the Airline Terminal.

RITTER: **Und jetzt sehen Sie hier die Votivkirche.**
Oont yetst ZAY-*h'n Zee here dee Voh-*TEEF-*keer-kheh.*
And now you see here the Votive Church.

SCHMITT: **Warum heisst sie so?**
*Vah-*ROOM *highst zee zoh?*
Why is it called that?

RITTER: **Das ist eine schöne Geschichte. Kaiser Franz Josef**
Dahs ist EYE-*neh* SHUH-*neh Ggeh-*SHIKH-*teh.* KIGH-*z'r Frahnts* YOH-*zeff*
It is a nice story. Emperor Franz Joseph

wurde hier einst von einem Attentäter angefallen,
VOOR-*deh here* INE*'st fonn* EYE-*n'm* AH-*t'n-tay-t'r* AHN-*ggeh-fahll'n,*
was once attacked here by an assassin,

der ihn erdolchen wollte. Der Dolch blieb im
*dehr een air-*DOLL-*kh'n* VOLL-*teh. Dehr Dollkh bleep im*
who tried to stab him. The dagger got stuck

Uniformkragen des Kaisers stecken.
OO-*nee-form-krah-g'n dess* KIGH-*z'rs* SHTEKK-*'n.*
in the collar of the emperor's uniform.

Zum Dank für die wunderbare Rettung liess
Tsoom Dahnk fewr dee VOON-*d'r-bah-reh* RETT-*oonk leess*
Out of gratitude for this miraculous escape,

der Herrscher diese schöne Kirche bauen.
dehr HERR-*sh'r* DEE-*zeh* SHUH-*neh* KEER-*kheh* BAOU-*'n.*
the ruler had this beautiful church built.

Jetzt fahren wir die Währingerstrasse hinauf zum Gürtel.
Yetst FAH-*r'n veer dee* VAY-*ring'r-shtrah-sseh hin-*AOUF *tsoom* GEWR-*t'l.*
We are now driving along Währinger street to the Gürtel.

 NOTE to Student: *Stecken bleiben*—"to get stuck". *Der Schauspieler bleibt stecken*—"The actor gets stuck (in his lines); der Wagen bleibt im Morast stecken*—"the wagon gets stuck in the mud."

SCHMITT: **Verzeihen Sie, was ist der Gürtel?**
*Fair-*TSIGH-*h'n Zee, vahss ist dehr* GEWR-*t'l?*
Pardon me, what is the Gürtel?

RITTER: **Der Gürtel ist eine breite Strasse, die im Kreis**
Dehr GEWR-*t'l ist* EYE-*neh* BRIGH-*teh* SHTRAH-*sseh, dee im Krice*
The Gürtel is a broad street, which goes in a circle

um die äusseren Bezirke herumgeht.
oom dee OY-*ss'-ren Beh-*TSEER-*keh hair-*OOM-*gait.*
around the outer precincts.

Hier rechts sehen Sie die Volksoper, das zweitgrösste
Here rekhts ZAY-*h'n Zee dee* FOLLKS-*oh-p'r, dahs* TSVIGHT-*gruhss-tek*
Here at your right you see the People's Opera, the second

Opernhaus der Stadt. Schade, dass wir heute nicht
OH-*p'rn-haous dehr Shtaht.* SHAH-*deh, dahss veer* HOY-*teh-nikht*
largest opera in the city. Too bad we cannot go

nach Schönbrunn fahren können. Dort ist das herrliche
*nahkh Shuhn-*BROONN *FAH-r'n* KUH-*n'n. Dohrt ist dahs* HERR-*lee-kheh*
to Schönbrunn today. That is where the magnificent

Schloss mit dem wunderschönen Garten.
Shloss mit daim VOON-*d'r-shuh-n'n* GAHR-*t'n.*
castle with the wonderful garden is.

SCHMITT: **Mutter sang uns immer das Lied:**
MOOTT'*r zahnk oons* IMM'*r dahs Leet:*
Mother always used to sing us the song:

"Draussen im Schönbrunner Park...."
"DRAOU-*ss'n im Shuhn-*BROONN'*r Park...."*
"Out in Schönbrunner Park...."

RITTER: **So, hier biegen wir in die Cottage-Strasse ein;**
Zoh, here BEE-*g'n veer in dee Cottage-*SHTRAH-*sseh ine;*
So, here we turn into Cottage street;

hier wohne ich, in Nr. 64.—Halten Sie hier,
here VOH-*neh ikh, in* NOOM'*r* FEER-*oont-sekh-tsikh.—*HAHL-*t'n Zee here,*
I live here at No. 64.—Stop here,

Schofför! Wie hoch ist der Fahrpreis?
*Shoh-*FUHR*! Vee hohkh ist dehr* FAHR-*price?*
driver! What is the fare?

SCHOFFÖR: **85 Schilling.**
FEWNF-*oont-ahkh-tsikh* SHILL-*ink.*
85 shillings.

RITTER: **Hier sind 100 Schillinge. Es ist schon gut.**
Here zint HOON-*d'rt* SHILL-*een-ggeh. Ess ist shohn goot.*
Here are 100 shillings. That is all right.

SCHOFFÖR: **Danke schön, danke bestens.**
DAHN-*keh shuhn,* DAHN-*keh best'ns.*
Thank you, thanks very much.

NOTE: Have you noticed, that *Chauffeur* "the driver" is spelled *der Schofför* this time? There are many foreign words in the German language which, as in English, have been completely adopted.

THINKING IN GERMAN

(Answers on page 265)

1. Welche Gebäude sehen die Herren auf der Ringstrasse?
2. Wer hat in der Hofburg gewohnt?
3. Regieren die Habsburger noch?
4. Wie heisst das grösste Schauspielhaus Wiens?
5. Wer hat die Votivkirche bauen lassen?
6. Auf welchem Platz steht sie?
7. Wer wollte den Kaiser töten?
8. Was rettete ihn?
9. Wo ist der Gürtel in Wien?
10. An welchem Theater fahren die Freunde noch vorüber?
11. Können sie das Schönbrunner Schloss besichtigen?
12. Wo wohnt Herr Ritter?
13. Wohin fahren die Herren jetzt?
14. Was gibt Herr Ritter dem Schofför?
15. Nennen Sie einige Sehenswürdigkeiten Wiens!
16. Hat Herr Schmitt in Wien geschäftlich zu tun?
17. Hat er seine Verwandten schon besucht?
18. Was für Verwandte hat er in Wien?

ÜBUNG NR. 37

Mein Haus ist das Ihre
Mine Haous ist dahs EE-*reh*
My house is yours

RITTER: **(die Tür öffnend) Verzeihen Sie, wenn ich vorausgehe.**
(*dee Tewr* UHFF-*n'nt*) *Fair-*TSIGH-*h'n Zee, venn ikh fohr-*AOUS-*gay-heh.*
(opening the door) Excuse me, if I enter first.

Legen Sie, bitte, ab.
LAY-*g'n Zee,* BIT-*teh, ahp.*
Take off your coat, please.

SCHMITT: **Eine schöne Wohnung haben Sie da!**
EYE-*neh* SHUH-*neh* VOH-*noonk* HAH-*b'n Zee dah!*
A nice home you have here!

RITTER: **Machen Sie sich's bequem. Hier kommt meine bessere Hälfte.**
MAH-*kh'n Zee zikhs beh-*KVAIM. *Here kommt* MIGH-*neh* BESS'*reh* HELLF-*teh.*
Make yourself comfortable. Here comes my better half.

Edith, darf ich Dir meinen Freund Schmitt aus New York vorstellen?
*AY-deet, dahrf ikh deer MIGH-n'n Froint Shmitt aous New York
FOHR-shtell'n?*
Edith, may I present you my friend Schmitt of New York?

FRAU RITTER: **Ich habe schon so viel von Ihnen gehört.**
Ikh HAH-beh shohn zoh feel fonn EE-n'n ggeh-HUHRT.
I have already heard a lot about you.

Es freut mich unendlich, Sie bei mir begrüssen zu können.
Ess froit mikh oon-END-likh, Zee by meer beh-GREW-ss'n tsoo KUH-n'n.
I am pleased no end to welcome you at my house.

Tun Sie, als ob Sie zuhause wären.
Toon Zee, ahls opp Zee tsoo-HAOU-zeh VAY-r'n.
Make yourself entirely at home.

SCHMITT: **Das Vergnügen ist ganz meinerseits.**
Dahs Fair-GNEW-g'n ist gahnts MIGH-n'r-zights.
The pleasure is all mine.

NOTE ON POLITENESS: *Das Vergnügen ist ganz meinerseits* means literally "the pleasure is all on my side." You
may abbreviate to: *Ganz meinerseits*, which means the same.
Tun Sie, als ob Sie zuhause wären—literally "do as though
you were at home" or "make yourself at home."

Ich kann jetzt schon sagen, dass ich mich nicht
Ikh kahn yetst shohn ZAH-g'n, dahss ikh mikh nikht
I can say right now that I could not

besser fühlen könnte, wenn ich wirklich daheim wäre.
BESS'r FEW-l'n KUHN-teh, venn ikh VEERK-likh dah-HYME VAY-reh.
feel better if I were really at home.

FRAU RITTER: **Wie gefällt Ihnen unsere Wienerstadt?**
Vee ggeh-FELLT EE-n'n OON-z'-reh VEE-n'r-shtaht?
How do you like our city of Vienna?

SCHMITT: **Was ich bis jetzt gesehen habe, begeistert mich.**
Vahss ikh bis yetst ggeh-ZAY-h'n HAH-beh, beh-GUY-st'rt mikh.
What I have seen so far fascinates me.

Ihr Gatte hat mich ein bisschen herumgeführt.
Eer GAHT-teh haht mikh ine BISS-kh'n hair-OOM-ggeh-fewrt.
Your husband showed me around a little.

Ich hätte nie gedacht, dass Wien wirklich so schön sei!
Ikh HETT-teh nee gay-DAHKHT, dahss veen VEERK-likh zoh shuhn zigh!
I had never imagined Vienna was so beautiful!

(Ritters Kinder kommen herein)
(RITT'rs KIN-d'r KOMM'n hair-INE)
(Ritter's children enter)

IMPORTANT NOTE ON CONDITIONAL CLAUSES:
(Bedingungssätze): There are two different constructions
with "if"—wenn.

1.) The real condition: Wenn ich Hunger habe, so esse
ich.—"If I am hungry, I eat." They take the indicative
present.

2.) The contrary-to-fact condition takes the past subjunctive in the
clause after wenn—"if" and the conditional ich würde in the main clause.
Wenn ich hungrig wäre, würde ich essen. As in English, "If I were hungry,
I should eat." You may leave out the—wenn: Wäre ich hungrig, so
würde ich essen.—"Were I hungry, I should eat."

RITTER: **Da kommt der Nachwuchs!**
Dah kommt dehr NAHKH-vooks!
Here come the offspring!

Kinder, das ist Onkel Schmitt aus Amerika.
KIN-d'r, dahs ist OHN-k'l Shmitt aous Ah-MEH-ree-kah.
Children, this is your Uncle Schmitt from America.

Das ist Liesl, die Älteste, und das sind unsere Zwillinge
Dahs ist LEEZ'l, dee EL-teh-steh, oont dahs zint OON-z'reh TSVILL-ing-eh
This is Liesl, the eldest one, and these are our twins

Franzl und Betty. Macht einen Knicks, Mädels!
Frahnts'l oont BET-tee. Mahkht EYE-n'n Knicks, MAY-d'ls!
Frank and Betty. Make a curtsey, girls!

LIESL: **Küss die Hand!**
Kewss dee Hahnt!
Kiss your hand!

NOTE ON POLITENESS: The Viennese generally say:
Küss die Hand—"I kiss your hand" when greeting a lady.
It is a nice custom, so do not laugh when you hear it.
Children greet their elders the same way.

SCHMITT: **Das sind aber herzige Kinder!**
Dahs zint AH-b'r HAIR-tsee-ggeh KIN-d'r!
What charming children they are!

Sicher seid Ihr alle drei sehr brav!
ZIKH'r zight Eer AHL-leh drigh zair brahf!
All three of you must certainly be very good!

LIESL: **Der Franzl ist gar nicht brav, er ist ein schlimmer Bub!**
Dehr Frahnts'l ist gahr nikht brahf, air ist ine SHLIMM'*r Boop!*
Little Frank is not at all good, he is a naughty boy!

SCHMITT: **Ist das wahr, Franz? Du schaust aber gar nicht so aus!**
Ist dahs vahr, Frahnts? Doo shaoust AH-*b'r gahr nikht zoh aous!*
Is that true, Frank? You don't look it!

FRANZL: **Die Betty ist nur böse, weil ich sie gestossen habe!**
Dee BET-*tee ist noor* RUH-*zeh, vile ikh zee gay-*SHTOHSS'*n* HAH-*beh!*
Betty is only angry because I pushed her!

Es war aber nicht so arg. Sie ist nicht einmal umgefallen.
Ess vahr AH-*b'r nikht zoh ark. Zee ist nikht ine-*MAHL *oom-gay-fall'n.*
It was not so terrible though. She did not even fall down.

RITTER: **Also Kinder, geht schön in Euer Zimmer zum Fräulein!**
AHL-*zoh* KIN-*d'r, gait shuhn in* OY-*'r* TSIMM'*r tsoom* FROY-*line!*
Now, children, go back to your room to your governess!

(Die Kinder gehen)
(Dee KIN-*d'r* GAY-*h'n)*
(The children leave)

IMPORTANT NOTE: When Mr. Ritter speaks to his wife or his children, he does not use the formal *Sie*—"you" but the familiar *Du* (plural *Ihr*). The endings of this second person of the verb forms are *-st* and *-t*. The objective forms are *Dir* (indirect) and *Dich* (direct), plural: *Euch* (indirect and direct).

You use the familiar form when you talk to members of your family and your relatives, or to your intimate friends, school-mates and small children. It is even used when speaking to animals, such as horses, dogs, and cats.

RITTER: **Wollen Sie bitte hier eintreten, Herr Schmitt!**
VOLL'*n Zee* BIT-*teh here* INE-*tray-t'n, Herr Shmitt!*
Won't you please step in here, Mr. Schmitt!

Das Essen muss gleich fertig sein!
Dahs ESS'*n mooss glighkh* FAIR-*tikh zine!*
The dinner will be ready in a minute!

SCHMITT: **Danke schön! Das Zimmer ist wirklich sehr gemütlich!**
DAHN-*keh shuhn! Dahs* TSIMM'*r ist* VEERK-*likh zair ggeh-*MEWT-*likh!*
Thank you! The room is really very comfortable!

A WORD TO REMEMBER: *Gemütlich* is a famous German word, which defies translation. It means leisurely, comfortable, debonair, generous and easy going, all in ONE word. Many people use the word, as is, in English. You will soon feel its meaning if you go to Germany or Austria.

RITTER: **Haben Sie auch Kinder, Herr Schmitt?**
HAH-*b'n Zee aoukh* KIN-*d'r, Herr Shmitt?*
Have you also children, Mr. Schmitt?

SCHMITT: **Nein, ich bin noch nicht mal verheiratet.**
*Nine, ikh bin nohkh nikht mahl fair-*HIGH-*rah-tet.*
No, I am not even married yet.

Wenn man Ihr Familienleben sieht,
*Venn mahn Eer Fah-*MEE-*lee-ehn-lay-b'n zeet,*
When one sees your family life,

wünscht man, auch Familie zu haben.
*vewnsht mahn, aoukh Fah-*MEE-*lee-eh tsoo* HAH-*b'n.*
then one wishes also to have a family.

RITTER: **Was hindert Sie, unserem Beispiel zu folgen?**
Vahss HIN-*d'rt Zee,* OON-*z'rem* BIGH-*shpeel tsoo* FOLL-*g'n?*
What is preventing you from following our example?

SCHMITT: **Eigentlich nichts. Ich bin so gut wie verlobt**
EYE-*g'nt-likh nikhts. Ikh bin zoh goot vee fair-*LOHPT
Nothing, in fact. I am practically engaged

und werde nach meiner Rückkehr heiraten.
oont VEHR-*deh nahkh* MIGH-*n'r* REWK-*kair* HIGH-*rah-t'n.*
and I shall be married after my return.

 EXPRESSION to Remember: *Ich bin so gut wie verlobt*—"I am as good as engaged."

Hier ist das Bild meiner Verlobten.
Here ist dahs Bilt MIGH-*n'r Fair-*LOHP-*t'n.*
Here is the picture of my fiancee.

RITTER: **Das ist ja eine Schönheit!**
Dahs ist yah EYE-*neh* SHUHN-*hight!*
But she is a beauty!

Da kann man nur gratulieren, Sie Glückspilz!
*Dah kahn mahn noor grah-too-*LEE-*r'n, Zee* GLEWKS-*pilts!*
We can only congratulate you, you lucky fellow!

SCHMITT: **Ich wünschte, es wäre schon so weit!**
Ikh VEWNSH-*teh, ess* VAY-*reh shohn zoh vite!*
I wish that it were already over!

NOTE to Student: *Ich wünschte, es wäre so weit!*—"I wish
that it were already over!" The subjunctive expresses the
desire. *Ich wünschte, ich wäre reich!*—"I wish I were rich!"
That is an unreal wish, because you are not rich—so use
the subjunctive! Or are you?

FRAU RITTER: **Schade, ich wäre sehr froh, wenn Sie Ihre Braut hier hätten.**
SHAH-*deh, ikh* VAY-*reh zair froh, venn Zee* EE-*reh Braout here* HAITT'*n.*
It's too bad, I should be very glad if you had your fiancee here.

DAS DIENSTMÄDCHEN: **Das Essen ist aufgetragen!**
Dahs DEENST-*mait-kh'n: Dahs* ESS'*n ist* AOUF-*ggeh-trah-g'n!*
The Maid: Dinner is served!

FRAU RITTER: **Danke schön, Klara! Bitte, Herr Schmitt, nehmen Sie hier
Platz!**
DAHN-*keñ shuhn,* KLAH-*rah!* BIT-*teh, Herr Shmitt,* NAY-*m'n Zee here
Plahts!*
Thank you, Clara! Please, Mr. Schmitt, take this seat here!

SCHMITT: **Das ist ja der Ehrenplatz! Ich fühle mich sehr geschmeichelt.**
Dahs ist yah dehr AIR'*n-plahts! Ikh* FEW-*leh mikh zair ggeh*-SHMIGH-
kh'lt.
But this is the seat of honor! I feel very flattered.

Ich wusste nicht, dass ich eine so wichtige Persönlichkeit sei!
Ikh VOOSS-*teh nikht, dahss ikh* EYE-*neh zoh* VIKH-*tee-ggeh Pair*-ZUHN-
likh-kite zigh!
I did not know I was such an important personality!

FRAU RITTER: **Sie müssen schon entschuldigen, aber unser Essen ist**
Zee MEW-*ss'n shohn ent*-SHOOL-*dig'n,* AH-*b'r* OON-*z'r* ESS'*n ist*
You must excuse us, but our meal is

heute sehr bescheiden. Meine Köchin hat gekündigt
HOY-*teh zair beh*-SHY-*d'n.* MIGH-*neh* KUH-*khin haht ggeh*-KEWN-*dikt*
very modest today. My cook has resigned

und Klara hilft nur aus.
oont KLAH-*rah hilft noor aous.*
and Clara is only helping out.

NOTE FOR HOUSEWIVES: *Die Köchin hat gekündigt*—
"The cook has given notice" or "quit." *Ich muss die Wohnung kündigen*—"I must give notice to my landlord."

SCHMITT: **Aber die Spargelsuppe ist ausgezeichnet!**
AH-*b'r dee* SHPAHR-*g'l-zoo-peh ist* AOUS-*ggeh-tsighkh-net!*
The asparagus soup is excellent though!

RITTER: **Da warten Sie nur, bis das Backhuhn aufgetragen wird!**
Dah VAHR-*t'n Zee noor, bis dahs* BAHK-*hoon* AOUF-*ggeh-trah-g'n veert.*
Then wait till the baked chicken is served!

Das ist eine Spezialität in unserem Hause!
Dahs ist EYE-*neh Shpeh-tsee-ah-lee-*TAIT *in* OON-*z'rem* HAOU-*zeh!*
This is a specialty at our house.

SCHMITT: **Ein Wiener Backhähndel mit Häuptelsalat!**
Ine VEE-*n'r* BAHK-*hain-d'l mit* HOIP-*t'l-sah-laht!*
A Viennese baked chicken with lettuce salad!

Meine Mutter würde sich freuen, das zu hören!
MIGH-*neh* MOOTT'*r* VEWR-*deh zikh* FROY'*n, dahs tsoo* HUH-*r'n!*
My mother would be pleased to hear that!

Heimatklänge, würde sie sagen. Sie hat uns immer erzählt,
HIGH-*maht-kleng-eh,* VEWR-*deh zee* ZAH-*g'n. Zee haht oons* IMM'*r air-*
TSAILT,
Sounds from home, she would say. She always told us

es gäbe nichts Besseres, als ein paniertes junges Hähnchen.
ess GAY-*beh nikhts* BESS'-*ress, ahls ine pah-*NEER-*tess* YOON-*ggess* HAIN-
kh'n.
there is nothing better than a breaded young rooster.

RITTER: **Und dazu einen leichten Vöslauer Wein!**
*Oont dah-*TSOO EYE-*n'n* LIGHKH-*t'n Vuhs-*LAOU-*ehr Vine!*
And a light wine from Vöslau to go with it!

SCHMITT: **Ganz wie Mutter gesagt hat: Essen und**
Gahnts vee MOOTT'*r ggeh-*ZAHKT *haht:* ESS'*n oont*
Entirely as mother has said: Eating and

Trinken hält Leib und Seele zusammen!
TRINK'*n hellt Lipe oont* ZAY-*leh tsoo-*ZAHM'*n!*
drinking keeps body and soul together!

THINKING IN GERMAN

(Answers on page 266)

1. Ladet Herr Ritter Herrn Schmitt bei sich zum Essen ein?
2. Kennt Herr Schmitt die Gattin Herrn Ritters?
3. Wünscht er, ihre Bekanntschaft zu machen?
4. Was sagt Frau Ritter, als ihr Herr Schmitt vorgestellt wird?
5. Wieviele Kinder haben die Ritters?
6. Wie heissen sie?
7. Wieviele Schwestern hat Franz?
8. Glaubt Liesl, dass Franz ein braver Junge sei?
9. Ist Herr Schmitt auch verheiratet?
10. Hat er ein Bild seiner Braut bei sich?
11. Findet Frau Ritter die Verlobte des Herrn Schmitt schön?
12. Sind Sie verheiratet?
13. Haben Sie Schwestern oder Brüder?
14. Was sagt das Dienstmädchen, sobald das Essen fertig ist?
15. Wo wird Herr Schmitt hingesetzt?
16. Was gibt es bei Ritters zu essen?
17. Haben Sie schon Backhuhn gegessen?
18. Was für Salate essen sie gerne?

ÜBUNG NR. 38

Im Prater
Im PRAH-*t'r*
At the Prater

NOTE TO FUN-SEEKERS: The *Prater* in Vienna is the Coney Island of the Austrian Capital. One part of the *Prater*, though, is only for strollers and nature lovers while the *Wurstelprater* has all the gaudy features of the usual amusement parks.

RITTER. **Heute will ich Sie in den Prater führen.**
HOY-*teh vill ikh Zee in dain* PRAH-*t'r* FEW-*r'n.*
Today, I want to take you to the Prater.

Sie haben doch schon vom Prater gehört?
Zee HAH-*b'n dohkh shohn fom* PRAH-*t'r* ggeh-HUHRT?
You have already heard of the Prater, haven't you?

SCHMITT: **Natürlich. Meine Mutter hat nie aufgehört,**
*Nah-*TEWR-*likh.* MIGH-*neh* MOOTT'*r haht nee* AOUF-*ggeh-huhrt,*
Of course. My mother never stopped

242

davon zu sprechen. Besonders vom sogenannten Wurstelprater,
*dah-*FONN *tsoo* SHPREH-*kh'n. Beh-*ZONN-*d'rs fom* ZOH-*ggeh-nahn-t'n*
VOOR-*st'l-prah-t'r,*
talking of it. Especially of the so-called Wurstelprater

der so ähnlich sein muss, wie unser Coney Island.
dehr zoh AIN-*likh zine mooss, vee* OON-*z'r Coney Island.*
which must be like our Coney Island.

NOTE TO STUDENT: In the *Wurstelprater,* the children can see Punch and Judy booths which are called *Wurstel* in Viennese.

RITTER: **Oder wie der Luna-Park in Paris oder Berlin.**
OH-*d'r vee dehr* LOO-*nah-Park in Pah-*REES OH-*d'r Behr-*LEEN.
Or like the Luna Park in Paris or Berlin.

Diese Plätze werden oft verglichen.
DEE-*zeh* PLETT-*tseh* VAIR-*d'n offt fair-*GLIKH'*n.*
These places are often compared.

SCHMITT: **Komisch, dieser Platz, den wir eben überqueren,**
KOH-*mish,* DEE-*z'r Plahts, dain veer* AY-*b'n ew-b'r-*KVEH-*r'n,*
That's odd, this square which we are just crossing

erinnert mich sehr an den Columbus Circle in New York.
*air-*INN'*rt mikh zair ahn dain Koh-*LOOM-*boos* SUHR-*k'l in New Yor*k..
reminds me very much of Columbus Circle in New York.

RITTER: **Ja, das ist mir schon oft gesagt worden.**
*Yah, dahs ist meer shohn offt ggeh-*ZAHKT VOHR-*d'n.*
Yes, I have already been told that frequently.

Das ist der Praterstern mit dem Denkmal des Admirals
Dahs ist dehr PRAH-*t'r-shtairn mit daim* DENK-*mahl dess Ahd-mee-*RAHLÇ
This is the Praterstern with the monument of Admiral

Tegetthoff. Jetzt biegen wir in die Ausstellungsstrasse ein,
TEH-*ggeh-toff. Yetst* BEE-*g'n veer in dee* AOUS-*shtell-oonks-shtrah-sseh ine*
Tegetthoff. Now we turn to Exhibition Street,

die in den Wurstelprater führt.
dee in dain VOOR-*st'l-prah-t'r fewrt.*
which leads to the Wurstelprater.

Da oben fährt die Stadtbahn. Hier links ist das Busch-Kino.
Dah OH-*b'n fairt dee* SHTAHT-*bahn. Here links ist dahs* BUSH-*kee-noh,*
Up there goes the Stadtbahn. Here to the left is the Busch movie theatre.

Viele Jahre lang war das der Zirkus Busch.
FEE-*leh* YAH-*reh lahnk vahr dahs der* TSEER-*koos Bush.*
For many years this was the Busch Circus.

NOTE ON THE PRATER SQUARE: The *Praterstern* is a huge square at the entrance to the *Prater,* where 8 streetr meet and form a huge "star" (*Stern*).

SCHMITT: **Wurde nicht im Zirkus Busch auch Theater gespielt?**
VOOR-*deh nikht im* TSEER-*koos Bush aoukh Teh-*AH-*t'r ggeh-*SHPEELT?
Weren't plays shown in the Busch Circus as well?

IMPORTANT NOTE: The passive voice in which the subject is the receiver of a certain action, is formed in German by the auxiliary *werden*—"become" and the past participle. *Ich werde genannt*—"I am called", imperfect *ich wurde genannt*—"I was called", past tense *ich bin genannt worden*—"I have been called." The past participle of *werden*—"become, geworden*—"have become" loses the first syllable *ge* when used in the passive form. Note the difference between *der Brief ist geschrieben worden* —"the letter was written" and *der Brief ist geschrieben*—"the letter is written."

RITTER: **O ja! Von Max Reinhardt sind hier "König Ödipus",**
Oh yah! Fonn Max RINE-*hart zint here "*KUH-*nikh* UH-*dee-poos",*
Oh yes! "Oedipus Rex", "Everyman" and "The Miracle"

"Jedermann" und "Das Mirakel" gespielt worden.
*"*YAY-*d'r-mahn" oont "Dahs Mee-*RAH-*k'l" ggeh-*SHPEELT VOHR-*d'n.*
were played here by Max Reinhardt.

Die wurden später auch in New York gezeigt.
Dee VOOR-*d'n* SHPAY-*t'r aoukh in New York ggeh-*TSIGHKT.
They were also shown later in New York.

SCHMITT: **Das sieht aber genau so aus wie in Coney Island!**
Dahs zeet AH-*b'r ggeh-*NAOU *zoh aous vee in Coney Island!*
This looks exactly like Coney Island!

"Berg- und Talbahn" heisst hier, was dort "Scenic Railway"
"Bairk- oont TAHL-*bahn" highst here, vahss dohrt "Scenic Railway"*
Here they call "Mountain and Valley Railroad" what is called there

genannt wird. Und das hier?
*ggeh-*NAHNT *veert. Oont dahs here?*
"Scenic Railway". And this here?

RITTER: **Das ist die Drachenbahn, so genannt, weil**
Dahs ist dee DRAH-*kh'n-bahn, zoh* ggeh-NAHNT. *vile*
This is the Dragon-railway, so called because

statt der Lokomotive ein Drachen vorgespannt ist.
*shtaht dehr Loh-koh-moh-*TEE-*veh ine* DRAH-*kh'n* FOHR-*gay-shpahnt ist.*
instead of a locomotive, there is a Dragon harnessed in front.

Hier kommt Präuschers Panoptikum, mit den
Here kommt PROY-*sh'rs Pahn-*OHPP-*tee-koom, mit dain*
Here is Präuscher's Panopticum with the

Wachsfiguren aller Mörder aus der österreichischen
VAHKS-*fee-goo-r'n* AHL-*l'r* MUHR-*d'r aous dehr* UH-*st'r-righ-khee-sh'n*
wax figures of all the murderers in Austrian

Kriminalgeschichte. Mir hat es immer gegruselt,
*Kree-mee-*NAHL-*ggeh-shikh-teh. Meer haht ess* IMM'*r* ggeh-GROO-*z'lt,*
criminal history. It always gave me the creeps

wenn ich von meinem Vater hineingeführt wurde.
venn ikh fonn MIGH-*n'm* FAH-*t'r hin-*INE-*ggeh-fewrt* VOOR-*deh.*
when I was taken there by my father.

SCHMITT: **Jetzt kann ich schon das Riesenrad sehen!**
Yetst kahn ikh shohn dahs REE-*z'n-raht* ZAY-*h'n!*
Now I can see the Ferris Wheel!

Ist es wahr, dass es aus Paris hierher gebracht wurde?
*Ist ess vahr, dahss ess aous Pah-*REES *here-*HAIR *ggeh-*BRAHKHT VOOR-*deh?*
Is it true that it was brought here from Paris?

RITTER: **Ja, nach der Pariser Weltausstellung.**
*Yah, nahkh dehr Pah-*REE-*z'r* VELLT-*aous-shtell-oonk.*
Yes, after the Paris World's Fair.

Eine Zeit lang war es wegen Baufälligkeit geschlossen.
EYE-*neh* TSIGHT *lahnk vahr ess* VAY-*g'n* BAOU-*fell-ikh-kite ggeh-*SHLOSS'*n.*
For a while it was closed because of its dilapidated condition.

Jetzt ist es wieder in Betrieb gesetzt worden.
Yetzt ist ess VEE-*d'r in Beh-*TREEP *ggeh-*ZETST VOHR-*d'n.*
Now it has been put in operation again.

Wollen wir eine Fahrt auf dem Riesenrad unternehmen?
VOLL'*n veer* EYE-*neh Fahrt aouf daim* REE-*z'n-raht oon-t'r-*NAY-*m'n?*
Shall we take a ride on the Ferris Wheel?

SCHMITT: **Ich habe nichts dagegen. Da kann ich gleich**
Ikh HAH-*beh nikhts dah-*GAY-*g'n. Dah kahn ikh glighkh*
I have no objection. So I can take a look

ganz Wien von oben besichtigen.
gahnts Veen fonn OH-*b'n beh-*ZIKH-*tig'n.*
at all Vienna from up there.

RITTER: **Bezahlen wir unseren Fahrpreis**
*Beh-*TSAH-*l'n veer* OON-*z'ren* FAHR-*price*
Let us pay our fare

und gehen wir zur Abfahrtsplattform! Zwei hübsche
oont GAY-*h'n veer tsoor* AHP-*fahrts-plaht-form! Tsvigh* HEWP-*sheh*
and go to the platform! Two pretty

junge Damen warten auf denselben Waggon.
YOON-*ggeh* DAH-*m'n* VAHR-*t'n aouf dain-*ZELL-*b'n Vah-*GOHN.
young ladies are waiting for the same car.

SCHMITT: **Das finde ich reizend!**
Dahs FINN-*deh ikh* RIGH-*ts'nd!*
I find that charming!

Das nenne ich Gastfreundschaft, Herr Ritter.
Dahs NEN-*neh ikh* GAHST-*froint-shahft, Herr* RITT*'r!*
That is what I call hospitality, Mr. Ritter!

RITTER: **Hier kommt unser Waggon.**
Here kommt OON-*z'r Vah-*GOHN.
Here comes our car.

ANGESTELLTER: **Aussteigen lassen! So, danke,**
AHN-*ggeh-shtell-t'r:* AOUS-*shtigh-g'n* LAHSS*'n! Zoh,* DAHN-*keh,*
EMPLOYEE: Let them off! All right, thank you,

jetzt können Sie Ihre Plätze einnehmen!
yetst KUH-*n'n Zee* EE-*reh* PLETT-*tseh* INE-*nay-m'n!*
now you can take your places!

RITTER: **Ich hoffe, die Damen sind schwindelfrei!**
Ikh HOFF-*feh, dee* DAH-*m'n zint* SHVIN-*d'l-fry!*
I hope, the ladies are free from dizziness!

1. DAME: ***Ich* hoffe es auch!**
AIR-*steh* DAH-*meh:* *Ikh* HOFF-*feh ess aoukh!*
1ST LADY: I hope so too!

2. DAME: **Das wäre eine schöne Bescherung,**
TSVIGH-*teh* DAH-*meh:* *Dahs* VAY-*reh* EYE-*neh* SHUH-*neh Beh-*SHAY-*roonk,*
2ND LADY: That would be a nice predicament,

wenn uns da oben schlecht würde!
venn oons dah OH-*b'n shlekht* VEWR-*deh!*
if we got dizzy up there!

 NOTE TO STUDENT: *Bescherung*—is the ceremony of distributing gifts at Christmas, *Eine schöne Bescherung* means ironically "a nice kettle of fish"—"a disagreeable surprise."

RITTER: **Aussteigen könnten Sie hier oben nicht!**
AOUS-shtigh-g'n KUHN-t'n Zee here OH-b'n nikht!
You could not get off up here!

SCHMITT: **Jetzt wird die Aussicht schon schön!**
Yetst veert dee AOUS-zikht shohn shuhn!
Now the view is already getting beautiful!

Das ist wohl die Donau da unten.
Dahs ist vohl dee DOH-naou dah OON-t'n.
That is surely the Danube down there.

RITTER: **Ja, da zweigt der Donaukanal ab und**
Yah, dah tsvighkt dehr DOH-naou-kah-nahl ahp oont
Yes, there the Danube Canal branches off and

schlängelt sich durch Wien hindurch!
SHLEN-g'lt zikh doorkh Veen hin-DOORKH!
winds through Vienna!

SCHMITT: **Was ist das dort drüben auf dieser Seite?**
Vahss ist dahs dohrt DREW-b'n aouf DEEZ'r ZIGH-teh?
What is that over on this side?

RITTER: **Das ist das Strandbad "Gänsehäufel".**
Dahs ist dahs SHTRAHNT-baht "GGEN-zeh-hoy-f'l".
That is the Gänsehäufel bathing beach.

Das Familienbad ist berühmt und sehr schön!
Dahs Fah-MEE-lee-en-baht ist beh-REWMT oont zair shuhn!
The family bathing beach is famous and very beautiful!

SCHMITT: **So, das war sehr schön, wir kommen wieder unten an.**
Zoh, dahs vahr zair shuhn, veer KOMM'n VEE-d'r OON-t'n ahn.
There, that was very nice, we are coming down again.

Steigen wir aus! Ich glaube, wir müssen unseren
SHTIGH-g'n veer aous! Ikh GLAOU-beh, veer MEWSS'n OON-z'ren
Let's get off! I think we must break up our

Praterbesuch abbrechen. Ich muss meine Verwandten besuchen.
PRAH-t'r-beh-zookh AHP-breh-kh'n. Ikh mooss MIGH-neh Fair-VAHN-t'n beh-ZOO-kh'n.
visit to the Prater. I must visit my relatives.

Auf Wiedersehen, ich rufe Sie morgen an.
Aouf VEE-d'r-zay-h'n, ikh ROO-feh Zee MOHR-g'n ahn.
Good-bye, I shall call you tomorrow.

RITTER: **Auf morgen also!**
Aouf MOHR-g'n AHL-zoh!
Until tomorrow then!

THINKING IN GERMAN
(Answers on page 266)

1. Womit wird der Prater verglichen?
2. Was steht auf dem Praterstern?
3. Was ist die Drachenbahn?
4. Was wird in Präuschers Panoptikum ausgestellt?
5. Woher wurde das Riesenrad nach Wien gebracht?
6. Von wem wird der Waggon auf dem Riesenrad geteilt?
7. Sind Sie schwindelfrei?
8. Wird Ihnen oft schlecht?
9. Wer wird von Herrn Schmitt besucht?
10. Von wem wird Herr Ritter am nächsten Tag angerufen werden?
11. Welche Sprache wird von Ihnen hier gesprochen?
12. Welcher Fluss schlängelt sich durch Wien hindurch?
13. Wird Herr Ritter Herrn Schmitt wiedersehen?
14. Warum war das Riesenrad nicht in Betrieb?
15. Hat es Sie schon einmal gegruselt?

ANSWERS

ANSWERS TO THE QUESTIONS OF LESSON 1 ON PAGE 3

Ja, das ist das Buch.

Nein, das ist nicht der Bleistift.

Nein, das ist nicht der Tisch.

Das ist das Buch.

Ja, das ist die Schachtel.

Nein, das ist nicht das Fenster.

Nein, das ist nicht die Tür.

Das ist die Schachtel.

Ja, das ist der Schlüssel.

Nein, das ist nicht der Stuhl.

11. Nein, das ist nicht die Lampe.

12. Das ist der Schlüssel.

13. Ja, das ist der Bleistift.

14. Nein, das ist nicht die Schachtel.

15. Nein, das ist nicht der Schlüssel.

16. Das ist der Bleistift.

17. Ja, das ist der Tisch.

18. Nein, das ist nicht der Stuhl.

19. Nein, das ist nicht die Tür, das ist der Bleistift.

20. Das ist der Tisch.

249

ANSWERS TO THE QUESTIONS OF LESSON 2 ON PAGE 6

1. Das ist der Schuh.
2. Das ist der Schuh.
3. Das ist weder die Krawatte noch das Taschentuch, das ist der Schuh.
4. Das ist der Handschuh.
5. Das ist der Handschuh.
6. Nein, das ist nicht der Bleistift, das ist der Handschuh.
7. Das ist die Hose.
8. Nein, das ist nicht das Kleid, das i die Hose.
9. Nein, das ist nicht der Mantel, das i die Hose.
10. Das ist die Hose.
11. Nein, das ist nicht die Krawatte, da ist die Hose.
12. Das ist weder der Hut noch de Mantel, das ist die Hose.

ANSWERS TO THE QUESTIONS OF LESSON 3 ON PAGE 11

1. Nein, die Feder ist nicht blau.
2. Die Feder ist grün.
3. Nein, die Feder ist nicht rot, sie ist grün.
4. Die Feder ist weder weiss noch schwarz, sie ist grün.
5. Das ist der Bleistift.
6. Ja, das ist der Bleistift.
7. Nein, der Bleistift ist nicht rot, er ist gelb.
8. Nein, er ist nicht schwarz.
9. Er ist gelb.
10. Nein, das ist nicht der Tisch.
11. Nein, das ist nicht die Tür.
12. Das ist die Lampe.
13. Die Lampe ist blau.
14. Nein, die Lampe ist nicht rot.
15. Nein, die Lampe ist nicht grau.
16. Ja, die Lampe ist blau.
17. Das ist das rote Buch.
18. Ja, das ist das rote Buch.
19. Nein, das ist nicht das gelbe Buch.
20. Es ist rot.
21. Nein, das Buch ist nicht schwarz.

ANSWERS TO THE QUESTIONS OF LESSON 4 ON PAGE 15

1. Ja, das rote Buch ist lang.
2. Ja, es ist breit.
3. Ja, es ist gross.
4. Ja, das grüne Buch ist kurz.
5. Ja, es ist schmal.
6. Ja, es ist klein.
7. Das grosse Buch ist rot.
8. Das grüne ist das kleine Buch.
9. Das lange Kleid ist schwarz.
10. Das gelbe Kleid ist kurz.
11. Das kurze Kleid ist gelb.
12. Es ist weder schwarz noch blau, es i gelb.
13. Das breite Fenster ist blau.

Das rote Fenster ist schmal.

Nein, das blaue Fenster ist nicht klein.

Das kleine Fenster ist rot.

Das grüne Buch ist nicht breit.

Das grüne Buch ist schmal.

19. Das grosse Fenster ist blau.

20. Das gelbe Kleid ist klein und kurz.

21. Das grüne Buch ist kurz.

22. Das blaue Fenster ist breit.

23. Das rote Buch ist nicht kurz.

ANSWERS TO THE QUESTIONS OF LESSON 5 ON PAGE 19

Ich bin Herr.../Frau.../Fräulein...

Ja, ich bin Amerikaner (Amerikanerin).

Nein, ich bin nicht der Lehrer, ich bin der Schüler (die Schülerin).

Nein, ich bin nicht Deutscher (Deutsche).

Sie sind Herr Juhn, Sie sind der Lehrer.

Ja, Sie sind der Lehrer.

Ja, Sie sind Amerikaner. (Nein, Sie sind nicht Amerikaner.)

Nein, Sie sind nicht Spanier.

Marlene Dietrich ist Deutsche.

10. Nein, Sonja Henie ist nicht Italienerin.

11. Nein, Clark Gable ist nicht Deutscher, er ist Amerikaner.

12. Nein, ich bin nicht Engländer (Engländerin).

13. Maurice Chevalier ist Franzose.

14. Frau Chiang-Kai-Shek ist Chinesin.

15. Nein, Cripps ist nicht Amerikaner, er ist Engländer.

16. Nein, Carmen Miranda ist nicht Deutsche, sie ist Brasilianerin.

17. Dieser Hut ist klein.

18. Dieser Kragen ist schmal.

19. Ich bin der Schüler (die Schülerin).

ANSWERS TO THE QUESTIONS OF LESSON 6 ON PAGE 23

Das Buch ist auf dem Tisch.

Ja, das Buch ist auf dem Tisch.

Nein, es ist nicht unter dem Stuhl.

Die Feder ist in der Schachtel.

Nein, sie ist nicht auf dem Buch.

Das Fenster ist hinter mir.

Der Lehrer ist vor mir.

Nein, der Professor ist nicht unter dem Tisch.

Nein, er ist nicht vor dem Tisch, er ist hinter dem Tisch.

10. Das Fenster ist hinter mir.

11. Ja, die Tür ist in der Wand.

12. Ja, das Papier ist in dem Buch.

13. Die Schachtel ist unter dem Tisch.

14. Die Feder ist in der Schachtel.

15. Ja, der Schlüssel ist auf dem Tisch.

16. Dieses Buch ist gross.

17. Der Hut auf dem Stuhl ist gross.

18. Ja, Berlin ist in Deutschland.

19. New York ist in Amerika.

20. Ich bin in New York.

ANSWERS TO THE QUESTIONS OF LESSON 7 ON PAGE 29

1. Der Lehrer nimmt das Buch.
2. Ja, er nimmt es.
3. Nein, er legt es nicht hin.
4. Nein, er nimmt nicht die Schachtel.
5. Der Lehrer steht.
6. Nein, der Lehrer schliesst nicht das Fenster.
7. Er öffnet das Fenster.
8. Er öffnet nicht die Tür, er öffnet das Fenster.
9. Nein, ich schliesse nicht die Tür.
10. Sie schliessen die Tür.
11. Nein, der Lehrer liegt nicht u dem Baum.
12. Er steht nicht, er sitzt.
13. Nein, er sitzt nicht auf dem Baum
14. Der Lehrer sitzt unter dem Baum
15. Ich sitze auf dem Stuhl.
16. Ja, der Baum ist gross.

ANSWERS TO THE QUESTIONS OF LESSON 8 ON PAGE 35

1. Ich zähle von eins bis zehn.
2. Sie zählen von zwanzig bis zweiundzwanzig.
3. Hier sind (zwei) Stühle.
4. Der Lehrer zählt Geld.
5. Ja, hier ist ein Tisch.
6. Auf dem Tisch sind keine Bücher.
7. Ja, es ist eine Dame hier.
8. Der Lehrer sitzt hinter dem Tisch
9. Ich zähle zwei Füsse.
10. Der Hut kostet zehn Dollar.
11. Ja, das ist ein Rock.
12. Nein, es ist kein Taschentuch auf Tisch.
13. Zwei und zwei ist vier.
14. Ein Berlitz-Buch kostet zwei Do fünfzig.

ANSWERS TO THE QUESTIONS OF LESSON 9 ON PAGE 43

1. Ja, wir gehen in die Berlitz-Schule.
2. Ja, die Herren haben Hüte auf.
3. Ja, die Damen gehen ins Kino. (Nein, sie gehen nicht ins Kino.)
4. Nein, Herr Berlitz geht nicht ins Büro.
5. Nein, die Schüler machen die Augen nicht zu.
6. Ja, ich nehme einen Bleistift in die Schule.
7. Nein, ich nehme keine Bücher in Kirche.
8. Ja, Fräulein Gertrude kommt aus d Park. (Sie kommt nicht aus d Park.)
9. Nein, es liegen keine Hüte auf d Tisch.
10. Nein, ich habe nicht 3 Augen, habe zwei.
11. Ja, die Schüler kommen aus Schule.

Nein, Herr Berlitz geht nicht aus dem Haus in den Garten.

Ich gehe in den Garten und nicht in die Kirche.

14. Nein, ich habe kein Haus. (Ja, ich habe ein Haus.)

15. Nein, ich habe keinen Hut auf dem Kopf.

ANSWERS TO THE QUESTIONS OF LESSON 10 ON PAGE 49

Ich schreibe den Buchstaben A auf das Papier.

Sie schreiben das Wort Kino.

Herr Strump schreibt das A—B—C.

Ich lese den Satz: "Ich bin der Schüler".

Der Satz: "Der Lehrer geht in die Kirche" hat sechs Wörter.

Er hat acht Silben.

Ich lese Wörter und Sätze in dem Buch.

Sie lesen das A—B—C.

"Ich" ist kein Satz, es ist ein Wort.

10. Ich lese das deutsche A—B—C.

11. Nein, das A—B—C beginnt nicht mit P, es beginnt mit A.

12. Nein, H ist nicht der erste Buchstabe, A ist der erste Buchstabe.

13. Ja, ich schreibe in mein Heft.

14. Ich nehme mein Buch.

15. Nein, das Wort "Bleistift" hat nicht vier, es hat zwei Silben.

16. A ist der erste Buchstabe.

17. Auf Seite 35 lese ich Wörter.

18. Der Satz hat Wörter und Buchstaben.

19. Die Silbe hat keine Wörter.

ANSWERS TO THE QUESTIONS OF LESSON 11 ON PAGE 56

Das deutsche A—B—C hat 26 Buchstaben.

Ja, das C steht vor dem P.

Das A—B—C endet nicht mit W, es endet mit Z.

Wir haben fünf Selbstlaute. (Vokale)

K ist kein Selbstlaut.

Wir haben drei Umlaute.

Nein "Buch" ist nicht englisch, es ist deutsch.

Das ist ein deutsches Buch.

9. In Paris spricht man französisch.

10. Nein, in Berlin spricht man nicht französisch, man spricht dort deutsch

11. Ich schreibe Hände mit Umlaut a.

12. Sie sind der Lehrer.

13. Nein, der Lehrer antwortet nicht, er fragt.

14. Der Schüler fragt nicht, er antwortet.

15. Ja, das ist Ihr Bleistift. (Nein, das ist nicht Ihr Bleistift.)

16. Mein Mantel ist auf dem Stuhl. (Er ist zuhause.)

ANSWERS TO THE QUESTIONS OF LESSON 12 ON PAGE 63

1. Der Herr Lehrer hat mehr Geld als Frau Huber.
2. Nein, er hat weniger Geld als Vanderbilt.
3. Liese hat fünfzig Pfennig.
4. Ja, der Lehrer hat einen Bleistift hinter dem Ohr.
5. Ja, er hat mehr Bleistifte als Liese.
6. Nein, Liese hat mehr Bücher als der Herr Lehrer.
7. Frau Huber hat nicht viel Geld.
8. Frau Huber hat ihren Hut auf dem Kopf.
9. Lieses Rock ist kurz.
10. Ich habe nicht viel Geld.
11. Ich habe mehr Geld als Bleistifte.
12. In diesem Buch sind viele Seiten.
13. In dem Wort "Streichholz" sind Buchstaben.

ANSWERS TO THE QUESTIONS OF LESSON 13 ON PAGE 71

1. Ja, der Lehrer gibt Frau Huber ein Buch.
2. Der Lehrer gibt Liese Geld.
3. Frau Huber sagt: Danke, mein Herr!
4. Der Lehrer bekommt keinen Hut von Frau Huber.
5. Der Lehrer gibt Liese Geld.
6. Die Dame heisst Frau Huber.
7. Der Hund sitzt vor Frau Huber.
8. Schnucki sagt nichts.
9. Der Hund bekommt nichts.
10. Ja, Frau Huber sitzt auf dem Stuhl.
11. Ja, der Lehrer hat etwas in der Hand.
12. Frau Huber sitzt auf dem Stuhl.
13. Ich sage Ihnen nichts.
14. Der Lehrer gibt den Schülern eine deutsche Stunde.
15. Nein, der Hund spricht nicht englisch.

ANSWERS TO THE QUESTIONS OF LESSON 14 ON PAGE 77

1. Der Koch sitzt am Tisch.
2. Nein, der Braten ist auf dem Boden.
3. Nein, der Hund sitzt vor dem Ofen.
4. Der Braten liegt auf der Erde.
5. Er kommt aus dem Ofen.
6. Der Mantel ist im Schrank.
7. Der Koch geht vom Ofen zum Stuhl.
8. Der Kuchen liegt auf dem Tisch.
9. Nein, der Koch sitzt am Tisch.
10. Der Junge kommt vom Schrank.
11. Es liegt etwas auf dem Tisch.
12. Der Kuchen kommt aus der Bäckerei.
13. Der Junge bringt den Kuchen.
14. Nein, er ist nicht unter dem Tisch.
15. Nein, es sitzt niemand auf dem Ofen.

ANSWERS TO THE QUESTIONS OF LESSON 15 ON PAGE 82

Herr Vollmer sitzt am Klavier.

Fräulein Klara liest nicht in dem Buch.

Das Kätzchen sitzt auf dem Hut.

Fräulein Klara und Herr Vollmer sind im Zimmer.

Nein, das Glas steht auf dem Tisch.

Niemand sitzt am Fenster.

Nein, das Fenster ist hinter dem Sofa.

8. Das Radio steht auf einem Tisch.

9. Herr Vollmer kommt von der Tür.

10. Nein, Fräulein Klara liegt nicht auf dem Sofa, sie sitzt dort.

11. Nein, das Kätzchen sitzt auf dem Hut.

12. Ja, es ist etwas in dem Glas.

13. Herr Vollmer sitzt am Klavier.

14. Nein, er liest nicht in dem Buch.

15. Das Konzert kommt aus dem Radio.

ANSWERS TO THE QUESTIONS OF LESSON 16 ON PAGE 86

Ja, die Bluse ist in der Auslage.

Die Puppe ist in Lieses Hand.

Die Verkäuferin steht in der Tür.

Ja, er steht vor der Auslage.

Nein, die Handtasche ist in Frau Hubers Hand.

Die Verkäuferin bekommt von Frau Huber das Geld.

Sie nimmt das Geld aus der Handtasche.

8. Die Verkäuferin steht vor der Tür.

9. Der Hund trägt die alte Handtasche.

10. Ja, es ist Geld in der Handtasche.

11. Mein Taschentuch ist in der Tasche.

12. Sie gehen in die Schule.

13. Ich sitze nicht vor der Tür.

14. Sie haben nichts (etwas) in der Hand.

15. Nein, er hat keine Puppe in der Hand.

ANSWERS TO THE QUESTIONS OF LESSON 17 ON PAGE 93

Die Rose riecht gut.

Der Käse riecht nicht gut, er riecht schlecht.

Ja, Kaffee mit Zucker schmeckt gut.

Ja, ich nehme Milch zum Kaffee.

Ja, ich esse gern Blumenkohl mit Butter.

Nein, ich trinke nicht gern Limonade ohne Zucker.

7. Die Namen einiger Getränke sind: Kaffee, Tee, Bier, Wein, Wasser etc.

8. Ich kenne Fleisch, Gemüse, Suppe, Früchte, Brot etc.

9. Ich trinke nicht gern Wein. (Ich trinke gern Wein.)

10. Ja, ich spreche gern deutsch.

11. Ja, sie ist schön.

12. Nein, ich habe keine schöne Handschrift. (Ja, ich habe eine schöne
Handschrift.)

13. Ja, ich esse Brot zum Fleisch.

14. Ich esse mit dem Mund.

15. Wir gehen mit den Füssen.

16. Nein, ich sehe nicht mit gesch[...]
senen Augen.

17. Ich kenne die folgenden Gem[...]
Blumenkohl, Bohnen, Kohl, Kar[...]
feln, etc.

18. Ich sehe in diesem Zimmer ei[...]
Tisch, Stühle, Lampen, Bücher et[...]

ANSWERS TO THE QUESTIONS OF LESSON 18 ON PAGE 99

1. Vor dem Essen legt man ein Tischtuch und ein Besteck auf den Tisch.

2. Die Teller sind rund.

3. Man trägt die Speisen in Schüsseln auf den Tisch.

4. Wir essen Suppe mit dem Löffel.

5. Ich trinke Kaffee aus der Tasse und Wasser aus dem Glas.

6. Nein, ich schneide das Fleisch nicht mit der Gabel, ich schneide es mit dem Messer.

7. Das Fleisch liegt auf dem Teller.

8. Ich schmecke mit der Zunge.

9. Die Zitrone schmeckt sauer.

10. Ja, ich sehe gern, was schön ist.

11. Ja, das Pferd ist schöner als Krokodil.

12. Ja, die Venus von Milo ist schön

13. Tee ohne Zucker schmeckt bitter.

ANSWERS TO THE QUESTIONS OF LESSON 19 ON PAGE 104

1. Ja, ich kann ohne Brille sehen. (Nein, ich kann ohne Brille nicht sehen.)

2. Ja, ich kann hinausgehen.

3. Nein, man kann nicht ohne Bleistift oder Feder schreiben.

4. Er kann das Fleisch nicht ohne Messer schneiden.

5. Nein, ich kann den Himmel nicht berühren.

6. Ja, ich kann deutsch sprechen.

7. Ich kann das Buch nicht in die Ta[...]
stecken, weil sie zu klein ist.

8. Man kann ihn nicht sehen.

9. Ohne Mund kann ich nicht essen

10. Ich kann die Tür nicht ohne Schlü[...]
öffnen.

11. Ich kann meine Haare nicht zähle[...]

12. Ich kann den Stuhl berühren.

ANSWERS TO THE QUESTIONS OF LESSON 20 ON PAGE 109

1. Er kann nicht hinausgehen.

2. Er muss die Tür öffnen.

3. Er kann den Schirm nicht halten, wenn seine Hände nicht frei sind.

4. Ja, er muss die Tasche öffnen, um herauszunehmen.

5. Ich kann nicht sitzen, ohne ei[...]
Stuhl zu haben.

Ich brauche eine (keine) Brille, um zu sehen.

Der Koch muss Fleisch haben, um einen Braten zu machen.

Frau Huber muss Geld haben.

Ich muss eine Karte haben, um ins Theater zu gehen.

Ich gehe in die Berlitz School, um deutsch zu lernen.

11. Nein, man muss den Mund öffnen, um zu sprechen.

12. Wir essen, um zu leben.

13. Ja, ich kann das Fenster zerbrechen.

14. Weil ich nicht will.

15. Ich trinke keine Tinte, weil ich nicht will.

ANSWERS TO THE QUESTIONS OF LESSON 21 ON PAGE 114

Ich esse gewöhnlich um 1 Uhr und um 7 Uhr.

Ich nehme Früchte als Vorspeise. (Ich nehme keine Vorspeise.)

Ich will die Eier weich (hart) haben. (Ich will Rühreier (Spiegeleier) haben.)

Ich esse die Suppe mit dem Löffel.

Ja, es gibt kalte Suppen.

Ein Besteck besteht aus Löffel, Messer und Gabel.

Auf der Speisekarte finde ich die Speisenfolge.

Der Kellner bedient mich im Speisesaal.

Ich verlange die Speisekarte vom Kellner.

10. Ich trinke Wein (Wasser, Bier) zu meiner Mahlzeit.

11. Ja, ich nehme Zucker und Milch zum Kaffee.

12. Ich kenne Blumenkohl (Bohnen, Erbsen etc.).

13. Ja, ich nehme Obst als Nachspeise.

14. Nach dem Essen verlange ich die Rechnung.

15. Ich gebe dem Ober ein Trinkgeld.

16. In Amerika isst man mehr Entenbraten.

17. Ja, ich esse gern Fisch.

18. Im Frühling isst man Forellen.

19. Nein, der Geschmack ist verschieden.

20. Nein, nicht jedes Hotel hat einen Speisesaal.

ANSWERS TO THE QUESTIONS OF LESSON 22 ON PAGE 123

Ja, es ist eine Wanduhr in diesem Zimmer.

Sie befindet sich an der Wand.

Ja, (Nein) ich habe eine (keine) Armbanduhr.

Ich habe 3 Uhr vorbei.

5. Der Uhrmacher hat eine Uhr in der Hand.

6. Nein, sie geht nicht.

7. Eine Taschenuhr hat zwei (drei) Zeiger.

8. Ja, meine Uhr zeigt die Sekunden.

9. Das Kino fängt um 8 Uhr 30 an.

10. Es ist um 11 Uhr zu Ende.

11. Die Wanduhr zeigt 12 Uhr 50 Minuten.

12. Ich esse um 1 Uhr zu Mittag.

13. Ein Tag hat 24 Stunden.

14. Eine Minute enthält 60 Sekunden.

15. Meine Uhr geht (nicht) richtig.

16. Wenn meine Uhr vorgeht, stelle ich sie zurück.

17. Ich ziehe meine Weckuhr am Abend auf.

18. Ja, eine Kuckucksuhr ist grösser als eine Taschenuhr.

19. Nein, ich sehe keine Kirchenuhr.

20. Ja, die Schuluhr geht richtig.

21. Ja, das Fenster ist breiter als Stuhl.

22. Ja, die Damen haben längere H: als die Herren.

23. Ja, Damenhüte sind höher als I renhüte.

24. Ja, Wein ist besser als Wasser.

25. Nein, ich spreche nicht so gut deu wie englisch.

26. Ja, ich kann mit einer Brille be sehen als ohne Brille.

27. Ja, Rockefeller hat mehr Geld als

28. Ja, New York ist grösser als Berli

29. Ja, in Mexico ist es wärmer als Canada.

ANSWERS TO THE QUESTIONS OF LESSON 23 ON PAGE 131

1. In einem Jahr sind 365 Tage.

2. Ein Jahr hat 52 Wochen und 12 Monate.

3. Das Jahr fängt am ersten Januar an.

4. Es ist am 31. Dezember zu Ende.

5. Der erste Monat des Jahres ist der Januar, der achte Monat ist der August und Dezember ist der letzte Monat.

6. Der Februar hat 28 Tage.

7. Ein Schaltjahr hat 366 Tage.

8. März ist der dritte Monat.

9. Donnerstag ist der fünfte Tag der Woche.

10. Die sieben Tage der Woche heissen: Sonntag, Montag, Dienstag, Mittwoch, Donnerstag, Freitag, Sonnabend.

11. Die Frühlingsmonate heissen April, Mai und Juni.

12. Der Monat August dauert 31 Tag

13. Letzten Sonnabend war nicht der es war der . . .

14. Morgen ist das Jahr nicht zu E:

15. Wir sind jetzt im . . .

16. Nach dem Winter kommt der F ling.

17. Weihnachten ist kein gewöhnli Wochentag, es ist ein Feiertag.

18. Zu Ostern arbeite ich nicht.

19. Der Tag vor dem Sonntag h Samstag.

20. Jetzt ist es . . . Uhr.

21. Der 31. December fällt dieses Jahr einen . . .

22. Ja, ich habe einen Kalender.

23. Dezember ist der letzte Herbstmo

ANSWERS TO THE QUESTIONS OF LESSON 24 ON PAGE 137

Wir teilen die vierundzwanzig Stunden in Tag und Nacht ein.

Am Tage ist es hell, bei Nacht ist es dunkel.

Am Abend ist es nicht hell, es ist dunkel.

Das Tageslicht kommt von der Sonne.

Die Sonne scheint nicht während der Nacht.

Wir arbeiten bei Tage.

Wir gehen am Abend ins Theater.

Der Mond geht in der Nacht auf.

Wenn es dunkel ist, schalten wir das elektrische Licht ein.

Im Kino ist es dunkel.

Während der Nacht sehe ich den Mond und die Sterne am Himmel.

Im Sommer geht die Sonne früh auf.

Im Sommer sind die Tage lang.

Im Winter sind die Tage kurz, weil die Sonne spät auf- und früh untergeht.

Ja, die Nächte in den Wintermonaten sind länger als die Tage.

Ich zünde die Zigarette mit einem Streichholz an.

17. Ein Kind geht früh schlafen.

18. Ja, ein Kind schläft lang.

19. Ja, am Sonntag schlafe ich länger als an Wochentagen.

20. Man arbeitet 8 Stunden im Büro.

21. Ja, ich arbeite gern.

22. Ja, ich kann während des Tages schlafen.

23. Nein, das Licht des Mondes ist nicht so stark wie das der Sonne.

24. Nein, man kann die Sterne nicht zählen.

25. Ich sehe den Mond während der Nacht.

26. Die Sonne geht im Osten auf und geht im Westen unter.

27. Die vier Himmelsrichtungen heissen Osten, Westen, Süden und Norden.

28. Nein, ich frühstücke nicht am Abend, ich frühstücke am Morgen.

29. Jetzt ist es weder Abend noch Morgen, es ist Nachmittag.

30. Ja, die Sonne am Strand ist heiss.

31. Ja, ich nehme ein Sonnenbad.

32. Ich ziehe mich am Morgen an.

33. Ich kämme mich zweimal im Tage.

ANSWERS TO THE QUESTIONS OF LESSON 25 ON PAGE 145

Nein, mir ist nicht warm, machen Sie das Fenster nicht auf.

Ja, ich friere, wenn ich im Winter ohne Mantel ausgehe.

Bei schlechtem Wetter ist der Himmel grau.

4. Ja, es regnet, wenn der Himmel mit Wolken bedeckt ist.

5. Nein, wenn es friert, regnet es nicht.

6. Im Winter fällt Schnee vom Himmel.

7. Ich habe einen Regenschirm in der Hand, um mich gegen den Regen zu schützen.

8. Der Mantel schützt mich gegen die Kälte.

9. Ja, ich habe einen Regenmantel.

10. Das Wetter ist heute schön (hässlich).

11. Nein, hier ist es nicht zu warm.

12. Nein, im Hochsommer schneit es nie.

13. Nein, im Spätherbst ist es nicht warm.

14. Ja, mir ist manchmal im Frühling kalt.

15. Heute haben wir 50 Grad.

16. Man heizt die Zimmer, wenn es kalt ist.

17. Die Wärme kommt von der Sonne.

18. Nein, im Dezember scheint die Sonne nicht so warm wie im Juli.

19. Ich gehe im Sommer baden.

20. Im Winter ziehe ich dicke Kleider an.

21. Ja, im März ist es sehr windig.

22. Wenn meine Kleider und Schuhe s nass sind, ziehe ich sie aus und zi trockene an.

23. Ja, die Damen ziehen sich oft un

24. Ja, in Cuba ist es gewöhnlich heis

25. Wenn mir kalt ist, setze ich mich die Heizung.

26. Nein, die Sterne geben keine Wär

27. Ja, ich gehe manchmal bei schlech Wetter aus.

28. Nein, ich gehe bei Regenwetter n ohne Schirm aus.

29. Im Winter ziehe ich warme Kle an.

30. Kalt und trocken ist besser als w und nass.

ANSWERS TO THE QUESTIONS OF LESSON 26 ON PAGE 151

1. Die Beiden haben nicht gut geschlafen.

2. Der Briefträger bringt die Post.

3. Ja, (Nein) ich habe heute meine Zeitung (nicht) gelesen.

4. Ich habe vor einer Stunde das letzte Mal gegessen.

5. Es bleiben sechs Brötchen übrig.

6. Nein, ich habe noch nie einen deutschen Brief geschrieben.

7. Ja, (Nein) ich habe schon (noch nie) Sizilien besucht.

8. Ich habe mich kurze Zeit (lange Zeit, nicht) in Europa aufgehalten.

9. Ja, ich habe auch auf dem La gelebt.

10. Ja, (Nein) ich habe immer (n immer) gehalten, was ich versproc habe.

11. Nein, ich habe nicht alles behal was ich gelernt habe.

12. Nein, ich habe nicht vergessen, ich heisse.

13. Ja, ich habe alles verstanden, was gelesen habe.

14. Columbus hat Amerika entdeckt.

15. Ich habe bei Berlitz deutsch gele

ANSWERS TO THE QUESTIONS OF LESSON 27 ON PAGE 156

1. Fräulein Franzen ist im Sommer in Salzburg gewesen.

2. Ja, es ist ihr gelungen, mit wenig (einen schönen Sommer zu verbring

Die Tante hat sie eingeladen.

Ja, sie ist während der Festspiele dort geblieben.

Ja, die Reise hat sich gelohnt.

Ja, Richard Strauss ist hingekommen.

Ja, Herr Roth ist täglich baden gegangen.

Ja, (Nein) ich bin schon (noch nie) in Europa gewesen.

Im Jahre 1492 hat Columbus Amerika entdeckt.

10. Georg Washington ist 1799 gestorben.

11. Die Mayflower ist 1620 in Amerika angekommen.

12. Ja, (Nein) ich bin schon (noch nie) über den Ozean geflogen.

13. Ja, gestern Abend sind die Sterne am Himmel gestanden.

14. Nein, der Dreizehnte ist nicht auf einen Freitag gefallen.

15. Ich bin an meinem Geburtstag geboren.

ANSWERS TO THE QUESTIONS OF LESSON 28 ON PAGE 163

Liese denkt an ihre Zukunft.

Frau Huber denkt an den kommenden Abend.

Der Professor wird heute abend zu Frau Huber gehen.

Herr Krause ladet Herrn Dr. Peters zum Mittagessen ein.

Ja, dieser wird die Einladung annehmen.

Die Herren werden bei Herrn Krause speisen.

Herr Dr. Peters wird um sechs Uhr aufstehen.

Sie werden die Theaterkarten sofort nehmen.

Im Zwischenakt werden sie das Theaterfoyer besichtigen.

10. Herr Krause wird dem Herrn Eckner telegraphieren.

11. Ja, die Eckners werden aufs Land gehen.

12. Die Theatervorstellung wird zeitig (früh) aus sein.

13. Ich werde den Sommer (nicht) in der Stadt verbringen.

14. Herr Dr. Peters wird die Post lesen und telephonieren.

15. Er wird seine Kanzlei um ein Uhr verlassen.

16. Die Eckners werden in Frankreich französisch sprechen können, weil sie die Berlitz-Schule besucht haben.

ANSWERS TO THE QUESTIONS OF LESSON 29 ON PAGE 169

Die Pflanzen können sich nicht bewegen.

Die Tiere müssen atmen, trinken und essen, um zu leben.

3. Wir können nicht leben, ohne zu essen.

4. Ja, der Löwe muss trinken.

5. Wir brauchen Nahrung zum Leben. (um zu leben).

6. Die fünf Sinne heissen: Gesicht, Gehör, Geschmack, Geruch und Gefühl.

7. Das Organ des Geruchs heisst Nase.

8. Wir teilen die Tiere in Vierfüssler, Vögel, Fische, Reptilien und Insekten ein.

9. Die wichtigsten Haustiere heissen Hund, Katze, Pferd, Kuh, etc.

10. Die Vierfüssler können nicht fliegen und haben Haare.

11. Das Huhn ist nützlich.

12. Die Vögel fliegen mit den Flügeln.

13. Die Lungen sind die Atmungsorga

14. Wir verdauen mit dem Magen.

15. Ja, (Nein) ich bin (nicht) gesund.

16. Wenn unsere Atmungs-, Verdauu oder anderen Organe nicht nor sind, sind wir krank.

17. Nein, die Schlange fliegt nicht, kriecht.

18. Der Frosch lebt auf dem Lande im Wasser.

19. Ja, die Biene ist nützlich.

20. Ja, der Haifisch ist gefährlich.

ANSWERS TO THE QUESTIONS OF LESSON 30 ON PAGE 176

1. Nein, der Professor freut sich.

2. Er freut sich, weil er viel Geld hat.

3. Sie weint, weil ihre Puppe zerbrochen ist.

4. Nein, sie lacht nicht.

5. Sie ist traurig, weil sie allein ist.

6. Ja, der Mensch ist den Tieren überlegen.

7. Nein, ich denke nicht an sie, wenn ich nicht zuhause bin.

8. Nein, man kann nicht sprechen ohne zu denken.

9. Man weiss, was man gelernt hat.

10. Man kann, was man oft gemacht hat.

11. Ja, (Nein) ich kenne es (nicht).

12. Ja, Liese kann deutsch.

13. Ja, ich kann lesen.

14. Nein, ich weiss nicht, wieviele Zä Sie haben.

15. Nein, ich vergesse nicht schnell.

16. Nein, wir können die Sterne n zählen.

17. Ja, man liebt seine Mutter.

18. Ja, ich habe deutsche Musik gern.

19. Ich weine manchmal, wenn ich m sehr freue.

20. Ja, (Nein) ich habe (keine) Fur vor Katzen.

21. Nein, die Katze liebt den Hund ni

22. Ja, (Nein) der Winter gefällt (nicht).

23. Ja, ich bin ärgerlich, wenn es reg

24. Manche Tiere haben Verstand.

ANSWERS TO THE QUESTIONS OF LESSON 31 ON PAGE 185

1. Die grössten Städte Europas heissen: London, Paris und Berlin.

2. New York ist die grösste Stadt in Vereinigten Staaten.

3. Montreal liegt in Canada.

4. Ja, Berlin ist weit von London.

5. Ich reise am liebsten mit der Bahn (im Auto, im Flugzeug).

6. Ich kaufe die Fahrkarte am Schalter.

7. Wenn ich ein Abteil betrete, frage ich: Ist hier ein Platz frei?

8. Ich nehme Gepäck auf die Reise mit.

9. Ja, ich packe meine Koffer allein.

10. Ich nehme ein Taxi zur Bahn.

11. Ja, man reist im Flugzeug bequemer.

12. Ja, die Engländer reisen sehr viel.

13. In einer fremden Stadt wohne ich im Hotel.

14. Ja (Nein), ich verstehe (nicht) gut deutsch.

15. In einer grossen Stadt sehe ich viele Häuser und Menschen.

16. Fleisch kaufe ich beim Fleischer.

17. Macys und Gimbels sind New Yorks grösste Kaufhäuser.

18. Wenn ich mich verirre, frage ich einen Polizisten.

19. Im Hotel verlange ich ein Zimmer.

20. Wenn ich einen Hut brauche, sage ich zum Verkäufer: "Zeigen Sie mir bitte einige Hüte!"

21. Er fragt nach der Kopfweite.

22. Wenn der Preis zu hoch ist, frage ich: "Haben Sie nichts Billigeres?"

23. Nein, nicht jeder Hut passt mir.

ANSWERS TO THE QUESTIONS OF LESSON 32 ON PAGE 195

1. Die Herren befinden sich in Frankfurt.

2. Herr Ritter kommt von Wien.

3. Herr Schmitt ist seit einer Woche geschäftlich in Frankfurt.

4. Nein, Herr Ritter ist kein Deutscher, er ist Wiener.

5. Herr Schmitt stammt mütterlicherseits aus Wien.

6. Herr Schmitt will sich von Frankfurt nach Wien begeben.

7. Nein, Herr Schmitt wird sich nicht länger in Frankfurt aufhalten.

8. Nein, er ist noch nie in Wien gewesen.

9. Herr Ritter ladet ihn ein, mit ihm nach Wien zu reisen.

10. Ja, er nimmt seine Einladung an.

11. Ja, Herr Ritter wird das tun können.

12. Ich brauche in New York keinen Führer.

13. Die Herren gehen zum Hotel zurück, nachdem sie ihre Flugscheine gekauft haben.

14. Es ist gar nicht leicht, für denselben Tag eine Flugkarte zu bekommen.

15. Ich frage ihn: "Haben Sie noch eine Flugkarte nach Wien?"

16. Ich sage: "Geben Sie mir eine erste nach Wien!"

17. Es fliegt um 9 Uhr ab.

18. Sie wählen das 9 Uhr Flugzeug, um die Zwischenlandungen zu vermeiden.

19. Er macht Landungen in Stuttgart und München.

20. Es ist angenehmer zu fliegen, als im Expresszug zu fahren.

21. Herr Ritter nimmt keine Rückfahrkarte, weil er in Wien bleiben will.

22. Er verlangt sie, weil der Autobus sie abholen wird.

23. Ja, (Nein) ich wohne (nicht) in einer Grossstadt.

24. Ich wohne: (Adresse).

25. Der Autobus kommt die Herren um 6 Uhr früh abholen.

26. Ja, ich schlafe gern lang am Morgen.

27. Die Reisenden müssen zeitig aufstehen, um das Flugzeug nicht zu versäumen.

28. Ja, ich bin es, wenn ich sehr zeitig aufstehe.

ANSWERS TO THE QUESTIONS OF LESSON 33 ON PAGE 202

1. Ja, Herr Schmitt schläft, wenn der Fernsprecher läutet.

2. Die Telefonistin ruft ihn an.

3. Nein, er steht nicht gerne zeitig auf.

4. Der Hausdiener wird das Gepäck zum Auto bringen.

5. Herr Schmitt steht nach dem Telefongespräch auf.

6. Er lässt den Schlüssel in der Tür.

7. Er spricht mit dem Kassier im Hotelbüro.

8. Er lässt den Pagen nicht die Handtasche nehmen, weil er sie allein tragen will.

9. Die Passagiere dürfen 25 Kilo unentgeltlich mitführen.

10. Nein, er hat nichts gegessen, bevor er zum Fluggplatz gefahren ist.

11. Sie können nicht mehr am Flughafen essen, weil sie einsteigen müssen.

12. Er sagt, dass man im Flugzeug Essen serviert.

13. Ja, an Bord des Flugzeuges werden Mahlzeiten serviert.

14. Ja, Essen wird herumgereicht.

15. Ja, (Nein) ich bin schon (noch nie) geflogen.

16. Ich wiege . . . . Kilo (Pfund).

17. Ich wohne im zweiten Stock.

18. Ja, sie können es.

19. Sicher habe ich schon einmal verschlafen.

ANSWERS TO THE QUESTIONS OF LESSON 34 ON PAGE 213

1. Man sieht Berge, Flüsse und Städte von einem Flugzeug aus.

2. Nein, der Aeroplan kommt auf dem Flugfeld an.

3. Die Donau ist dort zu sehen.

4. Man muss den Reisepass bei der Passkontrolle vorzeigen.

5. Er fragt nach zollpflichtigen Sachen.

6. Ja, sie sind freundlich zu ihm.

7. Sie sind höflich, weil er Amerikaner ist.

8. Nein, Zollbeamte sind nicht immer höflich.

9. Herr Schmitt gedenkt nicht mehr als 2 Wochen zu bleiben.

10. Man kann sie in der Wechselstube wechseln.

11. Nein, er wird im Hotel wohnen.

12. Er will dort nicht seine Landsleute treffen.

13. Nein, er fährt allein nach Hause.

14. Ja, sie haben sich verabredet.

15. Er wünscht ein Strassenzimmer.

16. Man isst im Speisesaal des Hotels.

17. Der Hausdiener tut das.

18. Er will sich erst ein wenig herrichten.

19. Er hat seinen Schirm verloren.

20. Ja, ich habe meinen Schirm schon irgendwo stehen lassen.

21. Ich gebe ihm ein Trinkgeld.

22. Sein Doppelzimmer ist im ersten Stock.

23. Er erwartet Herrn Ritter am zeitigen Nachmittag.

24. Ich nehme Reiseschecks, weil sie sicherer sind.

25. Ja, sie sind praktischer.

ANSWERS TO THE QUESTIONS OF LESSON 35 ON PAGE 226

1. Sie beginnen ihren Spaziergang beim Hotel "Österreichischer Hof".

2. Der Strassenverkehr in Wien ist sehr stark.

3. Der Platz im Zentrum der Stadt ist der Stephansplatz.

4. Herr Schmitt kauft im Hutgeschäft Habig ein.

5. Der Verkäufer empfiehlt einen Borsalino.

6. Der Käufer hat Kopfweite 56.

7. Ja, er ist damit zufrieden.

8. Nein, Herr Schmitt behält ihn gleich an.

9. Ja, seine Mutter hat viel von der Wiener Oper erzählt.

10. Sie befinden sich auf dem Kärntnerring.

11. Er kauft noch Ansichtskarten ein.

12. Er fährt mit dem Taxi den Ring entlang.

13. Er kommt an den beiden Staatsmuseen vorbei.

14. Nein, er geht am Abend nicht ins Theater.

15. Er wird den Abend bei Ritters verbringen.

16. Ja, er nimmt sie mit Vergnügen an.

17. Sie werden einander am Abend wiedersehen.

18. Nein, sie geht im Kreise um die Innere Stadt herum.

19. Das Hotel Sacher ist wegen seiner Küche berühmt.

20. Man serviert dort die Sachertorte mit Schlagsahne.

21. Ja, (Nein) ich kenne sie (nicht).

22. Ja, man bekommt sie in einer Konditorei in der 72. Strasse West.

ANSWERS TO THE QUESTIONS OF LESSON 36 ON PAGE 233

1. Sie sehen die Sehenswürdigkeiten auf der Ringstrasse.

2. Die Habsburger haben dort gewohnt.

3. Nein, sie regieren nicht mehr.

4. Das grösste Schauspielhaus Wiens ist das Burgtheater.

5. Kaiser Franz Josef hat sie bauen lassen.

6. Sie steht beim Schottentor.

7. Ein Attentäter wollte ihn töten.

8. Sein Uniformkragen rettete ihn.

9. Der Gürtel geht um die äusseren Bezirke herum.

10. Sie fahren noch an der Volksoper vorüber.

11. Nein, sie können es nicht besichtigen.

12. Herr Ritter wohnt in der Cottage-Strasse.

13. Sie fahren zur Wohnung Herrn Ritters.

14. Er gibt ihm das Fahrgeld und ein Trinkgeld.

15. Die beiden Museen, die Hofburg, das Burgtheater, die Universität, die Votivkirche, usw.

16. Nein, er hat dort nicht geschäftlich zu tun, er ist zu Besuch in Wien.

17. Nein, er hat sie noch nicht besucht.

18. Er hat Kusinen in Wien.

ANSWERS TO THE QUESTIONS OF LESSON 37 ON PAGE 241

1. Ja, er hat ihn zum Essen eingeladen.

2. Nein, er kennt sie noch nicht.

3. Ja, er will sie kennenlernen.

4. Frau Ritter sagt, dass sie sehr erfreut sei.

5. Ritters haben 3 Kinder.

6. Sie heissen Liesl, Franz und Betty.

7. Franz hat 2 Schwestern.

8. Nein, sie glaubt nicht, dass er brav sei.

9. Nein, Herr Schmitt ist noch nicht verheiratet, aber er ist so gut wie verlobt.

10. Ja, er hat ein Bild seiner Braut bei sich.

11. Ja, sie findet sie sehr schön.

12. Ja, (Nein) ich bin (nicht) verheiratet.

13. Ja, (Nein) ich habe (keine) Schwestern und Brüder.

14. Sie sagt: "Das Essen ist aufgetragen!".

15. Herr Schmitt sitzt auf dem Ehrenplatz.

16. Es gibt Backhahn mit grünem Salat.

17. Ja, ich habe schon Backhuhn gegessen.

18. Ich esse gern grünen Salat.

ANSWERS TO THE QUESTIONS OF LESSON 38 ON PAGE 248

1. Der Prater wird mit Coney Island in New York, mit dem Lunapark in Berlin und Paris verglichen.

2. Das Tegetthoff-Denkmal steht dort.

3. Die Drachenbahn ist eine Bahn, die von einem Drachen gezogen wird.

4. Die Wachsfiguren der berühmten Verbrecher sind dort ausgestellt.

5. Es wurde von Paris nach Wien gebracht.

6. Der Waggon wird von 2 Herren und 2 Damen geteilt.

7. Ja, (Nein) ich bin (nicht) schwindelfrei.

8. Nein, mir wird nicht (oft) schlecht.

9. Herr Ritter wird von ihm besucht.

10. Er wird von Herrn Schmitt angerufen werden.

11. Es wird hier von mir deutsch gesprochen.

12. Die Donau schlängelt sich durch Wien hindurch.

13. Ja, er wird ihn wiedersehen.

14. Weil es baufällig war.

15. Ja, (Nein,) es hat mich (mir) schon (noch nicht) gegruselt.

GLOSSARY

A

A-B-C *n.* alphabet
abbrechen to break up
Abend *m.* evening
aber but
Abfahrt *f.* departure
Abfahrtsplattform *f.* departure
  platform
abfertigen to finish, to go through
  with
Abflug *m.* take-off
abgemacht agreed, "it's a deal!"
ablegen to take off (hat or coat)
abreisen to leave, depart
absteigen to get off, get down, stop
  (at hotel)
Abteil *n.* compartment
Abteilung *f.* department, section
abwesend absent
Abwesenheit *f.* absence
abzweigen to branch off
acht eight
Achtung *f* attention, "look out!"

achtzehn eighteen
achtzig eighty
Ader *f* artery
Admiral *m.* admiral
Affe *m.* monkey
ähnlich similar, alike
Alkohol *m.* alcohol
alle all
allerdings anyway, of course
allgemein general, common
Alpen *f. pl.* Alps
als as, than, when
also so, thus, then
alt old
altmodisch old-fashioned
Amerika *n.* America
Amerikaner *m.* American (male)
Amerikanerin *f.* American (female)
an at, to, near, by, next to
anbehalten to keep on (as clothing)

andere   other, others
anders   otherwise, differently
anempfehlen   to recommend
anfallen   to attack, assail
Anfang *m.*   beginning, start
anfangen   to start, begin
angekommen   arrived
angenehm   agreeable, pleasant
Angst *f.*   anxiety, fear
ankleiden, sich   to dress oneself
ankommen   to arrive
Anmeldeschein *m.*   registration slip
anrufen   to call up
anschliessen, sich   to join, attach
Ansichtskarte *f.*   picture postcard
Antwort *f.*   reply, answer
antworten   to reply, answer
anwesend   present
anzünden   to light, set aflame
Apfel *m.*   apple
Apfelbaum *m.*   apple tree
Apfelwein *m.*   cider
Appetit *m.*   appetite
applaudieren   to applaud
Apotheke *f.*   pharmacy
April *m.*   April
Arbeit *f.*   work, task
arbeiten   to work
arg   bad
Ärger *m.*   anger
ärgern, sich   to become angry
Arm *m.*   arm
arm   poor
Armbanduhr *f.*   wristwatch
Art *f.*   manner, kind, way
Asien *n.*   Asia
Atem *m.*   breath
atmen   to breathe
Atmung *f.*   breathing, respiration
Attentäter *m.*   assailant, assassin
auch   also, too
auf   on, upon, on top of
aufbrechen   to go on one's way, leave
Aufenthalt *m.*   sojourn, stop
auffallen   to draw attention, strike
Aufgabe *f.*   lesson, exercise
aufgehen   rise
aufhaben   to wear, have on
aufhalten, sich   to stay, remain
aufhören   to stop, cease, desist

aufmachen   to open
aufregend   exciting
aufrichtig   frank, sincere
aufstehen   to get up, rise
auftragen   to serve
aufziehen   to wind
Auge *n.*   eye
August *m.*   August
aus   from, out of, over
Ausbesserung *f.*   repair
ausfüllen   to fill out
ausgehungert   starved, famished
aushalten   to hold out, stand
aushelfen   to help out
auskleiden, sich   to undress
Auslage *f.*   display, show window
auslöschen   extinguish, put out
Ausnahme *f.*   exception
ausnahmslos   without exception
Aussicht *f.*   view, prospect
äusserer   outer
ausschalten   to switch off, put out
ausschauen   to appear, look
ausserdem   besides, moreover
aussteigen   to descend, get off
Auto *n.*   car, automobile
Autobus *m.*   bus

B

Bach *m.*   creek, brook, stream
backen   to bake, fry
Bäcker *m.*   baker
Bäckerei *f.*   bakery, cookies, pastry
Backhähndel *n.*   young fried (baked) chicken
Backhuhn *n.*   fried (baked) chicken
Bad *n.*   bath, resort, spa
baden   to bathe
Bahn *f.*   railroad, way
Bahnhof *m.*   railroad station
Bahnsteig *m.*   railroad platform
Bahnwärter *m.*   railroad watchman
bald   soon
Ball *m.*   ball
Bär *m.*   bear
Bärin *f.*   female bear
Bauch *m.*   abdomen, belly
bauen   to build

Bauer *m.* peasant, farmer
Baufälligkeit *f.* dilapidated condition
Baum *m.* tree
Beamte *m.* employee, clerk
bedauern to regret, feel sorry for
bedecken to cover
bedeckt covered
beehren to honor, do honor
befinden, sich *to* find oneself
begabt gifted, talented
begeistert fascinated, charmed
beginnen to begin, start, commence
Begriff *m.* conception, idea
begrüssen to welcome, greet, salute
behalten to keep, remember
bei at, by, with, according to
beide both
beim at the
Beispiel *n.* example
beissen to bite
bekannt known
bekommen to get, receive
belegen to reserve, retain
beliebt beloved, favorite
bellen to bark
benutzen to make use of
bequem comfortable
bereits already
Berg *m.* mountain
Bergziege *f.* mountain-goat
berühmt famous, famed
berühren to touch
beschädigt damaged
bescheiden modest
Bescherung *f.* distribution of presents
besetzt occupied, taken, busy
besichtigen to look over, inspect
besonders particularly, specially
besorgen to provide, see through, take care of
besser better
Besteck *n.* silverware
bestellen to order, convey
bestimmt sure, certain
Bestimmungsort *m.* destination, goal
Besuch *m.* visit
besuchen to visit, look up

Besuchszwecken, zu on a visit
betreten to enter
Betrieb *m.* function, operation
in Betrieb setzen to set into motion
Bett *n.* bed
bevor before, in front of
bewegen to move
bezahlen to pay (for)
Biene *f.* bee
Bier *n.* beer
Bild *n.* picture, painting, image
bilden to form, educate
billig cheap, inexpensive
Birne *f.* pear
Birnbaum *m.* pear tree
bis till, until, up to
bisschen a bit
bitte please
bitten to ask for, request
bitter bitter
blau blue
bleiben to stay, remain
Bleistift *m.* pencil
blühen to bloom, blossom
Blume *f.* flower
Bluse *f.* blouse
Blut *n.* blood
Blutkreislauf *m.* blood circulation
Boden *m.* bottom, floor, attic
Bohne *f.* bean
bös bad, evil
Brandgeruch *m.* burning smell
Braten *m.* roast
brauchen to need
braun brown
Braut *f.* bride, fiancee
brav good, obedient, well-behaved
breit wide, broad
brennen to burn
Brief *m.* letter
Briefträger *m.* mailman, letter carrier
Brille *f.* glasses
bringen to bring
Brot *n.* bread
Brötchen *n.* roll
Brust *f.* breast, chest
Bub, *m.* boy, lad
Buch *n.* book
Buchhandlung *f.* bookstore

Buchstabe *m.* letter (of the alphabet)
buchstabieren to spell
Burggarten *m.* castle garden
Burgtheater *n.* Court Theatre
Burgtor *n.* castle gate
Büro *n.* office, bureau
Bürste *f.* brush

C

Chauffeur *m.* driver
China *n.* China
Chinese *m.* Chinese (male)
Chinesin *f.* Chinese (female)
chinesisch Chinese
Cousin *m.* male cousin
Cousine *f.* female cousin

D

da here, there, then
dafür for it, instead of it
dagegen against it, on the other hand
daheim at home
Dame *f.* lady
Dank *m.* thanks
danken to thank
dann then, afterwards
daran at it, on it
das the, this, it, that (*art.* or *pron.*)
dass that, so that (*conj.*)
dauern to last, endure
dazukommen to get around to
dazwischen in between, meantime
Decke *f.* ceiling, cover, blanket
denken to think
Denkmal *n.* monument, memorial
denn for (*conj.*)
dennoch however, nevertheless
der the, this, it
derselbe the same
deshalb therefore
deswegen therefore
deutsch German
Deutsche (a) German

Deutschland *n.* Germany
Dezember *m.* December
Dichter *m.* poet
Dichterfürst *m.* prince of poetry
dick thick, fat
die the, this
dienen to serve
Diener *m.* servant
Dienstag *m.* Tuesday
Dienstmädchen *n.* maid, servant
diese ⎫
dieses ⎬ this, this one
dieser ⎭
Dimension *f.* dimension
Ding *n.* thing, object
direkt direct, straight
dirigieren to conduct
Doktor *m.* doctor
Dolch *m.* dagger
Dom *m.* dome, cathedral
Donau *f.* Danube
Donaukanal *m.* Danube canal
Donnerstag *m.* Thursday
Donnerwetter *n.* thunderstorm
Doppelzimmer *n.* double room
dort there
Drache *m.* dragon
Drachenbahn *f.* dragon railroad
draussen out there, in the open air
drei three
dreissig thirty
dreizehn thirteen
dritte third
drüben over there, on the other side
dulden to tolerate, suffer
dumm stupid, silly
dunkel dark
Dunkelheit *f.* darkness
dünn thin, loose, sparse
durch through, across, by way of
durchnehmen to go through (a lesson, assignment, etc.)
dürfen to be permitted to, be expected to

E

eben even, right now, just
Ehre *f.* honor

Ehrenplatz *m.* seat of honor

Ei *n.* egg

Eierspeise *f.* food made of eggs, scrambled eggs

eigentlich in fact, really, as a matter of fact

Eile *f.* hurry, haste

eilen to hurry, speed, run fast

ein one, a

einander each other, one another

einbiegen to turn into, take a turn

einfach simple, simply

einführen to introduce, import

Eingang *m.* entrance

einige a few, some

Einkauf *m.* purchase

einladen to invite

Einladung *f.* invitation

einmal once

einnehmen to take in, take

einpacken to pack, wrap up

einrechnen to count in, include

eins one thing, one o'clock

einschalten to switch on

einsperren to lock in, lock up

einsteigen to mount, get on, get aboard

einstellen to turn on (radio)

einteilen to divide

Eintritt *m.* entrance, admission

Eintrittskarte *f.* admission ticket

einverstanden agreed upon, "it's a deal!"

einwechseln to exchange, trade

einziehen to move in

Eis *n.* ice, ice-cream

Eisbär *m.* polar bear

Eisen *n.* iron

Eisenbahn *f.* railroad

Elefant *m.* elephant

elegant elegant

elf eleven

empfehlen to recommend

Empfindung *f.* sensation, sentiment

Ende *n.* end, finish

enden to end, finish, stop

endlich finally, in the end

Endstation *f.* terminal, last stop

energisch energetic, energetically

England *n.* England

Engländer *m.* Englishman

Engländerin *f.* English woman

englisch English

Ente *f.* duck

enthalten to contain, comprise

entlang along

Entschluss *m.* decision

entschuldigen to excuse, forgive

Entschuldigung *f.* excuse, apology

entwickeln to develop

er he, it

erblicken to catch sight of

Erbse *f.* pea

Erdbeere *f.* strawberry

erdolchen to stab to death

Ereignis *n.* event

erinnern, sich to remember

Erlebnis *n.* event, occurrence

erledigen to finish, achieve

erst first, in the first place

erste (the) first

erstklassig first class, first rate

erwarten to expect

erzählen to report, tell, relate

erzeugen to produce

es it

Esel *m.* donkey, jackass

essen to eat

etwas something

Eule *f.* owl

Europa *n.* Europe

Europäer *m.* (a) European

europäisch European

F

fahren to ride, drive, travel

Fahrkarte *f.* railroad ticket, travel ticket

Fahrpreis *m.* fare

Fahrschein *m.* ticket

Fahrt *f.* ride, trip

fallen to fall

Familie *f.* family

Familienleben *n.* family life

famos famous, excellent

Farbe *f.* color

fast almost, nearly

faul lazy, rotten

Februar *m.* February
Feder *f.* pen, feather, spring
federleicht light as a feather
Feiertag *m.* holiday
fein fine
Feld *n.* field
Fell *n.* skin, fur
Fenster *n.* window
Fensterbrett *n.* windowsill
Ferkel *n.* piglet
Fernsprecher *m.* telephone
fertig ready, complete, finished
Festland *n.* firm ground
Festspiele *n.pl.* festival
fett fat
Feuer *n.* fire
Film *m.* motion picture
finden to find
Finger *m.* finger
Fisch *m.* fish
Flasche *f.* bottle
Fleisch *n.* meat
Fleischer *m.* butcher
Fliege *f.* fly
fliegen to fly
fliessen to flow
Flosse *f.* fin
Flug *m.* flight
Fluggesellschaft *f.* airline
Flugplatz *m.* airport
Flugzeug *n.* aircraft, airplane
Flugzeugabsturz *m.* airplane crash
folgen to follow, obey
Forelle *f.* trout
Form *f.* form, figure
fort away
fortgehen to go away, leave
fortschrittlich progressive
Frage *f.* question
fragen to ask, inquire
Frankreich *n.* France
Franzose *m.* Frenchman
Französin *f.* French woman
französisch French
Frau *f.* woman, wife
Fräulein *n.* miss, young lady, governess
frei free
Freitag *m.* Friday
freigeworden vacated
fremd foreign, alien

Fremde stranger
Fremdenführer *m.* guide
fressen to eat (used for animal only)
freuen, sich to be glad, joyful, happy
Freund *m.* friend, gentleman friend
Freundin *f.* friend, lady friend
frieren to freeze
froh glad, joyful, pleased
fröhlich gay, merry
Frucht *f.* fruit
früh early
Frühe *f.* early morning
Frühstück *n.* breakfast
frühstücken to have breakfast
Fuchs *m.* fox
fühlen to feel, sense
fühlen, sich to have the feeling, the sensation
führen to lead, conduct
Fundbüro *n.* lost-and-found bureau
fünf five
fünfzehn fifteen
fünfzig fifty
funktionieren to function
Furcht *f.* fear
fürchten to fear
fürchten, sich to be afraid
Fuss *m.* foot

G

Gabel *f.* fork
Gans *f.* goose
Gänseblümchen *n.* daisy
ganz entire, complete
garantieren to guarantee, vouch for
Garten *m.* garden
Gas *n.* gas
Gast *m.* guest
Gastfreundschaft *f.* hospitality
Gebäck *n.* pastry, cookies
Gebäude *n.* building
geben to give
Gedanke *m.* thought
Gedeck *n.* place setting

gedenken to intend, plan, have in mind
Geduld *f.* patience
gefährlich dangerous, perilous
gefallen to please
gefallen fallen
Geflügel *n.* fowl
Gefühl *n.* feeling, sentiment
gegen against, toward, versus
Gegenstand *m.* object, matter
Gegenteil *n.* opposite, contrary
gegenüber in front of, opposite
gehen to go
Gehirn *n.* brain
Gehör *n.* hearing, ear
gehören to belong, to be owned
gekocht cooked
gelb yellow
Geld *n.* money
Gelegenheit *f.* opportunity
gelingen to succeed
gemeinsam common, together
Gemse *f.* chamois
Gemüse *n.* vegetable
gemütlich comfortable, leisurely
genannt called, named
genau exactly
General *m.* general (mil.)
genug enough, sufficiently
Gepäck *n.* baggage
Gepäckschein *m.* baggage check
Gepäckwage *f.* baggage scale
gerade even, just
Geräusch *n.* noise
gern gladly
gern haben to like, love
Gerüst *n.* scaffolding
Geschäft *n.* store, shop, business
geschäftlich commercial, business-wise
geschehen to happen
Geschenk *n.* gift, present
Geschichte *f.* story, history
geschlossen closed, locked
Geschmack *m.* taste
geschmeichelt flattered
Gesicht *n.* face, sight
gestatten to permit
gestattet permitted
gestehen to confess
gestern yesterday

gesund healthy, sound
Getränk *n.* beverage
Getreide *n.* wheat
gewesen been
gewiss certain, sure
gewogen weighed
gewöhnlich usual, general
Gewürz *n.* spice, seasoning
gibt, es there is, there are
giessen to pour
Giraffe *f.* giraffe
Glas *n.* glass, tumbler
glauben to believe
gleich alike, at once, on the spot
gleichzeitig at the same time, simultaneously
glücklich happy, fortunate, lucky
Glückspilz *m.* lucky fellow
Gold *n.* gold
golden golden
Gott *m.* God
Gras *n.* grass
gratulieren to congratulate
grau gray
gross large, big, great, tall
grossartig magnificent
Grösse *f.* size, greatness, magnitude
grün green
Grünzeughändler *m.* greengrocer
gruseln to shudder
Gruss *m.* greeting, regard, salute
grüssen to greet, salute
Gürtel *m.* belt
gut good, well
Guten Tag! Good day!

H

Haar *n.* hair
haben to have
Hahn *m.* rooster
Hähnchen *n.* little rooster, young chicken
Haifisch *m.* shark
halb half
Hälfte *f.* half
Halle *f.* hall, lobby
Hals *m.* neck
haltbar durable

halten   to hold, keep
halten, für   to deem, regard as
Hand *f.*   hand
Handschuh *m.*   glove
Handtasche *f.*   handbag
hängen   to hang
hart   hard
Hase *m.*   hare
hässlich   ugly
Haupt *n.*   head
Häuptelsalat *m.*   head of lettuce
Hauptstadt *f.*   capital
Haus *n.*   house
Hausdiener *m.*   servant
Haustier *n.*   domestic animal
Hecht *m.*   pike
Heft *n.*   notebook
Heim *n.*   home
Heimat *f.*   country of origin, homeland
heimgehen   to go home, return
Heimatsklang *m.*   memory of home
heiraten   to marry
heiss   hot
heissen   to be named, to mean
heizen   to heat
Heizung *f.*   heating, radiator
hell   light, clear, bright
Hemd *n.*   shirt
herabfallen   to fall down
heran   closer, near to
heraus   out of here
herausnehmen   to take out
Herbst *m.*   fall, autumn
hereinlegen   to fool (someone)
Herr *m.*   gentleman, Mister, master, sir
herrichten   to repair, freshen up
herrlich   gorgeous, magnificent
Herrscher *m.*   emperor
herum   around, in a circle
Herz *n.*   heart
herzig   cute, neat
herzlich   hearty
heute   today
hier   here
hierbleiben   to stay here, remain in place
hierher   here, to this place
Himmel *m.*   sky, heaven

Himmelsrichtung *f.*   direction (N-S, E-W)
hin und zurück   there and back, round trip
hinausgehen   to go out, leave
hindern   to hinder, hamper
hindurch   across, through, right through
hingehen   to go (to a place), go there
hinlegen   to lay down, put down
hinstellen   to set down, stand (something) up
hinten   in the rear
hinter   behind, in back of
hinüber   over there
hinunter   down there, under there
Hirn *n.*   brain
hoch   high
höchstens   the highest, most
höchstwahrscheinlich   in all probability
Hochzeit *f.*   wedding
Hof *m.*   court, courtyard
Hofburg *f.*   imperial castle
hoffen   to hope
Hoffnung *f.*   hope
Höhepunkt *m.*   highlight, peak
holen   to fetch, pick up, get
Holz *n.*   wood
hören   to hear
Hose *f.*   trousers
Hotel *n.*   hotel
hübsch   pretty
Hügel *m.*   hill
Huhn *n.*   chicken
Hund *m.*   dog
hundert   hundred
Hunger *m.*   hunger
hungrig   hungry
Hut *m.*   hat
Hutgeschäft *n.*   hat store
hüten   to watch, guard

I

ich   I
Idee *f.*   idea, thought
ihm   to him, to it

ihn him, it
ihnen them, to them
Ihnen you, to you
ihr her, to her, to it, their
Ihr you, your
Imbiss *m.* snack
immer always, ever
in in, into
intelligent intelligent
interessant interesting
irgendwelcher any, anyone
irgendwo somewhere, anywhere
irren to err, be mistaken
Italien *n.* Italy
Italiener *m.* Italian (male)
Italienerin *f.* Italian (female)
italienisch Italian

J

ja yes
jagen to hunt, chase
Jahr *n.* year
Jahreszeit *f.* season
Jahrhundert *n.* century
Januar *m.* January
Japan *n.* Japan
Japaner *m.* Japanese (man)
Japanerin *f.* Japanese (woman)
japanisch Japanese
jedenfalls anyway, in any case
jeder everybody, each
jedermann everyone
jedoch however
jemand somebody, someone
jener that, that one
Jugend *f.* youth
jung young
Junge *n.* young animal
Junge *m.* boy

K

Kaffee *m.* coffee
Kaiser *m.* emperor
Kaiserin *f.* empress
Kalb *n.* veal
Kalender *m.* calendar

Kamel *n.* camel
Kamm *m.* comb
kämmen to comb
Kanada *n.* Canada
Kaninchen *n.* rabbit
kann, ich I am able to, I can
Kanzlei *f.* office
Karpfen *m.* carp
Karte *f.* card, ticket, map
Kartoffel *f.* potato
Käse *m.* cheese
Kasse *f.* cash, box office
Kassier *m.* cashier, treasurer
Kätzchen *n.* kitten
Katze *f.* cat
kaufen to buy
Kaufhaus *n.* department store
kein not any, none
keineswegs in no way, not at all
Kellner *m.* waiter
Kellnerin *f.* waitress
kennen to know, to b. acquainted
  with
Kilo *n.* kilogram
Kind *n.* child
Kinder *n.pl.* children
Kino *n.* movie house
Kiosk *m.* kiosk, newsstand
Kirche *f.* church
Kirsche *f.* cherry
Kirschbaum *m.* cherry tree
klagen to complain, sue
klar clear, pure, serene
Klavier *n.* piano
Kleid *n.* dress, clothing
klein small, little
Kleinigkeit *f.* small thing, detail
klingen to sound
klingeln to ring
Kloss *m.* dumpling
klug clever, intelligent
Knicks *m.* curtsy
Knödel *m.* dumpling
Koch *m.* cook, chef
Köchin *f.* female cook
Koffer *m.* suit case, trunk
Kohl *m.* cabbage
Kohle *f.* coal
Komfort *m.* luxury, comfort
komisch funny, comical, queer
kommen to come

komplett complete
Konditorei *f.* pastry shop
können to be able to, know how to
Konzert *n.* concert
Kopf *m.* head
Kopfweite *f.* head-size
Körper *m.* body
kosten to cost, taste
Kragen *m.* collar
krähen to crow
krank sick, ill
Krawatte *f.* necktie
Kreide *f.* chalk
Kreis *m.* circle
kreisen to circulate
kriechen to crawl, creep
Kriechtier *n.* reptile
Kriminalgeschichte *f.* criminal history
Krokodil *n.* crocodile
Krone *f.* crown
Küche *f.* kitchen, cuisine
Kuchen *m.* cake
Kuckucksuhr *f.* cuckoo-clock
Kuh *f.* cow
kündigen to give notice
Kunstmaler *m.* painter (artist)
Kurs *m.* exchange rate, course
kurz short
küssen to kiss

L

lachen to laugh
lächeln to smile
Lage *f.* position, situation
Lampe *f.* lamp
Land *n.* land, country
landen to land
Landsleute *m.pl.* compatriots
Landsmann *m.* compatriot
lang long
langsam slow
laufen to run
Laut *m.* sound
laut loud, aloud
lauten to sound
Leben *m.* life
leben to live

lebend alive, living
Lebewesen *n.* a being
legen to lay, to put down
lehren to teach
Lehrer *m.* teacher (male)
Lehrerin *f.* teacher (female)
Leib *m.* body
leicht easy, light
leichtsinnig foolish, lighthearted
leider unfortunately, to my regret
Leopard *m.* leopard
lernen to learn
lesen to read
letzte last, recent
Leute *pl.* people, men
Licht *n.* light
licht bright, clear, light
Liebe *f.* love
lieben to love
liebenswürdig lovable, genteel, kind
lieber rather, preferably
Liebling *m.* darling, pet, favorite
Liebste dearest one
Lied *n.* song
liegen to lie, to be situated
Literatur *f.* literature
Löffel *m.* spoon
lohnen, sich to be worthwhile
Lokomotive *f.* locomotive
los loose, amiss
lösen to solve, to buy (a ticket)
Luft *f.* air
Lunge *f.* lung

M

Magen *m.* stomach
Mahlzeit *f.* meal
Mai *m.* May
Makrele *f.* mackerel
man one, they, you
mancher someone, some
manchmal sometimes
Mann *m.* man, husband
Mantel *m.* coat, overcoat
Mark *f.* Mark (money unit)
Marke *f.* brand
Marmor *m.* marble

März *m.* March
Maul *n.* mouth (of an animal)
Maus *f.* mouse
Medikament *n.* medicine, remedy
Mehl *n.* flour
mehr more
mehrere several
mein my
meinen to think, to mean
meinerseits from my viewpoint, for my part
meistens mostly
Mehlspeise *f.* pastry
Mensch *m.* man (in general)
merken to notice, remember
messen to measure
Messer *n.* knife
Metall *n.* metal
mich me
Mietauto *n.* taxicab
Milch *f.* milk
Minute *f.* minute
Minutenzeiger *m.* minute hand
mir to me
missfallen to displease
mit with
mitgehen to go with
Mittag *m.* noon
Mittagessen *n.* lunch
mitteilen to communicate
Mittelpunkt *m.* center, focal point
mitten in in the middle of
Mittwoch *m.* Wednesday
modern modern, fashionable
mögen to like
möglich possible
Moment *m.* moment, instant
Monat *m.* month
Mond *m.* moon
Montag *m.* Monday
Mord *m.* murder
Mörder *m.* murderer
morgen tomorrow
Morgen *m.* morning
morgens in the morning
Morgenschlummer *m.* morning slumber
Morgenübung *f.* morning exercise
müde tired
Mund *m.* mouth (of human beings)

munden to taste good
Murmeltier *n.* marmot
Musse *f.* leisure
müssen to be obliged, must
Mut *m.* courage, mood
mutig courageous, unafraid
Mutter *f.* mother

N

nach after, behind, according to
nachholen to make up for something, catch up
nachlegen to throw on (coal, wood, etc.)
nachmachen to imitate
Nachmittag *m.* afternoon
nachsehen to look after, look into
Nachspeise *f.* dessert
nächste next
Nacht *f.* night
Nachtisch *m.* dessert
Nachwuchs *m.* offspring
nahe near, close to
Nähe *f.* nearness, vicinity
nähen to sew
nähern, sich to approach, near
Nahrung *f.* nourishment, food
Name *m.* name
nämlich namely
Nase *f.* nose
nass wet
Nationalbank *f.* National Bank
Natur *f.* nature
natürlich naturally, of course
naturhistorisch having to do with natural history
nehmen to take
nein no
Nelke *f.* carnation
nennen to call, name
Nerv *m.* nerve
nett neat, nice
neu new, recent
Neujahr *n.* New Year
neun nine
neunzehn nineteen
neunzig ninety
Neuzeit *f.* modern times

nicht not
nichts nothing
nie never
niemals never
niemand nobody, no one
Niere f. kidney
noch still, yet, again
Norden m. North
Nordpol m. North Pole
normal normal
Notizbuch n. notebook
November m. November
nun now
nur only
nützlich useful

O

ob if, whether
oben up there, above, upstairs
Ober m. waiter
Oberkellner m. headwaiter
Oberlehrer m. headmaster
Obst n. fruit
oder or
Ofen m. oven, stove
öffnen to open
oft often
ohne without
Ohr n. ear
Oktober m. October
Oper f. opera
Opernhaus n. opera house
Ordnung f. order, tidiness
Organ n. organ
Ort m. place
Osten m. East
Ostern n. Easter
Österreich n. Austria

P

paar (a) few
Paar n. couple, pair
packen to pack
Palatschinken f.pl. thin pancakes
panieren to bread
Papagei m. parrot
Papier n. paper, document

paradox paradoxical
Parfüm n. perfume
Pariser m. Parisian
Pariserin f. Parisian woman
Park m. park
Parlament n. parliament
Pass m. passport
Passagier m. passenger
passen to fit, suit, be convenient
passieren to happen, occur
Passkontrolle f. passport control
Passrevision f. passport inspection
Person f. person
persönlich personal, personally, in person
Persönlichkeit f. personality
Pfannkuchen m. pancake
Pfau m. peacock
Pfennig m. penny
Pferd n. horse
Pfirsich m. peach
Pflaume f. plum
pflücken to pluck, pick
Piano n. piano
Platz m. place, seat, square
Polizei f. police
Polizist m. policeman
Portion f. portion, helping
Portrait n. picture
Porzellan n. china, porcelain
Post f. post-office, mail
Präsident m. president
Preis m. price, praise
prima first rate, first class
probieren to try, try out
Professor m. professor
Prüfung f. test, examination
Puppe f. doll

Q

Qualität f. quality

R

Radio n. radio
rasch fast, quick
raten to advise, guess

Ratgeber *m.* advisor, counselor
Rathaus *n.* City Hall
Raubtier *n.* beast of prey
Raubfisch *m.* rapacious fish
rechnen to count, calculate
Rechnung *f.* bill
recht right
rechts to the right, on the right
Regen *m.* rain
Regenschirm *m.* umbrella
regieren to reign, govern
regnen to rain
Rehbraten *m.* roast venison
reif ripe, mature
reifen to ripen, mature
rein clean, pure, unadulterated
Reisebüro *n.* travel office
reisen to travel
Reisepapier *n.* travel document
reizend charming, enchanting
rennen to run
Restaurant *n.* restaurant, inn
Rettung *f.* rescue
Richter *m.* judge
richtig correct
Richtung *f.* direction
riechen to smell
Riesenrad *n.* ferris wheel
Rind *n.* beef
Ring *m.* ring
Rock *m.* coat, jacket, skirt
Rose *f.* rose
rosig rosy
rot red
Rückfahrkarte *f.* round trip ticket
Rückkehr *f.* return, homecoming
rufen to call
Ruhe *f.* calm, quiet, rest
ruhen to rest
Ruhetag *m.* day of rest
rund round
Rundfahrt *f.* round trip
rupfen to pluck, fleece
russisch Russian
Russland *n.* Russia

S

Sache *f.* thing, matter
saftig juicy

sagen to tell, say
Sahne *f.* cream
Samstag *m.* Saturday
Sänger *m.* singer (male)
Sängerin *f.* singer (female)
Satz *m.* sentence
sauer sour
Säule *f.* column, pillar
Schachtel *f.* box
Schaden *m.* damage
schädlich harmful
Schaffner *m.* trainman, conductor
Schalter *m.* ticket window
Schaltjahr *n.* leap-year
Schalttag *m.* February 29
scharf sharp, keen
schauen to look
scheinen to seem, shine
Scherz *m.* joke
schicken to send, ship
Schiff *n.* ship
Schinken *m.* ham
Schirm *m.* umbrella
schlafen to sleep
Schlange *f.* snake
schlängeln, sich to meander, twist, wind
schlau sly, clever
schlecht bad, evil
schliessen to close, finish
schlimm bad, evil, wicked
Schofför *m.* driver
Schöpfung *f.* creation
Schloss *n.* castle, lock
Schlüssel *m.* key
schmal narrow
schmecken to taste
schmutzig dirty
Schnee *m.* snow
schneiden to cut
schneien to snow
schnell fast, quick
schon already
schön beautiful
Schrank *m.* closet
schreiben to write
Schuh *m.* shoe
Schule *f.* school
Schüler *m.* pupil, student
Schülerin *f.* female pupil, student
Schüssel *f.* dish

schützen to protect
schwärmen to be enthusiastic
schwarz black
Schwein n. pig
Schweiz f. Switzerland
Schweizer m. Swiss (male)
Schweizerin f. Swiss (female)
schwer difficult, heavy
Schwierigkeit f. difficulty
schwimmen to swim
schwindelfrei not subject to giddiness
sechs six
sechzehn sixteen
sechzig sixty
Seele f. soul
Seelöwe m. sea lion
sehen to see
Sehenswürdigkeit f. sight (as in sightseeing)
sehr very
Seide f. silk
Seidenraupe f. silkworm
sein his
sein to be
seit since
Seite f. page, side
Sekunde f. second (unit of time)
selbstverständlich obviously
selten rare, seldom
September m. September
setzen, sich to sit down
sichtbar visible
sie she, it, they
Sie you
sicher sure, certain
sieben seven
siebzehn seventeen
siebzig seventy
Silbe f. syllable
Silber n. silver
silbern (of) silver
singen to sing
Sinn m. sense
sitzen to sit
so thus, so
Sofa n. sofa
sofort immediately, at once
sogenannt so called
sollen to be supposed to (do something)

Sommer m. summer
Sonnabend m. Saturday
Sonne f. sun
Sonntag m. Sunday
sorgen, sich to care, worry
sowas such a thing
sozusagen so to speak
Spanien n. Spain
Spanier m. Spaniard
Spanierin f. Spanish woman
spanisch Spanish
Spargel m. asparagus
Spargelsuppe f. asparagus soup
Spass m. joke, fun
spät late
spazierengehen to take a walk, stroll
Speise f. food
Speisekarte f. menu
Speisesaal m. dining room
Sperre f. gate, turnstile
Spezialitäten f.pl. specialties
Spiegelei n. fried egg
Spiel n. play, game
spielen to play, toy
Spinat m. spinach
Sprache f. language
sprechen to speak
Sprichwort n. proverb
Staatsmuseum n. state museum
Stadt f. city, town
Stahl m. steel
Stall m. stable
ständig steady
Standuhr f. floor clock
Stange f. rod, perch, post
statt instead of
stattfinden to take place
Statue f. statue
stechen to sting
Stechmücke f. mosquito
stecken to stick, put in
stehen to stand
stehlen to steal
steigen to climb, mount
stellen to put up, stand up
stempeln to stamp, obliterate
sterben to die
Stern m. star
Stiefmütterchen n. pansy
Stier m. steer, bull

stimmen   to be exact, correct
Stock m.   stick, cane, story (of a building)
stören   to disturb
stossen   to push, toss, prod
Strandbad n.   bathing beach
Strasse f.   street
Strauss m.   ostrich
Streichholz n.   match
Streifen n.   stripe
Stück n   piece
studieren   to study
Stuhl m.   chair
Stunde f.   hour, lesson
stundenlang   for hours
suchen   to look for, seek
Süden m.   South
Suppe f.   soup
süss   sweet

T

Tafel f.   blackboard, table
Tag m.   day
Tageslicht n.   daylight
Tal n.   valley, dale
Tante f.   aunt
tapfer   brave, courageous
Tasche f.   pocket, bag
Taschentuch n.   handkerchief
Taschenuhr f.   pocket-watch
Tasse f.   cup
Tastsinn m.   sense of touch
tausend   thousand
Taxi n.   taxicab
Tee m.   tea
Teil m.   part, portion
Telefongespräch n.   telephone conversation
telegraphieren   to telegraph
Teller m.   plate
Teppich m.   carpet
teuer   expensive, dear
Theater n.   theatre
Tier n.   animal
Tierart f.   class of animal
Tiger m.   tiger
Tisch m.   table
Tischchen n.   small table
Tischglocke f.   table bell

Tischtuch n.   table cloth
Tischuhr f.   table clock
Topf m.   pot
Torte f.   cake
tragen   to carry, wear
treffen   to hit, meet
treffen, sich   to meet with
trennen   to separate, cleave
trinken   to drink
Trinkgeld n.   tip
trocken   dry
Tropfen m.   drop
Truthahn m.   turkey
tun   to do
Turm m.   tower
Tür f.   door
typisch   typical

U

über   over, across, about
überall   everywhere
Übergewicht n.   overweight
Übergang m.   crossing, transition
überlegen   superior
überqueren   to cross
Überraschung f.   surprise
Überschuh m.   overshoe
übertreiben   to exaggerate, overdo
übrig bleiben   to remain
Übung f.   exercise, practice
Uhr f.   watch, clock
um   at, around
um zu   in order to
umbauen   to rebuild
umfallen   to fall down
umfassen   to comprise, embrace
umsteigen   to change trains
umziehen, sich   to change clothes
unangenehm   disagreeable, unpleasant
unbedingt   at any rate, undoubtedly
und   and
unendlich   infinite, unending
unerträglich   intolerable
Unfug m.   nuisance
ungefähr   around, about, approximately

ungeduldig impatient
unglaublich incredible
Universität f. university
uns us
unser our
unten downstairs, below
unter under, beneath
untergehen to go down, set
unternehmen to undertake
unverzüglich without delay, at once
unzählbar innumerable

V

Vater m. father
Vaterland n. fatherland, mother country
Veilchen n. violet
Vene f. vein
verbreiten spread out
verbringen to spend (time)
verdanken to be grateful for
verdauen to digest
Verdauung f. digestion
Verehrung f. veneration
Vereinigten Staaten m. United States
verfolgen to persecute, follow closely
Vergangenheit f. past
vergehen to pass by
vergessen to forget
Vergissmeinnicht n. forgetmenot
vergleichen to compare
Vergnügen n. pleasure
verheiraten to marry
verirren, sich to get lost, lose one's way
verkaufen to sell
Verkäufer m. salesman
Verkäuferin f. saleslady
Verkehr m. traffic
verlangen to ask, demand
verlassen to leave, forsake
verlieren to lose
verlobt engaged, affianced
vermeiden to avoid
vernehmen to perceive, hear

verpflichten to engage, commit
verraten to betray, to give away
Vers m. verse
verschieben to put off, delay
verschieden different
verschlafen to oversleep
versehen to provide
versprechen to promise
Verstand m. sense, brains
verstehen to understand, comprehend
vertreiben to chase away
Verwandten pl. relatives
Verzeichnis n. list, file
Verzeihung f. forgiveness, pardon
viel much
vielleicht perhaps
vier four
viereckig square, four-cornered
Vierfüssler m. quadruped
Viertel n. quarter (¼)
vierzehn fourteen
vierzig forty
Vogel m. bird
vor before, in front of
vorausgehen to precede, go before
vorbereiten to prepare
Vordergrund m. foreground
vorfallen to occur, happen
vorhaben to have in mind, intend
vorher beforehand
vorige preceding
vorlegen to show, lay out
vormittag in the forenoon
vornehmen to undertake, perform
vorspannen to attach, put in front
Vorspeise f. appetizer
Vorstadt f. suburb
vorstellen to introduce, personify
Vorstellung f. performance
vorweisen to show
vorzüglich excellent

W

Wachsfigur f. wax image, figure
Wagen m. car, wagon
wahr true
während during

wahrnehmen to perceive
Wald *m.* forest, woods
Wand *f.* wall
Wanduhr *f.* wall clock
wann when
Warenausgabe *f.* wrapping-
 counter
Warenhaus *n.* department store
warm warm
wärmen to warm up
warten to wait
warum why
was what
was für ein what kind of, which
waschen to wash
Wasser *n.* water
Wechselgeld *n.* change (money)
wechseln to change, exchange
Wechselstube *f.* change booth
wecken to wake up
Weckuhr *f.* alarm clock
weder ... noch neither ... nor
Weg *m.* way
weg away
weggehen to go away
wegkommen to get away with
wegwerfen to throw away
wegziehen to move away
weich weak, soft
Weihnachten *n.* Christmas
weil because
Wein *m.* wine
Weinbrand *m.* brandy
weiss white
weitaus by far
welche which
Welt *f.* world
Weltausstellung *f.* world's fair
weltberühmt world famous
wem to whom
wen whom
Wendung *f.* turn
wenig little
weniger less
wenigsten, am the least
wer who
werden to become
wessen whose
Weste *f.* vest
Westen *m.* West
Wetter *n.* weather

wichtig important
wie how, as
wieder again, back
wiegen to weigh
Wiese *f.* meadow
wieviel how much
wild wild, ferocious
Wind *m.* wind
windig windy
Winter *m.* winter
wirklich real, in fact
wissen to know
wo where
Woche *f.* week
woher whence, from where
wohin whither, to where
wohl well, indeed
wohnen to live, dwell, stay
Wohnung *f.* apartment, dwelling
Wohnzimmer *n.* living room
Wolf *m.* wolf
Wolke *f.* cloud
wollen to wish, want
womöglich if possible
woraus out of what
Wort *n.* word
wunderbar marvelous
wunderschön wondrously beautiful, gorgeous
Wunsch *m.* wish
wünschen to wish
Wurst *f.* sausage
Wut *f.* fury, rage
wütend furious, in a rage

Z

Zahl *f.* number
zahlen to pay
zählen to count
zahlreich numerous
Zahnbürste *f.* tooth brush
zehn ten
zeigen to show, point out
Zeiger *m.* hand (of the clock)
Zeit *f.* time
zeitig early
Zeitung *f.* newspaper
zentral central

Zentrum *n.* center
zerbrechen to break up
zerreissen to tear up
zerschneiden to cut to pieces
Ziegenbock *m.* billy-goat
Zigarre *f.* cigar
Zigarette *f.* cigarette
Zimmer *n.* room
Zitrone *f.* lemon
Zoll *m.* customs duty
zollfrei free of duty
Zollinspektor *m.* customs inspector
Zolluntersuchung *f.* customs inspection
Zollrevision *f.* customs inspection
zornig angry, irate
zu at, to, too
zufrieden satisfied, contented
Zug *m.* train, draft
Zucker *m.* sugar
zuhause at home
zuhören listen (to)
Zukunft *f.* future

zukünftig future, belonging to the future
zum at the, to the
zumachen to close, shut
Zunge *f.* tongue
zurück back
zurückbekommen to get back (something)
zurückfliegen to fly back
zurückgehen to go back, return
zurückhalten to hold back, keep back
zusammen together
zusammenhalten to keep together
zustossen to occur
zwanzig twenty
zwar though, however
zwei two
zweite second (of a series)
Zwillinge *pl.* twins
zwischen between
Zwischenakt *m.* intermission
Zwischenlandung *f.* stop-over
zwölf twelve